Aspects of Bilingual Aphasia

Jean-Albert Pitres (1848-1928)
Dean of the Faculty of Medicine of Bordeaux
Member of the French Academy of Medicine

ASPECTS OF
BILINGUAL APHASIA

edited by

MICHEL PARADIS
McGill University

INTERNATIONAL ASSOCIATION
OF LOGOPEDICS AND PHONIATRICS

PERGAMON

U.K.   Elsevier Science Ltd, The Boulevard, Langford Lane, Kidlington, Oxford OX5 1GB, U.K.

U.S.A.   Elsevier Science Inc., 660 White Plains Road, Tarrytown, New York 10591-5153, U.S.A.

JAPAN   Elsevier Science Japan, Tsunashima Building Annex, 3-20-12 Yushima, Bunkyo-ku, Tokyo 113, Japan

First edition 1995

Library of Congress Cataloging in Publication Data

Aspects of bilingual aphasia/ editor, Michel Paradis.
p. cm.
Includes index.
1. Aphasia. 2. Bilingualism. I. Paradis, Michel.
[DNLM: 1. Aphasia. WL 340.5 A838 1995]
RC425.A84 1995
616.85'52 – dc20
DNLM/DLC
95-13571

British Library Cataloguing in Publication Data

A catalogue record for this book is available from the British Library

ISBN 0 08 042570 4

Printed and bound in Great Britain by Galliard (Printers) Ltd, Great Yarmouth

Contents

List of Contributors

Maria De Agostini, C.N.R.S. (U 169), Villejuif, France.

Ria De Bleser, Institute for Linguistics, University of Potsdam, Potsdam, Germany.

Frauke Bürk, Sanderson Center of Speech Therapy, Gosforth, United Kingdom.

Nina Dronkers, Audiology and Speech Pathology Service, V.A. Medical Center, Martinez, California, and Departments of Linguistics and Neurology, University of California, Davis, U.S.A.

Alan C. Evans, McConnell Brain Imaging Center, Montreal Neurological Institute, McGill University, Montreal, Canada

Franco Fabbro, Laboratory of Higher Brain Functions, Università di Trieste, Trieste, Italy.

Carme Junqué, Escola de Patologia del Llenguatge, Servei de Neurologia, Hospital de la Santa Creu i Sant Pau, Barcelona, Spain.

Denise Klein, Cognitive Neuroscience Unit, Montreal Neurological Institute, McGill University, Montreal, Canada.

Helgard Kremin, C.N.R.S. (U 302), Hôpital de la Salpêtrière, Paris, France.

Yvan Lebrun, Neurolinguistiek, Akademisch Ziekenhuis, Vrije Universiteit Brusscl, Brussels, Belgium.

Ernst Meyer, McConnell Brain Imaging Center, Montreal Neurological Institute, McGill University, Montreal, Canada.

Brenda Milner, Cognitive Neuroscience Unit, Montreal Neurological Institute, McGill University, Montreal, Canada.

Reza Nilipour, Department of Speech Therapy, College of Rehabilitation Sciences, Tehran, Iran.

Loraine K. Obler, Speech & Hearing Department, City University of New York Graduate School and Boston V.A. Medical Center, U.S.A.

Michel Paradis, Department of Linguistics, McGill University, and Laboratoire de neuroscience de la cognition, Université du Québec à Montréal, Montreal, Canada.

Hea Suk Park, Yonsei University College of Medicine, Seoul, Korea.

G. Webster Ross, V.A. Outpatient Clinic, Honolulu, and University of Hawaii, Honolulu Heart Program, Hawaii.

Martha Taylor Sarno, Department of Rehabilitation Medicine, New York University School of Medicine and Rusk Institute of Rehabilitation Medicine, New York, U.S.A.

Sumiko Sasanuma, Department of Language and Cognition, Tokyo Metropolitan Institute of Gerontology, Tokyo, Japan.

Luise Springer, School of Logopedics, Faculty of Medicine, RWTH, Aachen, Germany.

Nicole Stadie, Institute for Linguistics, University of Potsdam, Potsdam, Germany.

Josep Vendrell, Escola de Patologia del Llenguatge, Servei de Neurologia, Hospital de la Santa Creu i Sant Pau, Barcelona, Spain.

Pere Vendrell, Escola de Patologia del Llenguatge, Servei de Neurologia, Hospital de la Santa Creu i Sant Pau, Barcelona, Spain.

Lon White, Honolulu Heart Program and National Institute on Aging, Hawaii.

Debra A. Wiener, Rusk Institute of Rehabilitation Medicine, New York University Medical Center, New York, U.S.A.

Yumi Yamasaki, Department of Linguistics, State University of New York, Buffalo, N.Y., U.S.A.

Robert J. Zatorre, Cognitive Neuroscience Unit, Montreal Neurological Institute, McGill University, Montreal, Canada.

Preface

At its August 1992 meeting in Hanover, Germany, on the occasion of the XXIInd Congress of the International Association of Logopedics and Phoniatrics, the Aphasia Committee undertook to prepare a report on bilingual aphasia to be published on the occasion of the 100th anniversary of Pitres' (1895) monograph on aphasia in polyglots, the first systematic study of the neurolinguistic aspects of bilingualism. Each member set out to study a specific aspect of bilingual aphasia. A first draft of these investigations was discussed by the members of the Aphasia Committee at a meeting held in Bordeaux, France, Pitres' birthplace, where he wrote his seminal paper on aphasia in polyglots, and where he is buried. After a thorough discussion of each contribution, authors wrote a final report which will be presented at the IALP XXIIIrd Congress in Cairo, Egypt, in August 1995, and is published in this volume. Hence all chapters have been written specifically for this book by members of the IALP Aphasia Committee and their collaborators.

The purpose of this work is to focus the attention of language pathologists around the world, and most particularly in areas traditionally assumed to be unilingual, on the pervasiveness of bilingualism in their communities. The various chapters illustrate why it is not sufficient to assess patients in only one of their languages, regardless of its premorbid relative degree of fluency. New cases of bilingual aphasia are described, including acquired childhood aphasia, subcortical aphasia, and various types of dissociations and shifts of dominance, whose characteristics could not be predicted on the basis of age or manner of second language acquisition, context of use or degree of mastery. Bilingual patients reported here speak a variety of languages ranging from structurally very similar (Catalan-Spanish, Friulian-Italian, Japanese-Korean) to structurally quite distant (English-Farsi, English-Japanese). Practical issues related to diagnosis, prognosis and therapy, as well as more theoretical issues of the organization of two or more languages in one brain, supported by a PET study, are also explored.

More specifically, the reader will find an account of Pitres' influence on the study of aphasia in bilinguals and polyglots over the 100 years following the publication of his 1895 monograph, focussing on what has come to be known as Pitres' Law, the influence of the language spoken in the patient's environment on the preferential recovery of a specific language, one's views on language representation in the brain, Pitres' contribution to an early theory of neuro-functional modularity with the characterization of memory as a variety of psychophysiologically distinct processes susceptible of selective impairment, the notion of inhibition vs. loss of language, specific bilingual phenomena, aphasia in deaf signers, and unilateral deficits (Chap. 1); an investigation of the neural substrates of bilingual language function, with an emphasis on proper task design for the interpretation of distributed patterns of cerebral activity, applying the PET-rCBF method to the study of bilingual individuals, with a view to finding similarities and/or differences in patterns of rCBF change for the first and second language tasks in order to determine whether the neural processes that subserve second language performance are the same as, or differ from, those that subserve first language performance (Chap. 2); a study of how cases of bilingual aphasia are managed in a U.S. urban rehabilitation hospital, with a view to ascertaining whether the services available to bilinguals were equivalent to those provided to the unilingual population, and to what extent, if any, the bilingual patients' benefit from treatment might be compromised by the necessity of arranging for translation, based on the 109 adult aphasic patients admitted for therapy and evaluated as either inpatients or outpatients by the Speech/Language Department in the year 1993, involving patients speaking a variety of different languages (Arabic, Armenian, Bulgarian, Chinese, Creole, Croatian, French, German, Greek, Hebrew, Hungarian, Italian, Lithuanian, Polish, Portuguese, Romanian, Russian, Spanish, Turkish, Ukrainian, Yiddish) in addition to English (Chap. 3); an exploration of the many parameters that could influence the assessment of bilingual aphasia, such as degree of bilingualism, context and manner of acquisition, the degree of dialect difference between patient and examiner, focussing on cases of multilingual Japanese-American patients living in the state of Hawaii, pointing out the extreme complexity of the linguistic and social issues surrounding the assessment, further complicated by the widespread use of Hawaiian Creole English, which makes the assessment of standard English somewhat problematic (Chap. 4), a description of the symptoms and pattern of differential impairment in a bilingual aphasic child, with more severe deficits in her native language (Friulian) that she had spoken until her ischemic stroke at the age of 7 and that continued to be the language of her home during recovery, than in her second language (Italian) that she had learned at school and used less frequently than Friulian before her cerebral accident, as assessed with a test battery equivalent in each of her two languages (Chap. 5).

The reader will also find a discussion of multilingual naming mechanisms with reference to the oral and written naming performance of a trilingual patient, with an analysis of whether intra- and inter-lingual errors occurred more frequently in any of the patient's languages, including a qualitative and quantitative analysis of stimulus sets in which the target name in two or all three languages shared phonemic/graphemic similarity with sets not having such similarity, and an interpretation in terms of higher semantic-phonological activation of the patient's improved naming performance in the presence of phonemic similarity for the foreign languages but not for the native language (Chap. 6); a report on two patients, one with differential picture naming in three languages and one with the unusual pattern of preserved picture naming in both languages in spite of severely impaired semantic comprehension, a condition explained in terms of a dual pathway model, one of which, the direct pathway for naming familiar pictures, bypasses the semantic system (Chap. 7); an examination of patterns of language impairment in two Korean-Japanese bilingual aphasic patients, using two equivalent comprehensive tests of aphasia, one in Korean and the other in Japanese, given to the first patient at 3 months post onset, and administered twice to the second patient, at 2.5 months post onset preceding a 3-month language therapy, and at 5.5 months post onset following the therapy, showing that the patterns of language deficits measured by the two tests at the initial evaluation were highly similar to each other in both patients, and a sizable improvement in all modalities in both languages of the second patient after therapy in Korean only, except in the writing modality in Japanese (Chap. 8); following a short description of relevant aspects of Farsi grammar, an analysis of the grammatical violations of three native speakers of Farsi who were also proficient speakers of English before they sustained cerebral damage and who, owing to the structure of each language, show qualitative differences in the patterns of deficits in their two languages, with mainly substitution of verb inflections in Farsi and omission of closed class words in English, thus demonstrating that types of possible deficits are determined by the structure of each language (Chap. 9); a characterization of subcortical aphasia symptoms, particularly following damage to the basal ganglia, as illustrated by one trilingual and three bilingual patients exhibiting different degrees of impairment in their native and non - native languages, with nonfluent speech, poor comprehension, and good repetition, and, in two of the patients, a unidirectional inability to translate into their native language (Chap. 10); and the results of a study to ascertain the presence and frequency of specific bilingual phenomena such as pathological mixing, switching or selective loss of access to one language, and possible correlations with linguistic, neurological and personal variables, on 50 adult Catalan-Spanish bilingual aphasic patients admitted to the Neuropsychology service of the Hospital de la Santa Creu i Sant Pau in Barcelona over an 18-month period (Chap. 11).

The considerable diversity of background of the various contributors (Language Pathologists, Linguists, Neurolinguists, Neuropsychologists, Neurologists, Neuro-physiologists, and Psychologists) attests to the multidisciplinarity and complexity of the issue of bilingual aphasia.

At their Bordeaux meeting, the contributors to this volume agreed to refrain from using "monolingual" (an ill-formed hybrid word, with a Greek prefix on a Latin root) and to use "unilingual" instead, in conformity with the accepted usage of "multi-lingual" and "polyglot" (rather than "polylingual", "multiglot" or "uniglot").

Thanks are due to John Matthews for his careful copy editing of the text, and his expert technical assistance in the preparation of indexes and the production of the camera-ready copy.

References

Pitres, A. 1895. Etude sur l'aphasie chez les polyglottes. *Revue de médecine*, **15**, 873-899.

Introduction: The need for distinctions

Michel Paradis

Too often, over the past 100 years, that is since Pitres' (1895) monograph, investigators of the organization of two or more languages in one brain in general, and of aphasia in bilinguals and polyglots in particular, have suffered the consequences of a failure to make a number of distinctions, namely, between (1) the linguistic and neurolinguistic levels of description (or domains of discourse); (2) lexical and conceptual representations; (3) language *qua* grammar (or system, or code) and language use (the grammar plus pragmatics); and (4) implicit linguistic competence and explicit metalinguistic knowledge. Once these distinctions are taken into consideration, one realizes that the controversies are resolved and that most of the differences that have been reported between bilingual and unilingual subjects are quantitative rather than qualitative.

Linguistic and neurolinguistic levels of description

It has often been mistakenly supposed that the organization of the neural substrate is in some way modified as a consequence of the differential organization of language structure. It has thus been assumed that a compound organization of an individual's linguistic system (a linguistic construct) would necessarily result in a cerebral organization (a neurolinguistic construct) different from that of individuals with a coordinate system. Yet, while *the contents* of the grammar differ from language to language and from one bilingual to another (depending on the degree and kind of deviance from the unilingual norm of each language), there is no necessary effect on *how* the grammar is subserved (at least in early bilinguals), and so far none has been documented. In other words, the internal structure of the grammar may differ, but it is subserved by the brain as a grammar, irrespective of its specific contents, hence irrespective of the number of illicit borrowings.

Evidence from aphasia has failed to support Lambert & Fillenbaum's (1959) conjecture that compound bilinguals (i.e., those who have acquired both their languages at the same time, in the same contexts) would store their languages in ways that are more neurofunctionally similar, while coordinate bilinguals (i.e., those who have learned their second language in a different environment) would store their two languages in more neurofunctionally separate ways. Lambert and Fillenbaum's (1983) own evidence does not support their hypothesis. Junqué, Vendrell and Vendrell (this volume) also report cases of bilinguals who had acquired both their languages at the same time in a bilingual environment but who exhibit differential deficits, and patients who had acquired a second language long after the first, in a different context, who show comparable deficits in their two languages. The same situation of parallel recovery prevails for the two patients described by Sasanuma and Park (this volume) who had acquired Korean at home in Korea and Japanese later at school as the language of instruction, and in one case, also in Japan.

One linguistic consequence of early bilingualism in some individuals may be a systematic deviance with respect to the unilingual norm at some or all levels of language representation (e.g., some degree of compoundness in voice onset time or vowel quality, the idiosyncratic use of a certain preposition in some contexts, or the peculiar use of some expressions) without any consequence with respect to the way in which (the mechanisms according to which) the grammar is subserved by neural substrates. A grammar rule (or whatever implicit process results in the systematic verbal behavior of the speaker) is processed as a grammar rule (or whatever), and a phoneme or syllable is processed as a phoneme or a syllable, whether it is a legitimate element or one that properly belongs to another language and is improperly incorporated. There is no reason to believe that there should be one way to process legitimate elements and another way to process illigitimate ones. Improper borrowings are processed as if they were legitimate, inasmuch as they are believed to be so by the speakers, and have been incorporated into their implicit linguistic competence. It is often an historical accident that in reality they are not legitimate. The actual number of shared elements between English and French is contingent upon such historical accidents —they are not necessary and could easily be different. In fact, they continue to change over time.

The fluency and accuracy of the languages spoken by an individual are independent of the manner in which they are processed by the brain. An early bilingual may process closed class words in the same way as unilingual speakers, even though the use of some of these closed class words may be deviant with respect to the norm (e.g., the systematic use of preposition "of" instead of preposition "to" in some contexts), while a late bilingual may use language with native-like accuracy, though processing closed class words in a manner that differs from unilinguals' and early bilinguals' (Webber-Fox & Neville, 1992). Thus the contents of implicit linguistic competence, as observed through performance, may be independent of the various cerebral processes that subserve them. Different processes may yield the same linguistic output; the same cerebral process may yield different linguistic outputs (i.e., outputs that differ from the unilingual norm and between bilingual individuals).

Linguistic and neurolinguistic domains of discourse bear on different objects, the nature and internal structure of which are independent of each other, and hence the particular form of the linguistic elements has no bearing on the neural principles that govern its substrate. What happens at a higher level does not condition the ways of functioning at a lower level. The domain of the linguistic level is the structure of language, implicit linguistic competence, the grammar. The domain of the neurolinguistic level pertains to the anatomical areas, brain mechanisms and physiological processes involved in the storage and use of language. The neurobiological level is concerned with the properties of cells and the actions of chemicals, hormones, enzymes, vitamins, cell metabolism and the like. The molecular level is concerned with the nature of particles that are at the basis of brain matter, and their motion.

Each level is subserved by the level below it. There is no language without a cerebral substrate. The cerebral substrate for language is made up of systems of neurons that function in accordance with their own neurophysiological laws. The internal structure and functioning of each level is necessarily different from those of the next level since each level concerns different types of entities that are subject to different laws. The laws of particle motion are different in kind from those that underlie physiological processes. The rules of syntax and phonology are of a different nature from those of neurophysiology, which themselves are independent of the nature of particle physics.

While it is indeed the case that language, eventually, rests on a bunch of particles in motion which form atoms that aggregate into molecules which underlie the various components of its neural substrate and serve as the basis for the various neurotransmitters, hormones, and cell protoplasm, the laws that preside over the distribution of type of particles and their motion are different in nature and bear on different objects than the rule that governs the agreement of the past participle with its preceding direct object in French. Irrespective of whether this rule, or one different from it, is part of a speaker's implicit linguistic competence, its implementation will be effected in the same way by the neural substrate that underlies language in accordance with its own mode of functioning. The laws that drive cell behaviour are different from those that control the working of systems of neurons, *a fortiori* from those that determine language behaviour.

What makes a particular item (word, inflection, syntactic construction) available depends on the activation threshold of its underlying neural substrate, which in turn depends on the frequency of activation of that particular item. But the grammatical nature of the item is irrelevant to the mechanisms that regulate the distribution of neural impulses, or the metabolism that supports the activity of the particular cells involved. Thus, each level has its own nature and *modus operandi*, and while it is, so to speak, at the service of the next level, the way it produces the goods it delivers is totally independent of how these goods are processed at the next level.

Lexical and conceptual representations

Another source of confusion has been a failure to distinguish between lexical semantics and nonlinguistic mental representations, or concepts. For the last four decades experimental psychologists have investigated whether bilingual speakers possess two linguistic memory stores or one (Kolers, 1963, 1968, 1977; McCormack, 1974). Eventually, the scope of the investigations was narrowed down from the linguistic system as a whole to the speaker's "internal dictionary" (Neufeld, 1973) or bilingual mental lexicon (Schreuder & Weltens, 1993).

The question, as first proposed by Weinreich (1953), can be formulated at the linguistic level, "do translation equivalents have the same meaning for a given speaker?" He had identified three types of organization of lexical units. Either (1) each word's meaning in the second language is that of the translation equivalent in the native language (subordinative bilingualism), thus exhibiting unidirectional interference; or (2) the meaning of the words in one of the languages and their translation equivalents in the other language is the same, i.e., an amalgam of the two (compound bilingualism), thus exhibiting bidirectional interference; or (3) each word and its translation equivalent has its respective meaning, without interference (coordinative bilingualism). (The terms "coordinative" and "subordinative" were soon replaced by "coordinate" and "subordinate" in subsequent literature.)

The following year, Ervin and Osgood (1954) shifted the question to the psycholinguistic level by relating type of organization of the lexicon (whether coordinate, compound, or subordinate) to the context of acquisition, hypothesizing that the acquisition of two languages in separate contexts would be conducive to coordinate bilingualism, whereas two languages learned in the same context or in school through translation would result in compound bilingualism.

The various investigations into the linguistic memory stores adopted the same general rationale. If subjects responded to translation equivalents in the same way as they responded to the repetition of the stimulus word, results were interpreted as supportive of the one-store hypothesis. If they responded to translation equivalents in the same way as they responded to altogether different words in the same language as the stimuli, results were interpreted as supporting the two-store hypothesis. Kolers (1968) examined the results of his own studies and concluded that they confirmed neither the one-store nor the two-store hypothesis. Responses were too similar across languages to support the two-store hypothesis, but not similar enough to support the one-store hypothesis. Translation equivalents triggered more or less the same response as synonyms in the same language.

These results are uninterpretable because of a number of confusions. Experimental studies designed to verify the organisation of languages in bilingual memory suffered from a quadruple lack of distinctions: (1) between different types of possible semantic organization in their bilingual subjects; (2) between stimuli that inherently overlap in meaning considerably between languages and those that do only minimally; (3) between semantic and conceptual levels of representation (lexical semantic constraints vs. nonlinguistic mental representations); and (4) between the language system (implicit linguistic competence) and the information acquired verbally (declarative memories). It is therefore not surprising that some experiments appeared to support the two-store hypothesis (Tulving & Colotla, 1970; Walters & Zatorre, 1978) while others tended to support the one-store hypothesis (Rose, Rose, King & Perez, 1975; McCormack, 1977). The problem at the level of type of bilingualism is twofold: (1) ignorance of the different types, but also (2) confusion among them when they are taken into consideration.

Experimental results are biased by whether the subjects' lexical semantics reflect the norms of each language (coordinate), exhibit bidirectional interference with the consequence that their lexical representations are fused and thus uniform for both languages (compound), or the lexical semantic representations for their second language are identical with those of their native language (subordinate). This diversity is reflected in the lack of consistence between results of various experimental studies.

The second problem is that when type of bilingualism *is* taken into consideration (i) subjects are put into one or the other category on the sole basis of the age of acquisition of their second language, with the consequence that coordinate bilinguals are grouped together with those who have learned their second language in school through translation on the grounds that both learned their two languages in different contexts; or (ii) compound bilinguals who have acquired both languages in the same context and subordinate bilinguals who have learned their second language through the first by translation are lumped together under the label "compound" (see Paradis, 1985, 1987, for details).

Results obtained were thus partly a function of linguistic rather than psycho-linguistic criteria: they varied as a function of the degree of overlap in meaning between the stimulus word and its translation equivalent. The more extensive the overlap in meaning, the greater the chances that the translation equivalent would trigger the same response as a repetition of the initial stimulus; the less extensive the overlap, the greater the chances that the translation equivalent would trigger a different response. These differences can be exacerbated by an increased overlap in meaning in the lexicon of compound and subordinate subjects.

One of the major problems, with many ramifications, has been the failure to distinguish between the meaning of words and nonlinguistic mental representations. The semantic field of each word is determined by language-specific constraints on its possible uses. Words share some but not all of the semantic features of their translation equivalents and will therefore not denote all of the same referents. The mental representation that corresponds to a word will thus differ to some extent from the mental representation corresponding to its translation equivalent. But the speaker has only one system of mental representations, which constitutes a third memory store, namely that of concepts (Paradis, 1980). Each language organizes the mental representations in accordance with its own lexical semantic constraints. This third cognitive system, phylogenetically and ontogenetically anterior to the language system(s) is independent of language and hence of the two languages, and remains available to the aphasic patient (Hécaen, 1968; Lecours & Joanette, 1980). Patients with jargonaphasia may nevertheless have normal scores on nonverbal intelligence tests (Beauvois & Dérouesné, 1976). Cognitive operations entailed in natural language persist despite severe aphasia (Gardner, Zurif, Berry & Baker, 1976). It is a common clinical observation that global aphasics who have no usable language and therefore no linguistic outlet for concepts nonetheless appear to control those concepts at nonlinguistic levels (Zurif & Blumstein, 1978). Even though an aphasic patient may have lost access to the word "mug" and "cup" and "glass", that person may nevertheless go to the store and buy a mug —not a cup. In spite of massive language loss global aphasic patients retain a rich conceptual system (Velletri, Gazzaniga & Primack, 1973).

We can thus distinguish between the lexical meaning of words, a part of the speaker's linguistic competence (a component of the lexical item, together with its syntactic features and phonological form), and hence vulnerable to aphasia, and conceptual representations which are outside of implicit linguistic competence and are not vulnerable to aphasia (but which are vulnerable to other forms of mental deterioration). Some concepts will be less easily verbalizable in one or the other of the patient's languages by virtue of the language system itself, and patients may find them all the more difficult to express in that language. But the conceptual system, where messages are elaborated before they are verbalized in the course of the encoding process, and where a mental representation is attained at the end of the decoding process, remains independent and isolable from the language systems.

Grammar and pragmatics

Bilinguals have been suspected of having their languages less asymmetrically represented in their cerebral hemispheres than unilingual speakers. That too has been shown not to be the case (Paradis, 1990, 1992, 1995a), if by language one refers to implicit linguistic competence, i.e., the grammar. Nevertheless, there is a sense in which individuals with a weaker second language (however acquired or learned) could enlist the participation of their right hemisphere (RH) for language functions to a greater extent than unilingual speakers. But in order to make such a claim, one must clearly distinguish between implicit linguistic competence (i..e, phonology, morphology, syntax, and the lexicon) on the one hand, and pragmatic aspects of language use (e.g., reliance on inferences from situational context, general knowledge, emotional prosody, mimicry, etc.) on the other. All clinical studies to date unambiguously point to the fact that implicit linguistic competence is subserved by areas of the left hemisphere (LH) of bilinguals in the same proportion as in unilinguals. On the other hand, there is increasing evidence from RH lesion studies to the effect that pragmatic and paralinguistic aspects of language use are subserved by areas of the RH. Hence it is not unlikely that, in order to compensate for their lacunae in implicit linguistic competence, speakers rely to a greater extent on pragmatic aspects (hence their RH) when using their weaker language, in the same way that children do during the acquisition of their native language (for further discussion, see Paradis, 1994a).

The failure to differentiate between grammar and pragmatics has resulted in a long drawn-out series of controversies as to whether there is a greater participation of the RH in processing language in bilinguals than in unilinguals. The answer seems to be an unqualified "yes" and "no", depending on what one means by "language". If by "language" one means the language system, the speaker's implicit linguistic competence, the answer seems to be clearly "no". Some bilinguals, like some unilinguals, may process some of their grammar in their RH and show subtle morphosyntactic and/or phonological deficits subsequent to a RH lesion (Joanette, Lecours, Lepage & Lamoureux, 1983). But there is no clinical evidence (such as a greater incidence of crossed aphasia) or neuropsychological evidence (such as Wada testing or electrical stimulation of the brain) indicating *greater* participation. If, however, "language" refers to the normal use of language, including pragmatics, then the answer is a qualified "yes" —only in the case of the use of a weaker language.

Linguistic competence and metalinguistic knowledge

It is equally important to distinguish between implicit linguistic competence and metalinguistic knowledge. The former is acquired incidentally, is stored in the form of procedural know-how, without conscious knowledge of its contents, and is used automatically. The latter is learned consciously (possibly but not necessarily effortfully), is available for conscious recall, and is applied to the production (and comprehension) of language in a controlled manner. Implicit linguistic competence is acquired through interaction with speakers of the language in situational contexts. Metalinguistic knowledge is usually learned in school. The extent of metalinguistic knowledge about one's native language is generally proportional to one's degree of education. Very often, a foreign language is learned almost exclusively through metalinguistic knowledge and whatever linguistic competence develops subsequently does so through practice of the language in communicative situations. Considering that implicit linguistic competence is what is affected by aphasia, and that explicit knowledge is generally not impaired in aphasic patients, it is not unreasonable to expect that metalinguistic knowledge, together with all other items of episodic and encyclopædic declarative memory, remains available to aphasic patients. It is likewise not unlikely that some patients have been exposed to much more explicit metalinguistic knowledge during the learning of a foreign language than during the acquisition of their native language. Some patients may in fact have been schooled entirely in a second language, while continuing to use the first language in the home, a language in which they remain illiterate, and about which they may have little metalinguistic knowledge.

In such individuals, metalinguistic knowledge about their second and possibly weaker language may thus be more extensive than that about their native language. Subsequent to aphasia, they may lose access to their implicit linguistic competence equally in both languages but retain full access to their metalinguistic knowledge which, being more extensive in their non-native language, may give the impression of a preferential recovery of the language that was the least fluent before insult. While in reality, even though implicit linguistic competence is equally impaired in both languages, these patients have more metalinguistic knowledge to fall back on in their weaker language. And since they are aphasic, the fact that they speak slowly and control their production consciously and keep asking their interlocutor to slow down and/or repeat may go unnoticed, being masked by the fact that the patients, being aphasic, are expected to speak more effortfully anyhow (Paradis, 1994b).

Qualitative vs. quantitative differences

There is no linguistic function specific to the bilingual speaker. Borrowing, switching, mixing and translating from one language to another have their unilingual counterpart. Unilinguals, for instance, may use a formal expression in an otherwise familiar conversation. They may switch from one register to another (say, from speaking to one's infant to addressing the arresting officer about to hand out a ticket for jay walking or illegal parking). They may mix registers. They may paraphrase, that is they may say more or less the same thing using different words, different syntactic constructions, and, if paraphrasing into another sociolinguistic register, even different phonology —which are the very characteristics of translation. There is thus no need to postulate qualitative differences between the cerebral structures and/or mechanisms of bilinguals and unilinguals. Any difference in verbal behaviour would be a greater degree of reliance on pragmatics and/or metalinguistic knowledge, thus possibly involving to a greater extent the RH in the first instance and the declarative memory system in the second. But these are quantitative, not qualitative differences. Hence, as Pitres would have put it, there is no need to postulate any as yet undiscovered purely hypothetical neurofunctional substrate that would be specific to bilingual individuals and would have no homologue in uni-lingual brains (for further discussion, see Paradis, 1995b).

The only qualitative difference identified so far seems to be the cerebral processing of closed class words by individuals who have learned a second language after a certain age, as demonstrated by studies of event-related brain potentials (ERPs). Closed class words elicit identical ERPs in unilinguals and early bilinguals that are qualitatively different from those elicited in late bilinguals (Neville, Mills & Lawson, 1992, Webber-Fox & Neville, 1992; Webber-Fox & Neville, 1994). These studies would allow us to distinguish between bilingualism proper (or early bilingualism) from the ability to speak a second language, albeit with quasi native-like fluency and accuracy.

Once we are clear as to the ontological status of the claims we make, namely, whether we intend them as descriptive metaphors (like the various characterizations of implicit linguistic competence) or as the actual state of affairs in the real world in real time, or in other words, whether these claims are at the linguistic or at the neurolinguistic level of description; once we have distinguished between the language-specific meaning of words and alinguistic mental representations; once we have distinguished between implicit linguistic competence and pragmatic aspects of language use; and once we have distinguished explicit metalinguistic knowledge from implicit linguistic competence, then we are in a better position to examine the complex problems posed by aphasia in bilinguals and polyglots.

References

Beauvois, M.F., & Dérouesné, J. 1976. Un modèle de fonctionnement de la mémoire verbale, ses implications en pathologie cérébrale. *Buttetin de psychologie: la mémoire sémantique*. Numéro spécial annuel, 166-173.

Ervin, S., & Osgood, C.E. 1954. Second language learning and bilingualism. *Journal of Abnormal and Social Psychology*, **49** (supplement), 139-146.

Gardner, H., Zurif, E., Berry, T., & Baker, E. 1976. Visual communication in aphasia. *Neuropsychologia*, **14**, 275-292.

Hécaen, H. 1968. L'aphasie. In A. Martinet (ed.), *Le langage* (pp. 390-414). Paris: Gallimard

Joanette, Y., Lecours, A.R., Lepage, Y., & Lamoureux, M. 1983. Language in right-handers with right-hemisphere lesions: a preliminary study including anatomical, genetic, and social factors. *Brain and Language*, **20**, 217-248.

Kolers, P.A. 1968. Bilingualism and information processing. *Scientific American*, **218**, 78-86.

Lambert, W., & Fillenbaum, S. 1959. A pilot study of aphasia in bilinguals. *Canadian Journal of Psychology*, **13**, 28-34.

Lecours A.R., & Joanette, Y. 1980. Linguistic and other psychological aspects of paroxismal aphasia. *Brain and Language*, **10**, 1-23.

Neufeld, G. 1973. The bilingual's lexical store. *Working Papers in Bilingualism*, **1**, 35-65.

Neville, H.J., Mills, D.L., & Lawson, D.S. 1992. Fractionating language: different neural systems with different sensitive periods. *Cerebral Cortex*, **2**, 244- 258.

McCormack, P.D. 1974. Bilingual linguistic memory —independence or interdependence: two stores or one? In S.T. Carey (ed.), *Bilingualism, biculturalism and education* (pp. 115-118). Edmonton: University of Alberta Press.

McCormack, P.D. 1977. Bilingual linguistic memory —the independence-interdependence issue revisited. In P.A. Hornby (ed.), *Bilingualism* (pp.57-66). New York: Academic Press.

Paradis, M. 1980. Language and thought in bilinguals. In W.C. McCormack & H.J. Izzo (eds.), *The Six LACUS Forum* (pp. 420-431), Columbia, SC.: Hornbeam Press.

Paradis, M. 1985. On the representation of two languages in one brain. *Language Sciences*, **7**, 1-39.

Paradis, M. 1987. Bilinguisme. In J. Rondal & J.P. Thibaut (eds.), *Problèmes de psycholinguistique* (pp. 421-489). Bruxelles: Pierre Mardaga.

Paradis, M. 1990. Language lateralization in bilinguals: enough already! *Brain and Language*, **39**, 576-586.

Paradis, M. 1992. The Loch Ness Monster approach to bilingual language lateralization: a response to Berquier and Ashton. *Brain and Language*, **43**, 534-537.

Paradis, M. 1994a. Neurolinguistic aspects of simultaneous translation: the framework. *International Journal of Psycholinguistics*, **10**, 319-335.

Paradis, M. 1994b. Neurolinguistic aspects of implicit and explicit memory: implications for bilingualism and SLA. In N. Ellis (ed.), *Implicit and explicit learning of languages* (pp. 393-419). London: Academic Press.

Paradis, M. 1995a. Another sighting of differential language laterality in multilinguals, this time in Loch Tok Pisin: comments on Wuillemin, Richardson, and Lynch (1994). *Brain and Language*, **49**, (in press).

Paradis, M. 1995b. Bilingual aphasics, how atypical are they? In P. Coppens, Y. Lebrun & Basso (eds.), *Aphasia in atypical populations* (in press). Hillsdale, N.J.: Lawrence Erlbaum Associates.

Pitres, A. 1895. Etude sur l'aphasie chez les polyglottes. *Revue de médecine*, **15**, 873-899. [Translated in M. Paradis (ed.), *Readings on aphasia in bilinguals and polyglots* (pp. 26-49), Montreal: Marcel Didier.]

Rose, R.G., Rose, P.R., King N., & Perez, A. 1975. Bilingual memory for related and unrelated sentences. *Journal of Experimental Psychology: Human Learning and Memory*, **1**, 599-606.

Schreuder, R., & Weltens, B. 1993. *The bilingual mental lexicon*. Amsterdam: John Benjamins.

Tulving, E., & Colotla, V. 1970. Free recall of bilingual lists. *Cognitive Psychology*, **1**, 86-98.

Velletri, G., Gazzaniga, M., & Premack, D. 1973. Artificial language training in global aphasics. *Neuropsychologia*, **11**, 95-103

Walters, J. & Zatorre, R.J. 1978. Laterality differences for word identification in bilinguals. *Brain and Language*, **6**, 158-167.

Webber-Fox, C.M., & Neville, H.J. 1992. Maturational constraints on cerebral specialization for language processing: ERP and behavioral evidence in bilingual speakers. Paper presented at the 22nd Annual Meeting of the Society for Neuroscience, Anaheim, 26 October.

Webber-Fox, C.M., & Neville, H.J. 1994. Sensitive periods differentiate neural systems for grammatical and semantic processing: ERP evidence in bilingual speakers. Paper presented at the Cognitive Neuroscience Society inaugural meeting, San Francisco, 28 March.

Weinreich, U. 1953. *Languages in contact*. New York: Linguistic Circle.

Zurif, E., & Blumstein, S. 1978. Language and the brain. In M. Halle, J. Bresnan & G.A. Miller (eds.), *Linguistic theory and psychological reality* (229-245). Cambridge, MA.: MIT Press.

I. Theoretical and practical issues

1 The study of bilingual aphasia: Pitres' legacy

Yvan Lebrun

A hundred years ago, the French *Revue de Médecine* in its 15th volume (1895) published a paper which was to become a classic of the literature on aphasia in bi- and multilinguals. This article was entitled *Etude sur l'aphasie des polyglottes* and had been written by Pitres.

Jean-Albert Pitres was born in Bordeaux in 1848. He began studying medicine at the *Ecole Secondaire de Médecine* of his home-town. In 1870 he went to Paris and joined the army as an auxiliary physician. In 1872 he resumed his medical studies, this time in Paris, where he graduated. He came into contact with Jean Martin Charcot (1825-1893) who was busy establishing neurology as an autonomous discipline.

Pitres was for some time affiliated with the Collège de France and the Faculty of Medicine in Paris. With Charles Emile François-Franck (1849-1921) he initiated a series of experiments on the motor cortex. He defended a doctoral thesis on cardiac dilatation and soon thereafter was appointed professor of anatomy and histology at the newly created Faculty of Medicine in Bordeaux. Three years later, he began teaching clinical medicine. He made valuable contributions to histology, cardiology and pneumology, and later to neurology and neuropsychiatry. He published his *Leçons cliniques sur l'hystérie* and, with Régis, a volume on *Les obsessions et les impulsions*. Together with the anatomist Testut, he compiled an atlas entitled *Les nerfs en schéma*.

In 1885 Pitres became dean of the Faculty of Medicine in Bordeaux. He retained this position for 21 years. In 1898 he was elected to the French Academy of Medicine. During the first world war, he headed a department of neurology. In 1913 he was made *Commandeur de la légion d'honneur*. He died in his home-town on March 25, 1928 at 80 years of age.

Pitres' law

In his study of 1895 Pitres advocated the view that in bi- or multilingual aphasics, recovery usually takes place in the following manner: "After being general at the outset, aphasia regresses progressively. The patient first begins to understand, then to speak the language that was most familiar to him/her. Later on, s/he recovers the ability to understand and then to speak the other languages that s/he knew."

Pitres contended that "the most familiar language reappears first because it is the one that uses the most solidly established associations." By most familiar language Pitres meant the language which the patient used the most frequently and the most intensively before suffering cerebral damage. In many cases, this language is the patient's mother-tongue. There are cases, however, in which the most familiar language is a second language. This second language is then recovered before the mother-tongue.

This view of "the psycho-physical mechanism that determines the loss and ensures the return of the command of language in polyglot aphasics" has come to be known as Pitres' law.

Pitres' law is in fact a modification of the opinion put forward by Théodule Ribot in 1881 in his essay on *Les maladies de la mémoire*. Ribot had contended that following brain damage the language which was acquired first is less affected, or is recovered more quickly, than languages acquired later in life. Pitres changed Ribot's axiom by substituting the notion of intensiveness for the notion of antecedence.

The influence of the patient's linguistic environment

In the 20th century a sizeable number of cases have been reported which do not conform to Pitres' law. In some of the cases, the language that reappeared first was not the one which the patient had been most familiar with or had used most intensively. In others, of two equally familiar languages one was much better regained than the other.

One of the factors that play a part in the differential recovery of two equally well - mastered and frequently used languages seems to be the vernacular used by the people around the aphasic patient.

One of the first instances, if not the very first, of this sort to have been published, is the description which Lordat gave in 1843 of an aphasic priest. The patient lived in a small village called St. Guilhem-le-Désert, some 20 km from Montpellier, France. Following a stroke, he was for some time speechless but for the sound /i/ and an expletive which he uttered when he felt angry or frustrated. Eventually, he recovered the local dialect spoken by those around him, but not the French language, in which he had been fully conversant before his illness. Lordat commented: "Since his accident (...) he had only had occasion to speak with his domestics and with the country folk". This priest, then, recovered the dialect used by those around him but not French, which he had little opportunity to hear after he fell ill. In other words, his linguistic recovery was determined by his linguistic environment.

In several of the cases described by Pitres in his 1895 paper, the language spoken by the patient's caretakers also appears to have played a part in the recovery process. For instance, patient Nr. 3 had a very good command of Basque, French and the Bearn patois premorbidly. Following a stroke, she had right-sided hemiplegia and aphasia. She was cared for by relatives who spoke Basque and French indifferently. Eventually she recovered these two languages, but remained unable to express herself in the Bearn patois.

As for Pitres' patient Nr. 7, he premorbidly had a command of six different languages. Following a stroke, he lost all six languages. He was taken care of by his wife and by his family doctor. Both spoke French, and gradually the patient regained command of this language. He then went to stay with his mother and aunt, who always conversed in the Gascon patois. Within three days, the patient recovered the ability to use Gascon. Eventually he regained a limited command of his other four languages. Pitres remarked that "outside of his visits to the hospital, nobody spoke to him in any language other than French or the Gascon patois."

The influence of the language used to address and stimulate the patient may be so strong as to cause a foreign language to supersede the mother-tongue. Bychowski

Jean-Albert Pitres
1848-1928

(1919) reported the case of a Polish soldier who was serving in the Russian army. During a battle he was hit by a bullet in the left hemisphere and he became completely aphasic. He was admitted to a Russian hospital where a Russian nurse took special care of him. Ultimately, he recovered Russian far better than his mother-tongue.

In 1931 Veyrac reported the case of a female whose mother-tongue was English but who had used French daily since adolescence. She became aphasic following brain damage and eventually recovered French to a much greater extent than English. As Veyrac pointed out, the patient's environment was all French.

At times, the prevalence of a foreign language results from the patient's deliberate efforts to recover the vernacular of those around him. Halpern (1949) described a patient whose mother-tongue was American English. This man emigrated to Israel where he started using Hebrew daily. Following brain trauma, he initially had sensory aphasia that affected Hebrew more than English. Accordingly, when he left the hospital and returned home, he had difficulty interacting with his children, who knew only Hebrew. He felt so frustrated that he decided to relearn Hebrew at all costs. Eventually, he regained a fair command of that language, but at the expense, it would seem, of his mother-tongue whose recovery stagnated.

It appears, then, that the patient's linguistic environment and his desire to adjust to this environment may have a decisive influence on the way the various languages are recovered.

However, this is not always the case. In some instances, the patient's linguistic surroundings have little effect on the recovery process. In a paper by Ovcharova, Raichev, and Geleva (1968), a patient is described who had acquired German and Hungarian in childhood. He received his higher education in Hungarian. At age 30, he emigrated to Bulgaria, married a Bulgarian woman and used Bulgarian daily for 40 years. Following a stroke he was at first totally aphasic. Then he gradually and simultaneously regained command of German and Hungarian. The recovery of Bulgarian lagged far behind and remained partial, despite the linguistic environment and the fact that his wife understood only Bulgarian.

One may wonder why in some cases the linguistic surroundings influence the recovery process and why in others they do not. Apparently, the ages at which the polyglot acquired his various languages play a part in the differential effect of the linguistic environment. In the cases reported by Pitres the languages which were regained under the influence of the patient's caretakers had all been acquired in childhood.

It may be presumed that the priest of St. Guilhem-le-Désert described by Lordat acquired the Langue d'Oc when he was a child. Bychowski's patient had been exposed to the Russian language during childhood. In the case reported by Halpern, "Hebrew was (...) learned between the ages of 7 and 9 years from the Bible and prayer book."

By contrast, the patient of Ovcharova et al. seems to have been exposed to Bulgarian only after he emigrated to Bulgaria at age 30. Thus, he was an adult when he first acquired his third language. This may be the reason why he recovered it to a far lesser extent than his other two languages, even though he lived in an all-Bulgarian environment after he had become aphasic.

It would appear, then, that the influence of the patient's verbal surroundings on the recovery process is conditioned —at least in part— by the ages at which the patient acquired, or was first exposed to, his various languages. For the language spoken by the environment to have a decisive effect on the restitution of verbal skills, it seems necessary that the patient should have come into contact with this language before adulthood.

Language representation in the brain

Maybe a language which is acquired in childhood is stored in the brain differently from a language acquired in adulthood and for that reason may be more easily re-activated by the linguistic environment. Paradis (1994) has suggested that second languages which have been learned formally are subserved primarily by declarative memory, whereas the mother-tongue and second languages which have been acquired in conversational settings are sustained essentially by procedural memory. Paradis considers that these two memories are neurofunctionally and anatomically different and accordingly may be differentially affected by brain damage.

Verbal skills in childhood usually develop intuitively and implicitly. Permanent exposure to language in communicative situations fosters a linguistic competence which grows without deliberate and conscious efforts on the part of the child. In adults, on the contrary, language acquisition is conscious and requires much application. Moreover, it often takes place in a formal context.

It would seem that following brain damage, the linguistic environment can more easily revive languages which have been acquired in conversational settings than languages acquired in a more formal and self-conscious way.

Memory

Interestingly enough, at the end of the 19th century, Pitres realized that memory was not a unitary function and that various types of memories subserved the efficient use of language. In his 1895 study and even more so in his paper on *L'aphasie amnésique et ses variétés cliniques*, which was published in *Le Progrès Médical* in 1898, the Bordeaux scholar emphasized that the word "memory" refers to a variety of processes which are psychophysiologically distinct and which can be differentially affected by brain damage.

Loss and inhibition

Pitres also distinguished between loss and inaccessibility. He pointed out that in some cases brain lesions destroy linguistic knowledge, whereas in other cases they block the access to this knowledge. Inhibition rather than erasure must be assumed in polyglots who, like his patient Nr. 7, recover the use of one of their languages within a short period of time. Actually, in many cases of bilingual aphasia, patients are unable to mobilize part of their verbal knowledge, even though this knowledge is still present in their brain.

Similarly, monolinguals with amnestic aphasia have not lost their memories for words, but find it difficult to access items in their mental lexicon, unless they receive some external stimulation.

Comprehension versus expression

In his 1895 paper Pitres drew attention to the fact that in aphasics comprehension is often recovered before expression. If the patient knows several languages, these languages are usually recovered one after the other, comprehension returning before expression in each individual language.

At times, comprehension is restored to a large extent, while expression remains severely limited. It is as if the linguistic system is difficult to access, unless there is external stimulation.

Polyglot reactions

In none of the seven case studies which form the bulk of his 1895 paper did Pitres mention language mixing. His patients seem never to have shown linguistic interference. Occasionally they did react in a language different from the language in which they were addressed, but this shift was deliberate and due to their inability to actively use the language of their speech partner. But apparently they never confused their various languages.

This is surprising, as language mixing is very frequent in polyglot aphasics. *Polyglotte Reaktionen*, as the phenomena of mixing came to be called in the German literature of the 1920's and subsequently, have been repeatedly reported in investigations of bilingual aphasia.

At least three types of polyglot reactions can be distinguished. A first type comprises unexpected language switches. All of a sudden and for no apparent reason, the patient changes languages. For instance, a bilingual patient of Bálint's (1922) who had been requested in German to recite the names of the months, mentioned the first five names in German and then continued in Greek.

The second type of polyglot reaction consists of linguistic interferences. The patient's verbal output is a mingle-mangle of phrases, words and morphemes from different languages. An instance of this was reported by Kauders (1929). His patient's verbal output comprised German sentences interspersed with French, and to a lesser extent also English, phrases and idioms.

Mössner and Pilch (1971) described a woman who knew German and English and who, following brain damage, produced such sentences as "Ich kann nicht remember", "Krieg und peace", "Der Fahrer ist sober", "Ach du heaven nein".

At times, mixing occurs within words. A patient of Ilse and Karl Gloning (1965) who knew German and Hungarian, produced such blends as "zwettö" which resulted from the coalescence of German "zwei" and Hungarian "kettö", both of which mean "two".

In addition to lexical, there may also be syntactical interferences. The patient may form in one language sentences according to rules used in another language. For instance, a bilingual patient of Ovcharova et al. (1968) used Turkish sentence patterns in Bulgarian.

Polyglot patients may also spontaneously translate some of their utterances or they may translate verbal commands before, or instead of, executing them, as was observed by Veyrac (1931) in his first case.

Spontaneous translations may be observed not only in polyglots who have aphasia following left brain damage, but also in bi- or multilinguals who have suffered right brain damage and have no aphasia. Their spontaneous translations may occur in written as well as in spoken language. A right brain damaged patient whose mother-tongue was French but who knew Dutch well, would spontaneously translate some of the French words he was dictated or some of the written answers he gave (Lebrun, 1983).

This patient not infrequently deviated from the assignment he had been given. He would add words to the sentences he was to write to dictation or details to the drawings he was to reproduce. When asked afterwards why he had made uncalled for translations or additions, he would answer that he acted on the spur of the moment. He felt a sudden inclination to add something and he yielded to it.

As a matter of fact, right-brain damaged patients are prone to forget test instructions and to pursue their own inspiration. In a patient with right brain injuries, Poizner, Kaplan, Bellugi and Padden (1984) noted a tendency to supplement with written comments the drawings she had been requested to produce. In Albert's test of unilateral neglect, she omitted to cross out a number of lines on the left but added several lines of her own on the right.

When given two or three words and asked to form a sentence incorporating them, these patients not infrequently produce a story instead, but fail to use one or two of the given words. When requested to form a sentence containing the words *maison* (house) and *chat* (cat) a French-speaking patient of Hécaen, Dubois and Marcie's (1967) wrote "*Petite Christine fait* (sic) *attention au chat, ferme la porte, car sur la table j'ai laissé quelque chose qui pourrait le tenter*." This is a well-formed complex utterance, but it contains only one of the two words specified by the examiners.

In conversation, patients with right brain injuries often fail to answer to the point. They are inclined to wander from the topic and to indulge in digressions. A patient of Ross and Stewart (1981) who had a right frontal lesion, often drifted away from the subject of discussion.

Clinicians know how difficult it can be to obtain an accurate anamnesis from such patients, who tend to mention numerous irrelevant details and to follow the train of their thoughts instead of adhering to the subject-matter at hand. When questioned, Hécaen et al.'s (1967) patient would answer readily, interspersing her answers with digressions difficult to stop.

Cambier, Elghozi and Strube (1980) also observed garrulity and digressiveness in their patients with right-sided cerebral injuries. In patients who undergo right hemispherectomy because of intractable epilepsy, the operation may cause the verbosity to clear up, as was observed by Griffith and Davidson (1966).

Spontaneous translations in brain damaged polyglots have sometimes been construed as compulsive behaviours. In the case of patients with right-sided lesions it would seem that the behaviour proceeds from disinhibition rather than from compulsion.

The patients tend to disregard conversational rules and to adopt an egocentric verbal demeanour. They are not forced to translate, but do so because they feel like it, thereby waiving a number of conversational conventions. This can be viewed as a disorder of pragmatics.

The seven patients described by Pitres in 1895 all had, or had had, right-sided hemiplegia, testifying to damage suffered by their left hemispheres. The left-sided lesions accounted well for their aphasia.

Pitres does not mention any case of right-sided brain damage. Being interested in bilingual aphasia, he probably did not look for language deviances in right brain damaged people, as he lived at a time when it was assumed that the right hemisphere was "uneducated in words", at least in right-handers, who formed the vast majority of the population. It may be presumed that, like most of his contemporaries, Pitres did not expect lesions in the minor hemisphere to interfere with the use of language or to bring on deviant verbal behaviour.

Aphasia in deaf signers

In the literature on bilingual aphasia, aphasic deaf signers are only incidentally mentioned. Yet, many deaf signers are truly bi- if not trilingual. They are familiar with sign language and common written language, and may have some command of a foreign language in addition to their written mother-tongue. If they sustain brain damage, such signers often show deficits which can be compared, or contrasted, with what is observed in polyglot aphasics who are not deaf.

A review of the published cases of aphasia in deaf signers (Lebrun and Leleux, 1986) indicates that, as in hearing multilinguals, brain damage in deaf people may differently affect the various codes with which the patients are familiar. Indeed, even writing and fingerspelling may be disturbed to different degrees, although they both use the same system of orthography and are performed by the same hand. In a case reported by Critchley (1938), brain damage disturbed dactylology while sparing writing, whereas in a case reported by Tureen, Smolik and Tritt (1951) the reverse was observed.

Sarno, Swisher and Taylor Sarno (1969) once asked, "Is there a basic difference between the motor acts of moving a pen to produce a series of letters and manipulating one's fingers to produce the same letters?" Although what is meant by "basic difference" in this question is not quite clear, the cases reported by Critchley and by Tureen et al. show that writing and fingerspelling comprise sets of learned movements which may be selectively disturbed by brain damage despite the fact that both sets of movements are performed by the same limb and share the same symbolic values.

Unilateral deficit

It may also happen that writing and fingerspelling are affected to the same degree. When such is the case, the disorder —remarkably enough— may be unilateral. In 1896, one year after the publication of Pitres' paper on aphasia in polyglots, Joseph Grasset, whose career in Montpellier rather closely paralleled Pitres' in Bordeaux, gave a short description of a right-handed, congenitally deaf man who, following left cerebral infarction, lost the ability to write and to fingerspell with his right hand, while remaining able to do so with his untrained left hand. Reading and understanding of fingerspelling were unimpaired.

This case has been construed by later authors as an instance of peripheral pathology or of pure motor impairment. Grasset, however, who was an experienced neurologist and aphasiologist, insisted, in his description, that the disorder was of central origin and that the right upper limb, though paretic, could be efficiently used for all movements except those of writing and fingerspelling.

In all likelihood, then, Grasset's case is an example of unilateral agraphia affecting both ordinary writing and dactylology. It, therefore, can be compared with a case of unilateral right agraphia published by Pitres in 1884. Pitres' patient was a right-handed syphilitic wine merchant who following a cerebrovascular accident in the left hemisphere at first had right-sided hemiplegia and aphasia with reduced consciousness. After some time, his condition improved, and eventually he was left with right-sided hemianopia, slight paresis of the right leg and total inability to write with his right hand, despite the fact that this hand was no longer paralysed and performed normally in everyday actions including drawing. Except for the unilateral right agraphia, verbal skills had been completely recovered.

The patient could spell words aloud from memory but was unable to form the named letters with his preferred hand. He explained to Pitres: "I know perfectly well how the word 'Bordeaux' should be spelled, but when I try to write it with my right hand, I no longer know how to proceed."

The patient also found it impossible to write numbers. Nor could he turn script into block letters or vice versa. Copying was possible, but was slow and laborious. Actually, the patient drew from the model more than he transcribed it. He could recognize the short words which Pitres made him write passively in the air moving his right arm. Because he could no longer write with his right hand, this man trained his left hand. Eventually, his left-handed handwriting became regular and quite legible. Several months later, the patient was seen again, after he had made sustained but nevertheless fruitless efforts to relearn writing with his right hand. This, then, is a clear instance of right unilateral agraphia comparable to the one which was reported by Grasset at the end of the 19th century.

Ever since, few, if any, new cases of right unilateral agraphia have been reported. This, however, should not cast doubt on the reality of the syndrome and on the veracity of Pitres' and Grasset's observations. The dearth of reports may be due —at least in part— to the fact that clinicians do not systematically test writing with the non-preferred hand in brain damaged people. If the patient can no longer write with his preferred hand —usually the right one— though this hand is not paralyzed, he is often diagnosed as being agraphic, and left hand writing is not tested. In this way, a number of cases of unilateral right agraphia may have escaped notice.

Pitres in his 1884 paper compared his observation of agraphia with a case reported by his master Charcot in one of his lectures on aphasia. Charcot's patient was a Russian commissioned officer who premorbidly had had an excellent command of Russian, French and German. Following a stroke, he lost his ability to speak French and German, though he could still understand these languages. Eventually, he regained the capability of speaking French. The stroke is said to have also deprived the patient of his writing skills in his three languages. Apparently, however, writing with the non-preferred hand was not assessed. Therefore, one cannot be sure whether agraphia in Charcot's case was unilateral or bilateral.

Pitres himself does not seem to have been sensitive to the possible difference between his case and that of his master. He mentioned the two of them in the same breath, as two indisputable instances of what he calls pure motor agraphia. The fact that in his case agraphia was unilateral while in Charcot's case it may have been bilateral does not seem to have impressed him. Yet, it is plain that unilateral and bilateral agraphia, even if they are both observed in the absence of aphasia, cannot be accounted for in precisely the same way. In all likelihood, unilateral agraphia is not simply an attenuated form of bilateral agraphia. Pitres seems to have overlooked the difference.

Conclusion

Pitres, then, appears to have been particularly sensitive to the fact that brain damage may affect differently the various languages or codes with which an individual is familiar. In various publications he pointed out that a patient's verbal skills are seldom impaired or recovered uniformly. By doing so, he paved the way for a better and more precise nosography of communication disorders following brain injury. His papers testify to his keenness of observation and judgement. Furthermore, they are replete with notations that are still very instructive. His legacy should therefore be preserved and Pitres himself given a place in the pantheon of aphasiology.

References

Bálint, A. 1922. Bemerkungen zu einem Falle von polyglotter Aphasie. *Zeitschrift für die gesamte Neurologie und Psychiatrie*, **83**, 277-283.

Bychowski, Z. 1919. Ueber die Restitution der nach einem Schädelschuss verlorengegangenen Sprachen bei einem Polyglotten. *Monatsschrift für Psychiatrie und Neurologie*, **45**, 183-201.

Cambier, J., Elghozi, D., & Strube, E. 1980. Lésion du thalamus droit avec syndrome de l'hémisphère mineur. Discussion du concept de négligence thalamique. *Revue Neurologique*, **136**, 105-116.

Critchley, M. 1938. Aphasia in a partial deaf-mute. *Brain*, **61**, 163-169.

Gloning, I., & Gloning, K. 1965. Aphasien bei Polyglotten. Beitrag zur Dynamik des Sprachabbaus sowie zur Lokalisationsfrage dieser Störungen. *Wiener Zeitschrift für Nervenheilkunde*, **22**, 362-397.

Grasset, J. 1896. Aphasie de la main droite chez un sourd-muet. *Le Progrès Médical*, **4**, third series, 44.

Griffith, H., & Davidson, M. 1966. Long-term changes in intellect and behaviour after hemispherectomy. *Journal of Neurology, Neurosurgery, and Psychiatry*, **29**, 571-576.

Halpern, L. 1949. La langue hébraïque dans la restitution de l'aphasie sensorielle chez les polyglottes. *La Semaine des Hôpitaux*, **57**, 2473-2476.

Hécaen, H., Dubois, J., & Marcie, P. 1967. Aspects linguistiques des troubles de la vigilance au cours des lésions temporales antéro-internes droite et gauche. *Neuropsychologia*, **5**, 311-328.

Kauders, O. 1929. Über polyglotte Reaktionen bei einer sensorischen Aphasie. *Zeitschrift für die gesamte Neurologie*, **122**, 651-666.

Lebrun, Y. 1983. Cerebral dominance for language: A neurolinguistic approach. *Folia Phoniatrica*, **35**, 13-39.

Lebrun, Y., & Leleux, C. 1986. Central communication disorders in deaf signers. In Nespoulous, J.L., Perron, P., Lecours A. (eds.) *The biological foundations of gestures* (pp.255-269). Hillsdale, NJ.: Erlbaum.

Lordat, J. 1843. Analyse de la parole pour servir à la théorie de divers cas d'alalie et de paralalie (de mutisme et d'imperfection du parler) que les nosologistes ont mal connus. Leçons tirées du Cours de Physiologie de l'année scolaire 1842-1843. *Journal de la Société de Médecine Pratique de Montpellier*, 7, 333-353; 417-433; 8, 1, 17.

Mössner, A., & Pilch, H. 1971. Phonematisch-syntaktische Aphasie. Ein Sonderfall motorischer Aphasie bei einer zweisprachigen Patientin. *Folia Linguistica*, 5, 394-409.

Ovcharova, P., Raichev, R., & Geleva, T. 1968. Afaziia u poligloti. *Nevrologiia, Psikhiatriia i Nevrokhirurgiia*, 7, 183-190.

Paradis, M. 1994. Neurolinguistic aspects of implicit and explicit memory: Implications for bilingualism and SLA. In N. Ellis (ed.) *Implicit and explicit learning of languages* (pp. 393-419). London: Academic Press.

Pitres, A. 1884. Considérations sur l'agraphie. *Revue de Médecine*, 4, 855-873.

Pitres, A. 1895. Etude sur l'aphasie des polyglottes. *Revue de Médecine*, 15, 873-899.

Pitres, A. 1898. L'aphasie amnésique et ses variétés cliniques. *Progrès Médical*, 7 (3e série), 321-324; 337-340; 369-371; 401-404; 8, 17-23; 65-70.

Poizner, H., Kaplan, E., Bellugi, U., & Padden, C. 1984. Visual-spatial processing in deaf brain damaged signers. *Brain and Cognition*, 3, 281-306.

Ribot, T. 1881. *Les maladies de la mémoire*. Paris, Alcan.

Ross, E., & Stewart, M. 1981. Akinetic mutism from hypothalamic damage: Successful treatment with dopamine agonists. *Neurology*, 31, 1435-1439.

Sarno, J., Swisher, L., & Taylor-Sarno, M. 1969. Aphasia in a congenitally deaf man. *Cortex*, 5, 398-414.

Tureen, L., Smolik, E., & Tritt, J. 1951. Aphasia in a deaf mute. *Neurology*, 1, 237-244.

Veyrac, G. 1931. Etude de l'aphasie chez les sujets polyglottes. Doctoral thesis. Paris.

2 The neural substrates of bilingual language processing: evidence from positron emission tomography

Denise Klein, Robert J. Zatorre, Brenda Milner,
Ernst Meyer and Alan C. Evans

The cerebral localization of languages in the polyglot speaker has received a great deal of attention, both in the past, and over the last decade (Whitaker, 1989). The representation of multiple languages in the brain has been investigated by examining patterns of language impairment and recovery in polyglot aphasics (Paradis, 1977, 1989, 1993), by the mapping of sites where electrical stimulation alters naming in bilingual individuals (Penfield and Roberts, 1959; Ojemann and Whitaker, 1978; Ojemann, 1983), and by experimental studies with normal volunteer subjects (see Albert and Obler, 1978). Despite this research effort, it has proven difficult to determine conclusively whether different languages share the same neural substrate. Many investigators have argued against the view of separate neuronal mechanisms for each language (e.g., Penfield, 1953; Penfield & Roberts, 1959), but others have proposed differential language representation, and some have even gone so far as to suggest greater participation of the right hemisphere in the acquisition and use of a second language (e.g., Albert & Obler, 1978; Sussman, Franklin & Simon, 1982; Wuillemin & Richardson, 1994). Ojemann & Whitaker have also suggested that, as a language becomes more automatised, a less extensive area of cortex will subserve this language than would subserve a language in which one is less fluent, but this interpretation has been questioned for methodological reasons relating to the placement of electrodes during cortical stimulation (Paradis, 1993).

In recent years, positron emission tomography (PET) has been used to investigate the neuronal processes that underlie linguistic performance in normal unilingual volunteer subjects (see Raichle, 1994 for a review). The use of PET as a technique for measuring activity-related changes in regional cerebral blood flow (rCBF) provides new possibilities for resolving the question of bilingual language organization, and allows us to assess the similarities and differences in bilingual and unilingual processing. We describe a PET study in which we have used functional imaging techniques to investigate whether performance in a second language (L2) involves the same neural substrates as that of a first language (L1) in normal bilingual subjects who learned L2 after age five. In this chapter we outline the basic methodology adopted, discuss its application to language research involving unilingual subjects, and then provide a review of our bilingual study.

Positron Emission Tomography

Methodological considerations

Historically, the exploration of brain functional anatomy has used methods of clinicopathological correlation. Enormous difficulties and great uncertainty surround the interpretation of the signs and symptoms associated with damage or disease of localized brain regions (Porter, 1991). The introduction of non-invasive tools for the quantitative mapping of cerebral function in human subjects (e.g., cerebral blood flow measurement and positron emission tomography) in conjunction with detailed in vivo tomographic morphology (magnetic resonance imaging) has led to the development of a new form of neuroscience whose aim is to explore brain function directly in the human subject (Raichle et al., 1983; Fox & Raichle, 1984). These methods provide a precision of anatomical localization that far exceeds that attainable with human brain lesion studies. Moreover, the study of healthy subjects avoids possible confounding effects of brain lesions, such as compensatory reorganization of brain function. PET-CBF studies have already identified several cortical areas involved in higher-order cognitive tasks. [For general reviews of PET technology and methodology, see Raichle (1989) and Stytz & Frieder (1990)].

The basic rationale for using PET activation studies is that the performance of any task places specific information processing demands on the brain. These demands are met through changes in neural activity in various functional areas (Posner et al., 1988). Changes in neuronal activity produce changes in local blood flow (Raichle 1989; Frostig et al., 1990), which can be measured with PET.

A principal method for measuring rCBF using PET involves bolus injections of oxygen-15 (O^{15}). Because the half-life of O^{15} is only 123 sec, these methods allow repeated scans spaced 12-15 min apart. Once the images have been obtained, a proportional scaling system is used to transform the tomographic location coordinates into coordinates within Talairachís stereotactic atlas of the human brain (Talairach & Tournoux, 1988). Superimposition of the magnetic resonance images (MRI) of brain anatomy onto the PET image allows for even more direct localization of anatomical landmarks (Evans et al., 1991a). Numerous factors concerning the counting of radioactivity, image reconstruction and kinetic model-fitting contribute to statistical noise (Worsley et al., 1992). Several methods have been developed to reduce this noise. The most common is image smoothing, which reduces noise at the cost of reducing spatial resolution. A second method of noise reduction is that of scan averaging, either within or between subjects. This averaging procedure is made possible by converting all scans to Talairach coordinates and interpolating values for pixels that fall between images. Because of interindividual variability in the precise location of rCBF activations, the magnitude of activations is reduced by this method, but the noise reduction achieved far outweighs activation diminution, resulting in dramatically improved signal-to-noise ratios.

The most powerful experimental designs exploit the ability to obtain multiple scans in individual subjects. Pairs of scans can be contrasted by subtracting one scan, pixel by pixel, from another. Central to PET studies of cognitive functions is the subtraction method, which consists of the use of successive and complementary tasks that comprise similar mental operations, except for one or a few component operations that differentiate the tasks from one another (Posner et al., 1988). By comparing activation in two such tasks, it is theoretically possible to isolate the activated areas uniquely associated with the operations that distinguish the two tasks, and thus to identify and localize the neural substrates underlying the performance of these operations. Although the subtraction method has heuristic value, and offers a way of comparing performance and neural activation between two closely related tasks, there are some limitations inherent in this method. Such an approach is exposed to difficulties, particularly because, in the case of verbal stimuli, processing may unfold automatically, or implicitly, to include operations that are not necessarily requested by the task demands. Also, the pattern of activation derived by a subtraction is relative, and is critically dependent on the chosen control task. That is, the difference in activation, representing the added task-processing demands, varies as a function of the actual operations performed in the control task and depends on the extent to which the control and the experimental tasks share common underlying processes. It is therefore incumbent upon the investigator to be aware of such processes in interpreting the data. Factors intrinsic to the design of experimental tasks, such as the rate of stimulation, degree of attentional demands, practice, and difficulty could all have significant effects on the distribution of activated brain regions. These issues imply that the proper design of tasks is critical to the interpretation of the distributed patterns of cerebral activity.

Language-activation studies in unilingual volunteer subjects

Language is perhaps the most studied process in brain-imaging research (Haxby et al., 1991). Prior to our studies, this research has been conducted exclusively in unilingual normal volunteer subjects. Using measurements of changes in local brain blood-flow obtained with PET as a marker of changes in local neuronal activity, investigators have examined the processing of single word stimuli (e.g., Petersen et al., 1988, 1989; Wise et al., 1991, Frith et al., 1991, Zatorre et al., 1992; Demonet et al., 1992; Raichle et al., 1994). These studies have revealed the distributed, modular nature of these processes, and have provided some preliminary insights into the substrates subserving different linguistic functions.

In studies designed to examine, at several levels, the processing of single words, Petersen et al. (1988, 1989) identified several regions potentially involved in lexical processing and provided a framework for the development and interpretation of subsequent PET investigations of language processing. They looked at three levels of change: simple presentation of common English nouns compared with no presentation; repetition aloud of nouns compared to simple presentation; and generation aloud of a verb appropriate to the presented noun, compared with repetition. The active state from one level acted as the control for the next level of analysis. Each of these levels was assessed in one set of scans with visual input and in another set of scans with auditory input. The auditory mode of presentation is most relevant to our discussion, but we shall briefly present the overall findings.

Passive presentation of words appeared to activate modality-specific primary and extraprimary sensory-processing areas. When words were presented visually, several areas of extrastriate visual cortex were activated in both hemispheres. The auditory presentation of words activated areas bilaterally along the superior temporal gyrus (STG), as well as a left-lateralized area in the temporoparietal cortex. When the repeat-aloud tasks were compared to the passive tasks, similar areas of activation for auditory and visual presentation were found (as would be expected, because the sensory-specific activation would be subtracted away). For both auditory and visual cues, speech output produced activation in areas that have been implicated in some aspects of motor programming, including primary sensorimotor mouth cortex, the supplementary motor area (SMA), and regions of the cerebellum. Several areas in the Sylvian-opercular cortex and a left-lateralized region on the lateral surface of the frontal cortex were also activated. The final subtraction in the Petersen et al. (1988) study, that of generating a verb compared to repeating a word aloud, made additional processing demands; two foci in the anterior cingulate cortex were activated, as well as several regions of the left anterior inferior frontal cortex and the right inferior lateral cerebellum.

The results concerning early visual and auditory processing, as well as some relating to higher cognitive processes, have found support from subsequent PET studies and relate well to what is known about the brain from the lesion literature. Marrett et al. (1990), Wise et al. (1991) and Petersen et al. (1990) have shown extrastriate activation with the presentation of visual words. Activation near Heschlís gyrus and the middle portion of the STG has been found for a wide range of auditory stimuli, including clicks, noise, tones, words, orthographically regular nonwords and real words played backwards (Lauter et al., 1985; Wise et al., 1991; Zatorre et al., 1992, 1994), which suggests a localization to primary and surrounding extraprimary auditory cortex. Simple repetition of visual and auditory words has been found to activate Sylvian-opercular and premotor regions bilaterally.

Most of the findings relating to primary sensory processing and motor output reported above have been uncontroversial., but the localization of higher cognitive functions and their interpretation (e.g., areas activated when subjects perform phonological and semantic operations) have given rise to more debate (see Demonet et al., 1993; Liotti et al., 1994). In the context of the study we report, we will focus on the controversy concerning the neural substrates involved in semantic processing. The activation of the left anterior inferior frontal gyrus (LIFG) in the noun-verb generation task (Petersen et al., 1988), and in a second semantic task requiring subjects to note the presence of dangerous animals in a list of words (Posner et al., 1988), has led to the suggestion that this region is related to a semantic network supporting the type of word associations involved in generation and monitoring tasks (Petersen et al., 1988; Posner et al., 1988). On a covert noun-verb generation task, however, Wise et al. (1991) observed left posterior temporal activation, and suggested that it is this region that primarily relates to word comprehension and semantic processing. Frith et al. (1991) advanced a different interpretation, because they observed left prefrontal cortex activation on a task that did not require semantic analysis (generating words starting with f or s), and failed to find frontal activation in an antonyms task, in which subjects were required to produce a meaning opposite to the word they heard. Moreover, there has been some discrepancy between some of the functional imaging results and many clinical views on the location of semantic association. From the aphasia literature it would be expected that the posterior superior temporal region should be involved in semantic processing, but instead it has been the LIFG that has been activated in most functional imaging studies involving word-generation tasks (e.g., Petersen et al., 1988, Frith et al., 1991). There are many reasons for the conflicting findings. From a methodological point of view, in functional imaging, the choice of activation and baseline tasks will determine the areas of rCBF change observed. Thus, if repetition is used as a baseline task, some aspect of semantic processing should be eliminated in the subtraction, because it is likely that hearing a familiar word will automatically involve some level of comprehension. Thus, if posterior STG is part of the semantic system, the participation of this region may not be revealed in a comparison of two tasks that both involve the semantic system, such as synonym generation and repetition of familiar words. Moreover, these tasks may tap only one specific aspect of semantic processing, whereas a different type of semantic computation, involving the integration of the processing and production of structured word-strings may activate different brain regions. A third important possibility is that the LIF region is not specifically engaged in semantic processing, but codes stimulus-response associations independent of the type of response required. If it is the processes of lexical search and retrieval that are dependent on the activity of this region, then one would expect that the LIFG would be activated by all tasks that require generation, irrespective of whether they involve synonym or rhyme generation or an across-language translation. In a comparison of rhyme and synonym generation, we have found this to be the case and thus have concluded that the LIFG is involved in search and retrieval processes in general, rather than being specific to semantic processing (Klein et al., 1994b,c).

Although the exact interpretation of the role of the LIFG and its relation to semantic processing has been called into question, it now seems plausible to suppose that when unilingual subjects make a verbal response selection, two distinct circuits are called into play. An apparent reciprocal relationship has been found, such that the left prefrontal cortex becomes active when speaking an appropriate verb for a heard noun, but becomes reduced during the repetition of a heard noun. In contrast, the Sylvian-insular cortex is active bilaterally when repeating a heard noun, but reduced in terms of its rCBF pattern when subjects produce a verb for a heard noun (Raichle et al., 1994). This has led to the postulation of (1) a pathway for non-automatic processing involving the anterior cingulate, left prefrontal and left posterior temporal cortices and right cerebellar hemisphere; and (2) a pathway for automatic processing involving areas of Sylvian-insular cortex bilaterally (Raichle et al., 1994).

In the PET studies involving unilingual subjects reported above, it has been assumed that responses to these associative generation tasks reflect lexical organisation. In the bilingual, this type of task can provide a window on the degree of separation or commonality of the two lexical systems. For example, we may ask how translation equivalents are stored and how such storage compares to storage of synonyms in the same language of given bilingual subjects. In this chapter we report how these hypotheses about bilingualism were tested by applying PET techniques in the context of a cognitive neuroscience approach.

Language activation in bilingual volunteer subjects

The PET studies reported above have constrained their language tasks to the investigation of single lexical items. In our study, we maintained the use of single-word stimuli because we believe that tasks such as repeating a heard word, or generating a synonym or a translation, require the interplay of a complex and highly specialized network of distinct brain regions, and are likely to engage many if not all portions of such networks. We took advantage of these seemingly simple tasks to investigate whether comprehension and production of L2, learned after age five, would activate identical regions to those involved in the repetition and generation of a word in the native language (L1).

We used PET to investigate word-generation in English-dominant subjects (who were also proficient in French), when they performed a semantic search, either within one of their languages or across-languages by means of translation. Two control tasks required word repetition in each language. It was hypothesized that such an investigation would provide opportunities for ascertaining whether storage of translation equivalents is the same or different from storage in the same language for given bilingual subjects; and whether the same neural substrates subserve the second language as those that subserve the first.

Twelve right-handed native speakers of English (L1), all of whom were proficient in French (L2), gave informed consent to undergo PET scanning, which was performed according to institution-reviewed medico-ethical guidelines. The mean age of the group was 22 years (6 male, 6 female) and each subject had acquired French after the age of five. The mean age of L2 acquisition was 7.3 years. Our sample included a wide range of ages of acquisition, but we took care to obtain bilinguals with roughly equivalent language competence. To the extent that the second language was learned later, after the first language had been acquired, and in a second-language setting, we hypothesized that any differences observed in cerebral representation of these subjects, would be elicited by the chosen subtractions.

rCBF was measured by the $H_2{}^{15}O$ intravenous bolus method with inter-subject averaging, and co-registration of magnetic resonance and PET images (Fox et al., 1985; Raichle et al., 1983; Fox & Raichle, 1984; Evans et al., 1991a,b and 1992). This was performed according to the method carried out at the Montreal Neurological Institute (see Klein et al., 1994 a & b for a more detailed description). The subjects were scanned under seven conditions of testing (Klein et al., 1994b). Six of the conditions are relevant to this discussion. The results of the seventh condition (rhyme generation), which was performed last in each subject, are reported elsewhere (Klein et al., 1994b) and will not be discussed here. In each condition, the subjects heard stimulus words, presented binaurally through insert earphones, and were required to give a single word response. The stimuli were matched item by item across each list on a range of psycholinguistic variables, such as length, syllable number, frequency and part-of-speech. Previous pilot testing of normal volunteer subjects not used in the actual PET study ensured that all lists were matched for difficulty and latency in producing the responses.

Table 1. Activation conditions

TASK		EXAMPLE	
		Cue	*Response*
1. Repeat English Words	(L1REP)	contestant	contestant
2. Repeat French Words	(L2REP)	pardessus	pardessus
3. Generate Synonym English	(L1SYN)	beverage	drink
4. Generate Synonym French	(L2SYN)	converser	parler
5. Translate English-French	(L1TRAN)	forget	oublier
6. Translate French-English	(L2TRAN)	réussir	succeed

In the baseline conditions, repetition of a presented item was required. The subjects then performed generation tasks involving a semantic search in each language; and translation from English to French and vice versa. The sensory input and motor output were similar in the stimulated (generation) and control (repetition) conditions, since all tasks involved listening to a single word and producing a single spoken response. L1 repetition was used to control for all tasks where input was in L1; L2 repetition was used for all tasks where the input was in L2. We hypothesized that subtraction of word-repetition from each of the respective word-generation tasks would allow us to observe the intended differences between the tasks: the generation of a semantic associate in L1 and L2 and the search and retrieval of a translational associate from L1 to L2 and vice-versa. Table 1 illustrates the task design.

In the behavioral data, there were no differences in accuracy or latency of response to the two language lists for repetition or translation; but subjects were significantly slower and less accurate at generating a synonym in L2 than in L1 ($p < 0.01$).

The regions of significant rCBF increase in the LIFG are shown across conditions in Figure 1 for purposes of comparison. In addition to the foci shown here, we observed distinct foci in the LIFG and immediately adjacent posterior dorsolateral frontal cortex in each of the word-generation tasks, as compared to the appropriate baseline repetition task. Across all the task subtractions, there was considerable overlap in the frontal activations observed, independent of the search requirement (synonym or translation), and irrespective of whether the search took place in the first or second language. The left-hemisphere contribution to these tasks was impressive, and no right-hemisphere cortical activations were observed. The various generation tasks used in our study did not differ substantially in the distribution of rCBF activation they elicited, although they appear to differ in their cognitive demands. As a further test of this observation, we directly compared L1-synonym to L1-translate and to L2-synonym and no significant activation (t(3.5) in the frontal lobe was detected. Similarly no significant frontal activations were observed when L2-synonym was compared to L2-translate. Thus, despite the slightly different configurations of rCBF visible across tasks in Figure 1, the underlying frontal-lobe activations were essentially identical. The activations in the LIFG across all our generation tasks were similar to those reported in the study of Petersen et al. (1988) and subsequently confirmed by other investigators (Raichle et al., 1994).

With regard to the posterior speech region, and its relation to semantic processing, we did not observe a superior temporal activation on our task, probably due to the fact that the control task of word repetition also activates the semantic system, and therefore the posterior temporal cortex. Semantic processing probably occurs automatically when subjects listen to words. For example, Wise et al. (1991) and Zatorre et al. (1992) , amongst others, have activated the superior temporal cortex in auditory word tasks with baseline control states that did not require word repetition, but Petersen et al. (1988) failed to observe a blood-flow response of significance in this area when they compared word generation with word repetition.

Interestingly, we did find a focus of significant activation in the left inferior temporal cortex in several of our subtractions during tasks requiring word generation. Using similar tasks and subtractions, Raichle et al. (1994) have also observed an inferior temporal activation, although 16.6mm superior to ours (Klein et al., 1994b). Raichle et al. have argued for two separate areas in the temporal cortex responsible for the processing of words: a more dorsal area for auditorily presented words, and a

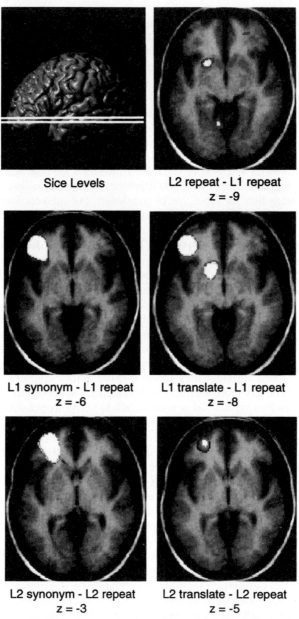

Sice Levels

L2 repeat - L1 repeat
z = -9

L1 synonym - L1 repeat
z = -6

L1 translate - L1 repeat
z = -8

L2 synonym - L2 repeat
z = -3

L2 translate - L2 repeat
z = -5

Figure 1. The figure shows the averaged PET subtraction image of rCBF increases in the left inferior frontal gyrus (LIFG) for all 12 subjects, superimposed upon the averaged MRI scans. The upper left panel shows a lateral view of the left hemisphere, the white lines indicate the lowest (z = −9) and highest (z = −3) levels for the cuts of each of the horizontal sections. The rest of the panels show a horizontal slice indicating the main finding for each subtraction. The subjectís left is on the left side in all the horizontal sections. Horizontal slices are taken through the most inferior of the left frontal peaks for each subtraction, and the z level (Talairach and Tournoux, 1988) is indicated for each section. The top right panel shows the subtraction of L2repeat − L1repeat. Note the single significant rCBF change in the left putamen. The middle panel shows L1synonym −'L1repeat and L1translate − L1repeat. Note the strong LIFG activations for both subtractions. Also visible is the strong left putaminal activation when L2 output is compared to L1 output in L1translate − L1repeat. The bottom two sections show L2-synonym − L2-repeat and L2-translate − L2 repeat. The left frontal activations are in similar positions to the previous images.

more ventral area for visually presented words; but our finding of a ventral activation in relation to auditory tasks casts doubt on such an interpretation.

For both synonym-generation tasks in either language and for across-language translation tasks, we also found evidence for the existence of an apparent reciprocal relationship between left prefrontal cortex (active when generating but reduced during repetition), and the Sylvian-insular cortices bilaterally (active when repeating heard words, but inactive when generating). Our findings confirmed Raichle et al.'s (1994) suggestion of two pathways that are distinguished by the degree to which the task at hand is learned or automatic, with word generation requiring the non-automatic pathway, and word repetition playing an important role in the automatic pathway for verbal response selection.

We also observed left parietal and right cerebellar activations, although the activations varied in strength across conditions, and did not always reach significance for our whole-brain tests. Nevertheless, nearly significant positive activations were observed in similar locations in all of these subtractions, making it likely that these areas have some computational process in common in all these tasks. The distributed neuronal networks observed here suggest that within- and across-language lexical searches are unlikely to be subsumed in a single enclosed localization, and that several types of coding must be coordinated to perform these computations.

The results of the subtractions suggest that within- and across-language searches involve similar distributed networks even when there are differences in the accuracy and latencies across the tasks, strongly suggesting that word generation in the two languages makes demands on overlapping neural substrates.

One additional unexpected activation emerged from this investigation. A strong rCBF activation in the left putamen (visible in Fig.1) was observed in the L1-translate–L1-repeat subtraction, but was not present in the equivalent L2-translate–L2-repeat subtraction, nor in the subtractions of L1-synonym–L1-repeat, L2-synonym–L2-repeat. What is specific to the L1-translate–L1-repeat subtraction is that the subject is required to produce a spoken response in L2. In an effort to determine whether output of response contributes to activation in the putamen we compared rCBF changes when subjects repeated words in L2 with repeating words in L1. The PET results demonstrated that the pattern of rCBF was strikingly similar across the two conditions, with only a single significant rCBF change in the vicinity of the left putamen. No other significant increases or decreases in rCBF were detected. This focus was in a similar position to the one observed in the L1-translate–L1-repeat subtraction (Klein et al., 1994a). The activation of the left putamen indicates that additional neural processes within this structure are required for production of L2 as compared to L1.

Previous PET studies of language-processing in unilinguals have not demonstrated subcortical activation sites. This does not necessarily mean that there is no subcortical contribution to language output, even in unilinguals, but that previous studies were not designed to elicit this particular component. The findings of this study allowed us to postulate that activation of the left putamen is a function of the increased articulatory demands imposed by speaking a language learned later in life. We hypothesized that this provides evidence for the contribution of the left basal ganglia in articulation, namely when the task requires precise timing of motor output (Klein et al., 1994a). Lesion studies of basal ganglia function concur with the interpretation that these structures subserve complex motoric processes involved in articulation and fine motor skills (Crosson, 1992; Volkmann et al., 1992). A complementary role for the right putamen in the motor control of prosody has also been suggested (Cohen et al., 1994).

Our interpretation of left putaminal involvement in articulatory processes in L2 finds support from studies of "foreign accent syndrome" (Blumstein et al., 1987; Gurd et al., 1988). Rarely, subsequent to left hemisphere damage, unilingual individuals develop articulatory difficulties that mimic a foreign accent, a symptom clearly distinct from dysarthrias or apraxias of speech. Although lesion sites in foreign accent syndrome vary, the left basal ganglia are often implicated (e.g., Blumstein et al., 1987; Gurd et al., 1988). However, strokes of the basal ganglia are not sufficiently focussed to discriminate between cortical disconnection and direct putaminal involvement. The observation of putaminal activation in our L2 repetition task adds support for the specific contribution of this structure in articulation, particularly in the precise timing of motor output. Our findings thus help to explain why lesions to the left basal ganglia may produce a foreign accent syndrome.

Comment

In this chapter we have described how developments in measuring local rates of rCBF in the brain have made it possible to investigate functional neuroanatomy in healthy unilingual subjects. PET-rCBF studies have already identified several cortical areas involved in higher-order cognitive processing, indicating that functional neuroimaging may reveal answers about human brain functioning that have so far proved elusive. We have also begun to apply this method to the study of bilingual individuals. Strikingly similar patterns of rCBF change were observed in the L1 and L2 tasks, suggesting that the same neural processes subserve second-language performance as subserve the first. At least on these particular tasks, we find no evidence to support the hypothesis that a language learned later in life is represented differently from the native language; nor do we find differences in the neural substrates that subserve within- and across-language searches. Moreover, translation appears to require similar processes to those necessary for accomplished performance within a single language.

Thus far, most of the functional imaging work with unilingual subjects has been performed with groups of subjects, using inter-subject averaging. The bilingual study we have implemented also makes use of group averaging. Our data cannot yet explain the phenomenon of selective patterns of recovery of the various languages of bilingual aphasic patients. Also, the issue of whether a wider area of cortex may be called into play when languages are less well known remains open (Ojemann, 1983). Nevertheless, even though specific methods are not currently available to evaluate the spatial extent of an activation pattern, on the basis of what we know about PET, one would expect that any differences between the two languages should be observed in the appropriate subtractions, but no such differences were found.

Inter-subject averaging studies of language activation are a necessary preliminary stage, but single-subject studies are critical if issues of anatomical and cognitive interindividual variability are to be addressed. Intra-subject averaging of individual anatomo-functional organization will allow for more meaningful comparisons to be made in relation to the patterns of recovery of the various languages of bilingual aphasic patients (Paradis, 1993) and the patterns of organization of the two languages, as indicated by cortical stimulation mapping during naming (Ojemann, 1983).

In addition, restrictions imposed by radiation dosage limit the number of activation states that can be sampled within a single study, and hence allow for only a small part of language to be examined at one time. Many more studies will thus be required in order to build up a comprehensive picture. There are still many questions about language processing, both as regards the unilingual individual and the polyglot, that remain unresolved and that will no doubt be the subject of future investigations. The study reported here examined only a single aspect of linguistic processing; it will be interesting in future to see if similar results are obtained for more complex linguistic tasks. It will also be important to study languages that are structurally more distinct than are English and French, and which may therefore call on different neural mechanisms. Despite these constraints, our results provide no support for the hypothesis that a language learned later in life is represented differently from the native language; nor do we find evidence in favor of a specific right-hemisphere contribution to bilingual processes. With regard to the question of the functional representation of multiple languages, speaking in L1 and L2 may differ in cognitive demands, but from this initial experiment, we conclude that the same specialized cerebral regions are active in both cases, except for the articulatory demands of L2, which may require additional processing in the left putamen.

Future studies involving individuals with varied linguistic histories, a diversity of languages, and a wider range of linguistic tasks will no doubt reveal more about the representation of the two languages of the bilingual. Such an approach also offers a unique vantage point from which to investigate verbal processes in general and has potential for constraining models of language processing.

Acknowledgements.

We thank Natalie Routhier and Pierre Ahad, together with the staff of the McConnell Brain Imaging Centre for their technical assistance. This work was supported by grants from the Medical Research Council of Canada (MT2624, SP-30 & MT11541), the McDonnell-Pew Program in Cognitive Neuroscience, and the Fonds de la Recherche en Santé du Québec.

References

Albert M., Obler L. K. (eds). 1978. *The Bilingual Brain*. New York: Academic Press.

Blumstein, S. E., Alexander, M. P., Ryalls, J. H., Katz, W. & Dworetzky, B. 1987. On the nature of the foreign accent syndrome: A case study, *Brain and Language*, **31**, 215-244 .

Cohen, M. J., Riccio, C. A., Flannery, A. M. 1994. Expressive aprosodia following stroke to the right basal ganglia: A case report. *Neuropsychology*, **8**, 242-245.

Crosson, B. 1992. *Subcortical Functions in Language and Memory*. New York: Guilford Press.

Demonet, J. F., Chollet, F., Ramsay, S., Cardebat, D., Nespoulous, J. L., Wise, R. et al. 1992. The anatomy of phonological and semantic processing in normal subjects. *Brain*, **115**, 1753-68.

Demonet, J. F., Price, C., Wise, R., Frackowiak, J. 1993. Language functions explored in normal subjects by positron emission tomography, *Human Brain Mapping*, **1**, 39-47.

Evans, A. C., Dai, W., Collins, L., Neelin, P., Marrett, S. 1991a. Warping of a computerized 3-D atlas to match brain image volumes for quantitative neuroanatomical and functional analysis. *Proceedings of the International Society of Optical Engineering (SPIE): Medical Imaging V.*

Evans, A. C., Marrett, S., Torrescorzo, J., Ku, S., Collins, L. 1991b. MRI-PET correlative analysis using a volume of interest (VOI) atlas *J. Cereb. Blood Flow Metab*. **11**, A69 - A78.

Evans, A. C., Marrett, S., Neelin, P., Collins, L. et al. 1992. Anatomical mapping of functional activation in stereotactic coordinate space. *Neuroimage*. **1**, 43-53.

Fox, P. T., Raichle, M. E. 1984. Stimulus rate dependence of regional cerebral blood flow in human striate cortex, demonstrated with positron emission tomography *Journal of Neurophysiology*, **51**, 1109-1120.

Fox, P. T., Perlmutter, J. S., Raichle, M. E. 1985. A stereotactic method of anatomical localization for positron emission tomography *Journal of Computer Assisted Tomography*, **9**, 141-153.

Frith, C. D., Friston, K. J., Liddle, P. F., Frackowiak, R. S. J. 1991. Willed action and the prefrontal cortex in man: a study with PET. *Proceedings of the Royal Society of London*, **29**, 1137-48.

Frostig, R. D., Lieke, E. E., Tsío, D. Y., Grinvald, A. 1990. Cortical functional architecture and local coupling between neuronal activity and the microcirculation revealed by in vivo high-resolution optical imaging of intrinsic signals. *Proceedings of the National Academy of Science*, *USA*, **87**, 6082-86.

Gurd, J. M., Bessell, N. J., Bladon, R. A. W. & Bamford, J. M. 1988. A case of foreign accent syndrome with follow-up clinical, neuropsychological and phonetic descriptions. *Neuropsychologia*, **26**(2), 237-251.

Haxby, J. V., Grady, C. L., Ungerleider, L. G., Horwitz, B. 1991. Mapping the functional neuroanatomy of the intact human brain with brain work imaging, *Neuropsychologia*, **29**, 539-555.

Klein, D., Zatorre, R. J., Milner, B., Meyer, E., Evans, A. C. 1994a. Left putaminal activation when speaking a second language: evidence from PET, *NeuroReport*. **17**, in press.

Klein, D., Milner, B., Zatorre, R. J., Meyer, E., Evans, A. C. Submitted 1994b. The neural substrates underlying word generation: A bilingual functional-imaging study.

Klein, D., Milner, B., Zatorre, R. J., Evan, A. C., Meyer, A. C. 1994c. Functional anatomy of language processing: A neuroimaging study of word-generation within and across languages, *Soc. NeuroSci Abstr*, **20**, 352.

Lauter, J., Herscovitch, P., Formby, C., Raichle, M. E. 1985. Tonotopic organization in human auditory cortex revealed by positron emission tomography. *Hear. Res*. **20**, 199-205.

Liotti, M., Gay, C. T., Fox, P. T. 1994. Functional Imaging and Language: Evidence from positron emission tomography, *Journal of Clinical Neurophysiology*, **11**, 175-190.

Marrett, S., Bub, D., Chertkow, H., Meyer, E., Gum, T. et al. 1990. Functional neuroanatomy of visual single word processing studied with PET/MRI. *Soc. Neurosci. Abstr*. **16**, 27.

Ojemann, G. A. 1983. Brain organization for language from the perspective of electrical stimulation mapping. *The Behavioral and Brain Sciences*, **6** (2), 189-230.

Ojemann, G. A. & Whitaker, H. A. 1978. The bilingual brain. *Archives of Neurology*, **35**, 409-412.

Paradis, M. 1977. Bilingualism and Aphasia. In H. Whitaker & H. A. Whitaker (eds.), *Studies in Neurolinguistics*, vol. 3. (pp. 65-121). New York: Academic Press.

Paradis, M. 1989. Bilingual and polyglot aphasia. In F. Boller & J. Grafman (eds.), *Handbook of Neuropsychology*, vol. 2. (pp.117-140). Amsterdam: Elsevier.

Paradis, M. 1993. Multilingualism and Aphasia. In G. Blanken, J. Dittmann, H. Grimm, J. C. Marshall, C. W. Wallesch, (Eds.), *Linguistic Disorders and Pathologies: An international handbook*, (pp. 278-288). Berlin: Walter de Gruyter.

Penfield, W. 1953. A consideration of the neuropshysiological mechanisms of speech and some educational considerations. *Proceedings of the American Academy of Arts and Sciences*, **82**, 201-214.

Penfield, W. & Roberts, L. 1959. *Speech and Brain Mechanisms*. (Princeton University Press).

Petersen, S. E., Fox, P. T., Posner, M. I., Mintun, M. A., Raichle, M. E. 1988. Positron emission tomographic studies of the cortical anatomy of single word processing. *Nature*, **331**, 585-589.

Petersen, S. E., Fox, P. T., Posner, M. I., Mintun, M. A., Raichle, M. E. 1989. Positron emission tomographic studies of the processing of single words. *Journal of Cognitive Neuroscience*, **1**, 153-70.

Petersen, S. E., Fox, P. T., Snyder, A. Z., Raichle, M. E. 1990. Activation of extrastriate and frontal cortical areas by visual words and word-like stimuli. *Science*, **249**, 1041-44.

Porter, R. 1991. Exploring brain functional anatomy with positron tomography, *Ciba Foundation Symposium*, **163**, 1-14.

Posner, M. I., Petersen, S. E., Fox, P.T., Raichle, M. E. 1988. Localization of cognitive operations in the human brain. *Science*, **240**, 1627-31.

Raichle, M. E. 1989. Developing a functional anatomy of the human brain with positron emission tomography. *Curr. Neurol.*, **9**, 161-78.

Raichle, M. E., Martin, W. R. W., Herscovitch, P., Mintun, M. A. & Markham, J. 1983. Brain blood flow measured with intravenous $H_2^{15}O$. II. Implementation and validation. *Journal of Nuclear Medicine*, **24**, 790-798.

Raichle, M. E., Fiez, J. A., Videen, T. O., MacLeod, A. K., et al. 1994. Practice-related changes in human brain functional anatomy during nonmotor learning. *Cerebral Cortex*, **4**, 8-26.

Raichle, M. E. 1994. Images of the mind: studies with modern imaging techniques. *Annual Review of Psychology*, **45**, 333-356.

Stytz, M. R. & Frieder, O. 1990. Three-dimensional medical imaging modalities: An overview. *Crit. Rev. Biomed. Eng.* **18**, 1-25.

Sussman, H. M., Franklin, P., Simon, T. 1982. Bilingual speech: Bilateral control. *Brain and Language*, **15**, 125-142.

Talairach, J. & Tournoux, P. 1988. *Co-Planar Stereotaxic Atlas of the Human Brain*. New York: Thieme.

Volkmann, J., Hefter, H., Lange, H. W. & Freund, H.-J. 1992. Impairment of temporal organization of speech in basal ganglia diseases. *Brain and Language*, **43**, 386-399.

Whitaker, H. A. 1989. Bilingualism and Neurolinguistics: A note on the issues. *Brain and Language*, **36**, 1-2.

Wise, R., Chollet, F., Hadar, U., Friston, K., Hoffner, E. et al. 1991. Distribution of cortical neural networks involved in word comprehension and word retrieval. *Brain*, **114**, 1803-1817.

Worsley, K. J., Evans, A. C., Marrett, S. & Neelin, P. 1992. A three-dimensional statistical analysis for CBF activation studies in human brain. *Journal of cerebral Blood Flow Metabolism*, **12**, 900-918.

Wuillemin, D., Richardson, B. 1994. Right-hemisphere involvement in processing later-learned languages in multilinguals. *Brain and Language*, **46**, 620-636.

Zatorre, R. J., Evans, A. C., Meyer, E., Gjedde, A. 1992. Lateralization of phonetic and pitch processing in speech perception. *Science*, **256**, 846-849.

Zatorre, R. J., Evans, A. C., Meyer, E. 1994. Neural mechanisms underlying melodic perception and memory for pitch. *The Journal of Neuroscience*, **14**, 1908-1919.

3 Speech/language management of the bilingual aphasic in a U.S. urban rehabilitation hospital

Debra Wiener, Loraine K. Obler and Martha Taylor Sarno

Introduction

Despite the fact that the United States is considered by many a unilingual English-speaking country, 14 percent of the population, by 1990 Census Reports, is bilingual. The major languages other than English spoken in the United States are Spanish (by 54.4 percent of bilinguals), French (5.4 percent), German (4.7 percent), Italian (4.1 percent), and Chinese (3.8 percent).

Urban areas such as New York City have disproportionately large numbers of bilinguals, as they provide points of entry for immigrants and are sophisticated cultural centers. The 1990 Census reported 41 percent of the New York City population as bilingual. The major foreign languages spoken in New York City, in order of frequency, are Spanish, Chinese, Italian, French, and Yiddish.

Yet, despite the frequency of bilingualism, the field of speech/language pathology has relatively little professional representation of bilinguals. Of the approximately 78,000 certified speech/language pathologists who are members of the American Speech/Language Hearing Association (ASHA), fewer than one percent report themselves to be bilingual. In its first major position paper on the clinical management of bilingual clients, written only in the last decade, ASHA recommended that the treatment of bilingual clients be administered by bilingual speech/language pathologists, but recognized that this was not always possible and that bilingual translators, family members, or friends might need to be utilized (ASHA, 1985).

Only in the last two decades has there been any discussion in the research literature of speech/language rehabilitation for bilingual patients with aphasia (see Fredman, 1975, and a review in Paradis, 1993). To our knowledge, there is no quantitative information available regarding how bilingual aphasic patients are characteristically managed.

Since two of the authors are on staff in the speech/language pathology department of a major New York City rehabilitation hospital, we were provided with the opportunity to study retrospectively how cases of bilingual aphasia have been managed. As is fairly typical, the staff consists of nine unilingual English-speaking speech/language pathologists, six of whom have limited knowledge of one or two foreign languages. Before conducting this study, it was our impression that a sizable number of the aphasic patients seen in the department were bilingual, perhaps one-quarter of the group. Due to the multiplicity of languages spoken, we anticipated that our ability to provide bilinguals with services equivalent to those provided to the unilingual population was compromised, and we wanted to document the extent to which this might be true. We expected that the bilingual patients would wait longer to be evaluated due to the necessity of arranging for translation, and that they would have less frequent treatment and for shorter durations. Most importantly, we were concerned that their benefit from treatment might be compromised.

In what follows, we first describe our subject selection criteria, the definitions of bilingualism that we employed, and the language backgrounds of our two bilingual patient groups. We then compare the two bilingual groups and the unilingual group demographically, neurologically, and with respect to their presenting speech/ language symptomatology. Finally, we review their speech/ language rehabilitation and treatment outcomes.

Methods

The subjects were all those adult aphasic patients evaluated as either inpatients or outpatients by the Speech/Language Pathology Department of the Rusk Institute of Rehabilitation Medicine (RIRM) in the year 1993. All patients who are seen in the department are referred by an attending physiatrist.

RIRM is a private, fee for service, 152 bed, university-affiliated rehabilitation center located in the borough of Manhattan in New York City. Approximately 20% of adult inpatients are aphasic. Inpatient admission to the Institute is based upon selection criteria which include medical stability, a need for inpatient nursing care, the potential to benefit from rehabilitation services within a reasonable amount of time, and sufficient insurance coverage or other financial resources to cover the cost of care. The average length of stay for a left or right hemisphere damaged CVA patient at RIRM in 1993 was 46 days. Outpatients are seen in the Speech/Language Pathology Department for a number of reasons including diagnostic evaluations, second opinions, and/or therapy. The length of treatment in recent years has been steadily decreasing as a result of a pattern of markedly decreased insurance reimbursement and escalating health service costs which makes self-pay prohibitive for the large majority of patients.

The subjects were diagnosed with aphasia on the basis of clinical observation and language examination conducted by either one of the two senior speech/language pathologists or the assistant director of the department. All three of these clinicians are unilingual English speakers, each with only a limited familiarity with one or two foreign languages. While there are no formal departmental mandates regarding the assessment and treatment of bilingual patients, the diagnosis of aphasia is based upon a patient's performance in his or her dominant language. Whenever possible, family members or friends who are fluent in both the patient's primary language(s) and English are engaged as translators in the evaluation process. The benefits of family involvement are viewed not only as an aid in translation when necessary, but in the provision of information regarding linguistic strengths and weaknesses relative to premorbid status. Further, the examiner is provided with the opportunity to educate the family for increased carry-over of treatment goals.

The department's computerized data base was reviewed by the first author, and the departmental charts of all those patients with a diagnosis of aphasia were retrieved from the inactive and active files. The data for this study come from speech/language therapists' reports, test materials, and other relevant documents contained in the patient charts.

In 1993, 114 adult patients with aphasia were evaluated at RIRM. Five of the patients were excluded from this study because their admission to RIRM was for reasons unrelated to their long history of aphasia (e.g., peripheral neuropathy, cardiac bypass surgery, onset of a right-hemispheric CVA, or a decrease in physical functioning with no new neurological onset diagnosed) or, as in the case of one patient, an initial impression of aphasia was changed to "nonlinguistic communication impairment" once treatment began.

Of the remaining 109 patients, 54 were classified as "unilingual" for purposes of this study, as neither the patients nor their significant others reported a premorbid history of fluency in a language other than English. The other 55 patients were classified as "bilingual," as they or their families reported premorbid fluency in a language other than English. This "bilingual" group was quite diverse and ranged from being premorbidly fluent in only one foreign language with no proficiency in English in the case of two patients, to being premorbidly fluent in English and at least one second language, but using English 100% of the time. We, therefore, divided the bilingual group into two groups: (1) bilingual patients with a limited English background, and (2) those with a strong English background. This division was based upon whether or not English was listed as the preferred language (or, in one instance, one of the two preferred languages). For nine patients, review of the departmental charts did not yield an indication of a preferred language. Therefore, these patients were or were not assigned to the English-preferred category based upon whether translation was required in the initial evaluation. Also, note that two of the "limited-English bilingual" group were actually not bilingual; rather, they were unilingual in a language other than English. We call this group "bilingual" because the vast majority of the patients in it were, and we include these two unilinguals in that group because we are interested in the treatment effects of not being premorbidly proficient in the language of the therapists.

The outcome of this categorization was: (1) 22 bilinguals with a limited English background, and (2) 33 with a strong English background. Consider, for example, bilingual subject #27 who is in the first category: a 59-year-old man, self-employed as a restaurant owner, who immigrated to the United States from Greece 34 years ago. His family reported that the patient had limited premorbid proficiency in English. They estimated that premorbidly, he spoke English 30% of the time. Greek was his preferred language and the language used mostly at work and in the home. Bilingual subject #18 is in the second category, a 53-year-old retired supermarket supervisor who immigrated to New York from Puerto Rico 33 years ago. While his native language is Spanish, premorbid spoken English usage was estimated at 95%, with the patient and his wife reporting English as his preferred language and the sole language used at home.

Descriptive Data

For data analyses involving nominal level data, a series of χ^2 analyses were conducted. For interval level data, a series of one-way ANOVAs was employed. Post-hoc analyses using the Bonferroni method were conducted for any significant one-way ANOVA findings.

Bilingual demographics

Table 1. Premorbid languages of the bilingual patients

	Native language	Home language	Preferred language	Second language
Arabic				1
Armenian	1	1	1	
Bulgarian	1			
Chinese	4	4	4	
Creole	1	1		
Croatian				1
English	12	34	28	41
French	1	1	1	7
German	5	1		4
Greek	4	2	2	
Hebrew				1
Hungarian	3	2	1	2
Italian	6	1	1	1
Lithuanian	1			
Polish	3	2	2	2
Portuguese	1	1		2
Romanian				1
Russian	1	1		3
Spanish	8	5	4	3
Turkish				1
Ukrainian	1	1		
Yiddish	8	5	3	3

ENGLISH AS NATIVE LANGUAGE

One hundred percent of the limited-English bilingual patients reported that English was not their native language. In comparison, 27.3% of the strong-English bilingual group reported English was their native language, 63.6% of this group reported that it was not, and 9.1% of these patients reported that English and one other language were their native languages. The difference between the two groups was significant, χ^2 (1, $N = 55$) = 10.23, $p < .001$.

ENGLISH USAGE IN THE HOME

Of the limited-English bilingual patients, 22.7% reported some use of English at home and 72.7% reported no use of English in the home (for 4.6% of these patients, this information was not available). In comparison, the findings for the strong-English bilingual patients were 87.9%, 6.1%, and 6.1%, respectively. The difference between the two groups was significant, χ^2 (1, $N = 52$) = 26.90, $p < .05$.

USAGE OF TWO LANGUAGES IN THE HOME

Of the limited-English bilingual patients, 31.8% reported that two languages are used at home, and 63.6% of the group reported that only one language is used at home. (The information was not available for 4.6% of the group.) In comparison, the findings for the strong-English bilinguals were 9.1%, 84.8%, and 6.1%, respectively. The difference between the two groups only approached significance ($p = .07$).

YEARS SINCE IMMIGRATION TO THE UNITED STATES

All of the limited-English bilingual patients were foreign-born. Information was unavailable regarding the number of years since immigration to the United States for 13.6% of the group. For the remaining patients ($n = 19$), the average number (M) of years since U.S. immigration was 43.7. In contrast, 33.3% of the strong-English bilinguals were born in the United States. For 9.1% ($n = 3$) of the strong-English patients, number of years since U.S. immigration was not available. Of the remaining patients in this group ($n = 19$), the average number of years since U.S. immigration was 38.8. The two groups did not differ significantly on this variable.

In summary, significant differences were found between the two bilingual groups for most of the variables by which language history and usage were examined. While this is not surprising given the fact that the bilingual subjects were initially subdivided based primarily on whether or not English was their preferred language, the results of further analyses elaborate on the differences between the two groups. English was the native language of significantly more of the strong-English bilingual patients than of the limited-English patients. In addition, while the home environments of the limited-English group tended to be more bilingual than those of the strong-English group, English was used in the homes of the limited-English group significantly less frequently than in the strong-English group. Although more of the limited-English bilinguals were immigrants than were the strong-English bilinguals, it is worth noting that the strong-English immigrants have been living in the U.S. for no longer than the limited-English group.

Demographics

AGE

The average age of the limited-English bilingual aphasics was 73.3 (standard deviation (SD) 11.8, range 56-93), that of the strong-English bilinguals was 67.4 (SD 14.2, range 21-86), and the average age of the unilinguals was 65.3 (SD 17.3, range 19-87). No significant age differences obtained among the three patient groups.

GENDER

Fifty percent of the limited-English bilinguals were male, as were 57.6% of the strong-English bilinguals and 51.8% of the unilingual patients. No significant differences in gender composition obtained.

HANDEDNESS

In the limited-English bilingual group, 95.4% of the patients were right-handed and 4.6% were left-handed. These findings compare with 97% right-handed and 3% left-handed in the strong-English bilingual group and 92.6% right- and 5.6% left-handed in the unilingual group (with the handedness of the remaining 1.8% of these patients unclear as this information was not included in their records). No significant differences obtained for handedness.

EDUCATION

Years of education were classified as either zero years, less than 6 years, or a specific number of years when it was 6 or greater. However, for some patients ($n = 16$), educational information was not available. While education was consistently reported for the limited-English bilingual group, findings do not account for 12.1% of the strong-English group and 22.2% of the unilingual group. Two measures of education demonstrate that the limited-English group had the least education. First, they are the only group with instances of either zero or fewer than 6 years of education, at 4.6% and 27.3%, respectively. Second, for patients with documented 6 years of education or greater in the three groups ($n = 15$, 29, and 42, respectively), the average years of education was 11.2 (SD 4.2), 13.2 (SD 3.5), and 14.2 (SD 3.8), respectively. Nevertheless, the highest number of years of education is similar at 18, 21, and 21, respectively. The overall ANOVA for mean years of education was significant ($F(2, 84)=5.21$, $p < .01$). Post-hoc comparisons revealed a significant difference between the limited-English bilingual and the unilingual group.

SOCIO-ECONOMIC STATUS

Socio-economic status was approximated for the patient groups by utilizing the Hollingshead scale (1977), which takes education and professional category of both the individual and his/her spouse into account for estimations of social status. However, due to limited information provided in some of the patient charts, our estimations do not include the patients' spouses' occupations and educational backgrounds. In addition, for a large percentage of patients (36.4% of each of the bilingual groups and 24.1% of the unilinguals), a score could not be calculated due to either no indication of occupation in the files (e.g., "retired"), a non-specific occupation being listed (e.g., "manufacturer"), no educational background or a non-specific educational background listed, or female patients' occupation listed as "homemaker." For the remaining patients in each group ($n = 14$, 21, and 40, respectively), there was a significant main-effect for socioeconomic status, $F(2, 72) = 7.92$, $p < .001$. Post-hoc comparisons revealed significantly lower socio-economic status among the limited-English bilingual group, $M = 29.4$, compared to either the strong-English bilingual group, $M = 45.7$, or the unilingual group, $M = 48.0$.

In summary, while no significant differences were found among the three patient groups regarding age, gender, or handedness, the limited-English bilingual group was significantly less educated than the unilingual group. Likewise, the estimated socio-economic status of the limited-English bilingual group was significantly lower than that of the strong-English bilingual group and the unilingual group.

Neurological non-aphasic background

ETIOLOGY

Figure 1 displays comparisons of the percentages of the four etiologies of aphasia for the three patient groups: CVA; brain tumor; CHI; and other (total n = 4: brain cyst/hydrocephalus; multiple TIAs; anoxia; and temporal lobectomy for seizure management). No significant differences obtained among the groups on this variable.

LESION SIDE

Figure 2 portrays comparisons of the percentages of the four lesion side ratings for the three groups: left; right; bilateral; and unknown/not listed in departmental chart. No significant differences obtained among those subjects for whom lesion side information was available.

PHYSICAL DISABILITY

Figure 3 displays comparisons of the percentages of the four types of physical disability documented in the three patient groups: right hemiparesis/hemiplegia; left hemiparesis/hemiplegia; none; and other (total n = 5: four instances of ataxia and one of cortical blindness). (For 6.1% of the strong-English bilingual group and 5.6% of the unilingual group, information regarding physical disability was unavailable.) No significant differences obtained among the patient groups.

PRIOR NEUROLOGICAL HISTORY

Figure 4 portrays the non-significant differences in the four types of neurological history in the three patient groups, prior to their most recent onset: none; CVA(s); TIA(s); and other (total n = 7: brain tumor (3 patients); progressive word-retrieval difficulty/disorientation (2 patients); meningitis/encephalitis/ seizures; and CHI).

In summary, the three patient groups were not found to differ neurologically, when etiology, lesion side, physical disability, and prior neurological history were examined.

Initial presenting speech/language symptomatology

Fluency

Aphasia type was categorized as either fluent or nonfluent following traditional guidelines (Benson, 1967; Geschwind, 1971; Goodglass & Kaplan, 1983). Figure 5 depicts the non-significant group differences in distribution of the percentages of the four ratings of fluency of the three patient groups: fluent; nonfluent; conduction aphasia; and information not available or not indicated. The high incidence of fluency data excluded from patients' speech/language diagnoses can be attributed to a number of factors: (1) an indication of fluency is frequently omitted from a diagnostic label of "global aphasia" due to the severity of the disorder; (2) fluency may be neither clearly

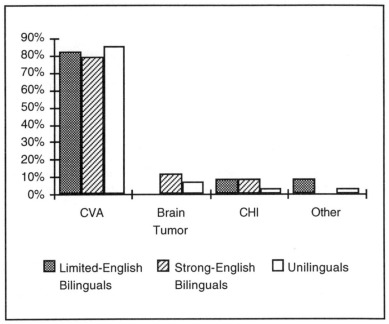

Figure 1. Etiology

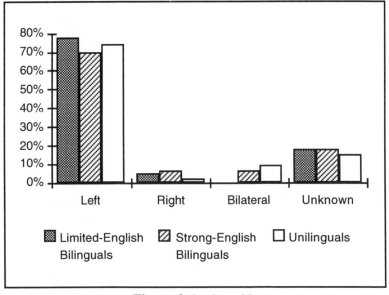

Figure 2. Lesion side

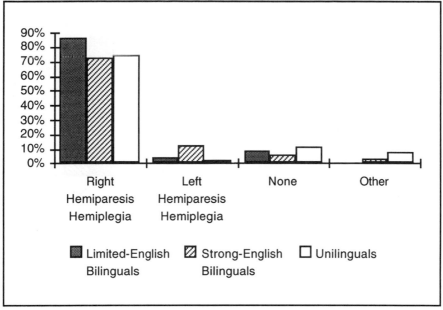

Figure 3. Physical disability

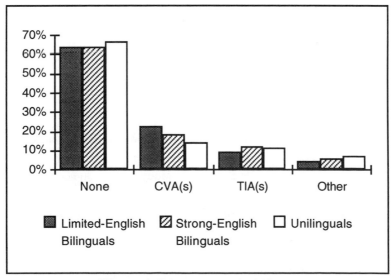

Figure 4. Prior neurological history

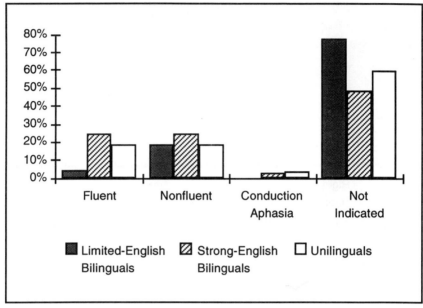

Figure 5. Fluency

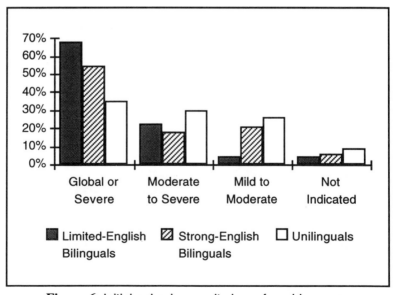

Figure 6. Initial aphasia severity in preferred language

fluent nor non-fluent but mixed, with "mixed" not specified in the diagnostic label; and (3) a reliable rating of fluency is at times difficult when assessment involves an intermediary translator.

Severity

Severity of aphasia categories was derived from a combination of clinical performance on formal language examination and an observation of patients' functional communicative performance. For our analyses, initial aphasia severity was categorized into seven degrees: (1) global; (2) global/severe; (3) severe; (4) moderate-severe; (5) moderate; (6) mild-moderate; and (7) mild. In Figure 6, these categories have been collapsed for ease of exposition into three categories: global or severe, moderate to severe, and mild to moderate. There was a significant main-effect for initial severity rating, $F(2,98) = 4.78$, $p < .01$. Post-hoc comparisons revealed significantly lower severity ratings for the limited-English bilingual group, $M = 2.4$, compared to the unilingual group, $M = 4.0$.

Accompanying peripheral dysarthria or dysphonia

Of the limited-English bilingual patients, 4.6% presented with an accompanying dysphonia or peripheral dysarthria, as compared to 9.1% of the strong-English bilinguals and 22.2% of the unilingual patients, χ^2 (2, $N = 109$) = 5.08, $p =.09$. This trend may reflect a hesitancy on the part of the clinicians diagnosing bilingual patients to ascribe dysarthria when a foreign accent is evident.

Accompanying cognitive impairment

The speech/language diagnoses of 27.3% of the limited-English bilingual patients included the presence of non-linguistic cognitive reductions in addition to aphasia which further compromised communicative function, as compared to 15.2% of the strong-English bilingual patients and 20.4% of the unilingual patients, a non-significant group difference. While the inclusion of cognitive impairment in the diagnosis does reflect apparent non-linguistic reductions, its absence does not necessarily imply preserved cognition, as non-linguistic cognitive measures are not included in the speech/language examination battery.

Speech/language rehabilitation

Patient status

In the limited-English bilingual group, 72.7% ($n = 16$) of the patients were evaluated by the Speech/Language Pathology Department as inpatients, 18.2% ($n = 4$) as outpatients, and 9.1% ($n = 2$) first as inpatients and then as outpatients. These percentages compare to 63.6% ($n = 21$), 30.3% ($n = 10$), and 6.1% ($n =2$), respectively, in the strong-English bilingual group and 57.4% ($n = 31$), 25.9% ($n = 14$), and 16.7% ($n = 9$), respectively, in the unilingual group.

Previous speech/language treatment

Of the limited- English bilingual patients, 36.4% had received prior speech/ language treatment either at another institution or at home, related to the recent neurological onset or a previous neurological event. This compares with 54.6% of the strong-English bilinguals and 44.4% of the unilingual patients. These group differences were not significant.

Interval from onset to RIRM speech/language evaluation

The average interval in weeks from onset of most recent neurological event to the RIRM inpatient or outpatient initial speech/language evaluation did not differ significantly across the groups. It was 30.6 (*SD* 66.7) for the limited-English bilingual group, 53.2 (*SD* 155.8) for the strong-English bilinguals, and 13.7 (*SD* 27.8) for the unilingual group.

Interval from inpatient admission to speech/language evaluation

Of the limited-English bilingual patients, 81.8% (*n* =18) were seen for an inpatient speech/language evaluation, as compared to 69.7% of the strong-English bilinguals (*n* = 23) and 74.1% of the unilingual patients (*n* = 40). The average number of working days, excluding week-ends and holidays, from date of admission to the initial evaluation was somewhat higher for the limited-English bilingual inpatients (*M* = 5.8), compared to the strong-English bilingual inpatients (*M* = 4.0) and the unilingual inpatients (*M* = 3.7). This trend was not confirmed in our post-hoc analyses.

Length of inpatient speech/language treatment

As of 1/1/94, 5.6% of the limited-English bilingual inpatients, 8.7% of the strong-English inpatients, and 12.5% of the unilingual inpatients were in the middle of their inpatient speech/language treatment program. Of the remaining inpatients, 94.4% (*n* = 17), 91.3% (*n* = 21), and 87.5% (*n* = 35), respectively, the average length of inpatient speech/language treatment in days was not significantly different at 41, 32, and 34.5, respectively. Of these limited-English patients, 88.2% were treated by the Speech/Language Pathology Department until discharge from inpatient hospitalization, as compared to 85.7% of these strong-English bilinguals and 100% of these unilingual patients. This difference in the treatment of the bilingual and unilingual groups only approached significance (*p* = .08).

The early termination of speech/language treatment for the two limited-English bilingual patients were the result of: (1) their family proved to be unavailable after the initial evaluation for educational purposes or to serve as translator for a patient who spoke solely Chinese premorbidly; and (2) a translator who was literate in Chinese could not be located for a patient with mild aphasia who spoke primarily Chinese, but who had been living with aphasia for five years and whose communication was functionally adequate. The early termination of the three strong-English bilingual patients was due to: (1) a patient refusing treatment immediately after the initial evaluation due to the relatively mild nature of aphasia; (2) a patient requesting termination of treatment at 8 days post-evaluation due to a combination of fatigue and the relatively mild degree of aphasia; and (3) the speech/language pathologist recommending termination at 22 days post-evaluation due to the severity of cognitive deficits and no linguistic gains evidenced.

Length of outpatient speech/language treatment

Of the limited-English bilingual patients, 27.3% ($n = 6$) were seen for an outpatient speech/language evaluation, as compared to 36.4% of the strong-English bilinguals ($n = 12$) and 42.6% of the unilingual patients ($n = 23$). Of these outpatients, 16.7%, 41.7%, and 43.5%, respectively, were still on outpatient program as of 1/1/94. Of the remaining outpatients, 83.3% ($n = 5$), 58.3% ($n = 7$), and 56.5% ($n = 13$), respectively, the average length of outpatient speech/language treatment in weeks was 7.4, 8.7, and 10.1, respectively. These group differences were not statistically different.

Individual and group therapy

After the initial inpatient or outpatient speech/language evaluation, four of the limited-English bilingual patients, four of the strong-English bilinguals, and three of the unilingual patients were not placed on a treatment program. The reasons for the limited-English bilingual patients were: (1) unavailable family/translator; (2) unavailable translator, as well as adequate functional communication and long duration of aphasia; 3) long duration of symptoms and maximized communicative function; and 4) family elected not to participate in outpatient educational program recommended for patient and family (prognosis for recovery was poor given long duration of symptoms and severity of both aphasic and non-linguistic deficits). The reasons for lack of further contact with the strong-English bilingual patients were: (1) patient attended evaluation for a second opinion/ interest in our department's non-fee aphasia group program/ on program elsewhere; (2) inadequate physical endurance for the evaluation; (3) patient refusal of treatment due to relatively mild nature of aphasia; and (4) insurance company denial of outpatient speech/language treatment reimbursement. The reasons for the unilingual patients were: (1) patient refusal due to busy cognitive remediation outpatient schedule; and (2) two patients never attending due to worsening of medical status.

Of the remaining 81.8% ($n = 18$) limited-English bilinguals, 87.9% ($n = 29$) strong-English bilinguals, and 94.4% ($n = 51$) unilingual patients, the average frequency per week (maximum days = 5) of individual therapy received was 2.3, 2.6, and 2.7 sessions for the three patient groups, respectively. Although none of the post-hoc comparisons were significant, the trend observed ($p = .06$) may have been due to the fewer sessions for the limited-English bilingual group. In terms of aphasia group therapy, the average frequency per week was 2.2, 2.0, and 1.9 sessions for the three patient groups, respectively. These group differences were not significant.

In lieu of treatment, 9.1% of the limited-English bilingual patients' families, 3.0% of the strong-English bilinguals' families, and 0% of the unilinguals' families participated in a formal educational consultation with the speech/ language pathologist. Group differences between the limited-English and the unilingual groups approached significance ($p = .08$).

Family education

Of all the patients evaluated, 100% of the limited-English bilinguals' families, 66.7% of the strong-English bilinguals' families, and 59.3% of the unilinguals' families received some amount of documented individual education regarding the nature of aphasia from the Speech/Language Pathology Department. The limited-English group received significantly more education than either the unilingual group, $\chi^2(1, N = 76) = 12.62, p < .001$, or the strong-English group, $\chi^2 (1, N = 55) = 9.12, p < .01$.

TRANSLATOR INVOLVED IN EVALUATION AND/OR TREATMENT

For the limited-English bilingual evaluations, a translator participated in 96.8% of the evaluations compared to 9.5% of the strong-English bilingual evaluations, a significant difference, $\chi^2 (1, N = 52) = 40.27, p <. 0001$. For the limited-English bilingual individual treatment contact, a translator was present for 55.6% of these patients, with a translator's absence in the remaining 44.4% of treated patients generally attributable to unavailability of a family member or friend and/or the patient's adequate usage of English for purposes of treatment. A translator was never present during the treatment of the strong-English bilinguals. This difference between the two bilingual groups was significant, $\chi^2 (1, N = 51) = 22.81, p < .0001$.

Outcomes

TREATMENT OUTCOMES

Improvements in speech/language function regarding aphasic symptomatology for those patients placed on a treatment program were examined in two ways. First, one of the authors (DW) reviewed evaluation, progress, and discharge reports and formal test data (when available) and subjectively rated degree of improvement on a 7-point scale: worsening condition; none; minimal; fair; good; excellent; and not applicable (which applied to only one patient in the limited-English bilingual group, a bilingual Yiddish/English speaker, where the focus of treatment was on family education given the long duration of symptoms). To determine inter-rater reliability, a second rater (MTS) rated 10% of the records. Agreement within one point on the 7-point scale was achieved in 10/12 (83.3%) of the cases. For the two cases where the judges differed by two points in their evaluation of progress, the reasons were as follows: In one case, the same patient was admitted twice during the year due to a deterioration of medical and communicative status; it was decided to include only the first admission in this study. In the second case, the first rater over-rated the progress of the patient based upon an improved clinical skill (e.g., oral reading) rather than functional communication. The first author then made a second pass through all the records to insure a consistent philosophy of what constituted improvement in communicative function.

Figure 7 displays comparisons of the degrees of improvement in the three patient groups. Ratings of "worsening status" and "excellent improvement" are absent from the graph, as they did not apply to any of the patients. There were no significant group differences for these ratings. Likewise, we found no significant group differences when ratings were combined for patients who showed no or minimal improvement compared to those who showed fair or good improvement. However, when patients who showed good improvement (total $n = 15$) were compared to those who showed no, minimal, or fair improvement, we found that the unilingual group had significantly more patients (23.5%) who showed good recovery, as compared to the limited-English bilingual group (0%), χ^2 (1, $N = 68$) = 4.86, $p <. 02$. Although statistical significance was not obtained for the comparison between the unilingual and the strong-English bilingual group, it should be noted that there were very few strong-English bilinguals ($n = 3$) who showed good improvement.

Improvement was also examined by comparing severity in speech/language diagnosis at the end of the study to that at the initial evaluation. The possible range of improvement is 0 to 6, with 6 representing improvement from global status (1) to mild status (7). No patient treated improved beyond 3 points.

The average "points" of improvement reflected in speech/language diagnoses for the limited-English bilingual group was .3 on the 7-point scale, as compared to .4 for the strong-English group and .6 for the unilingual group. Figure 8 portrays comparisons of points of improvement across the three patient groups. No significant group differences obtained by this measure, even when we compared the 3-point recoveries to all the rest. (As 18.2% of each of the bilingual groups and 14.8% of the unilingual group were either not seen for treatment or had diagnoses in which degree of severity was not specified, they are excluded from Figure 8.)

RECOMMENDATIONS POST RIRM CONTACT

Figure 9 displays comparisons between the three patient groups of therapists' speech/language recommendations post inpatient or outpatient contact, for those patients who were evaluated and discharged in 1993. It excludes 9.1% of the limited-English bilingual group, 21.2% of the strong-English bilingual group, and 27.8% of the unilingual group, since they were still receiving treatment on 1/1/94. The graph depicts the following five recommendations: (1) continued speech/language treatment; (2) no continued speech/language treatment; (3) future formal re-evaluation; (4) independent home program only; and (5) continued treatment only upon patient request. (For ease of exposition, the category of "other" was excluded from the figure, total $n = 4$, which included two instances where recommendations were not documented and two instances where therapeutic services other than speech/language treatment were recommended.) No significant group differences obtained for this variable.

REASON FOR RIRM SPEECH/LANGUAGE DISCHARGE

Comparisons of the reasons for discharge for the three patient groups are shown in Figure 10, once again for those patients who were evaluated and discharged in 1993: (1) inpatient discharge due to discharge from the hospital; (2) plateau/lack of gains; (3) patient moved/left for vacation and never returned; (4) patient refused therapy or requested termination; (5) family or translator were unavailable; (6) insurance problems, pertaining to outpatients only; (7) functional adequacy/good usage of compensatory strategies; (8) medical problems; and (9) other (total $n = 2$), which consists of one patient who came for an outpatient re-evaluation but was still receiving speech/language treatment at home and a second patient who came for an outpatient

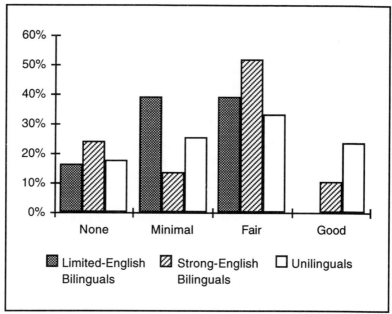

Figure 7. Speech/Language Pathology improvement ratings

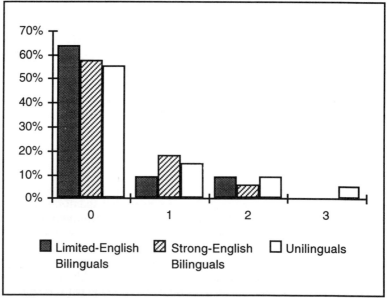

Figure 8. Points of improvement on a 7 point diagnostic scale

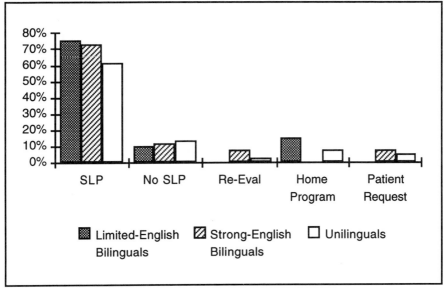

Figure 9. Recommendations post-RIRM

evaluation for a second opinion and with interest in the department's non-fee aphasia group socialization program. No significant differences obtained on this measure.

Discussion

Our review of the ASHA Council reports of the past nine years had led us to expect that bilingual patients with aphasia would be under-treated in the United States, especially in a speech/language pathology department with no explicit mandates or job-lines for bilingual speech/language pathologists. This retrospective study, to our knowledge the first which addresses the current management of cases of bilinguals with aphasia, countered such expectations in several regards.

Overall, the large number of similarities among the groups studied, especially with regard to demographics, treatment, and recovery, were not anticipated, although we had no reason to be surprised by the similarities of neurological phenomena. That the unilingual and bilingual groups were similar in age, handedness, and gender distribution was useful in permitting us to conduct simple comparisons of the dependent variables. The fact that the two demographic differences found among the groups were in education and the linked variable, socio-economic status, may be explained by the social ramifications of immigration. Educational attainment for immigrants to New York has historically been lower than that for American-born New Yorkers (Youssef, 1992). In addition, even highly educated immigrants frequently experience a decline in their socio-economic status upon immigration, particularly when knowledge of English is weak (Foner, 1987; Youssef, 1992). Both education and the consequences of immigration likely contributed to the pattern seen whereby unilinguals had the highest socio-economic status, limited-English bilinguals the

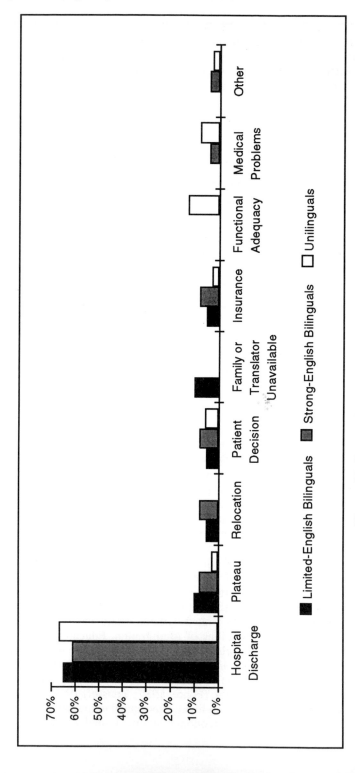

Figure 10. Reason for Speech/Language discharge

lowest, and strong-English bilinguals intermediate.

We had not predicted the equivalent frequency of individual and group aphasia treatment across the groups. Despite the potential difficulties of incorporating a limited English speaker in group therapy, we were pleased to find that the bilingual patient group was equally exposed to the communicative stimulation and peer support provided in our varied group program. We were also impressed that the limited-English bilinguals fared particularly well with respect to the departmental commitment to educate family members regarding patients' speech/language disabilities and methods to facilitate maximized communicative function, even though we initiated the family contact to obtain language background information for a valid diagnostic impression.

As to recovery, while there were no significant overall differences between the groups, it does appear that "good" recovery was less frequent among the limited - English bilingual group. In addition, the unilingual group was the only group that included patients who were discharged from the program primarily because they had achieved functional communicative adequacy. Currently, we do not know if our evaluations were biased such that good recovery went unrecognized in the limited-English group or whether, in fact, recovery in that group was somewhat more limited. Specifically, biases could have resulted from the assessment of function via an intermediary translator, where subtleties in improvement could be overlooked. Similarly, treatment that utilizes a translator may not be as effective as direct one-on-one intervention, despite the constant presence and direction of the speech/language pathologist. We considered that the greater degree of initial severity of the limited-English group may have accounted for their limited progress within our one-year study and, therefore, performed co-analyses of these two variables, and the interaction proved non-significant. Similarly, there was no significant interaction between improvements evidenced in the three patient groups and education and/or socio-economic status. One might argue that the spontaneous recovery inherent in the aphasic patient may be the sole contributor to the recovery patterns evidenced. However, this appears to be unlikely given recent demonstration of the overall efficacy of aphasia treatment based upon meta-analysis of language intervention studies involving large numbers of subjects and controls (Whurr, Lorch, & Nye, 1992; Robey, 1994). Further investigation of the impact of a translator's involvement in aphasia assessment and treatment is clearly indicated.

In a number of ways, this study must be seen as a first attempt to evaluate treatment and outcome in bilingual individuals with aphasia. Given the retrospective nature of the study, data were sometimes missing or incomplete. Furthermore, a part of the context in which these patients find themselves is quite culture-specific to both New York City and RIRM. In the field of rehabilitation medicine, RIRM holds a preeminent position and may attract a select patient population, making our sample not representative of all New Yorkers. Moreover, additional economic forces will change the 1993 picture reported here since marked changes are taking place in the delivery of all health services in the United States. Clearly, insurance coverage practices were a determining factor in the duration of therapy for both outpatients and, we assume, for a sizable group of inpatients. Nevertheless, we may report that in this study, bilingual patients showed recovery that was virtually equivalent to that of unilinguals.

Acknowledgements

Thanks are due to Dr. Kathy Flannery for her help with the data analysis and to Marjorie Nicholas for her editorial comments. We are grateful for John Shin's expertise in creating the graphics and Sendia Kim's helpfulness in locating the census data.

References

American Speech-Language Hearing Association. 1985. Clinical management of communicatively handicapped minority language populations. ASHA, June 1985, Vol. 27, No. 6.

Benson, D.F. 1967. Fluency in aphasia: Correlation with radioactive scan localization. *Cortex*, **8**, 373-394.

Bureau of the Census. 1990. *United States 1990 Census of Population: Social and Economic Characteristics of U.S. and New York City*. Washington, D.C.: U.S. Department of Commerce.

Foner, N. 1987. New immigrants and changing patterns in New York City. In Foner, N. (Ed.) *New Immigrants in New York* (pp. 1-33). New York: Columbia University Press.

Fredman, M. 1975. The effect of therapy given in Hebrew on the home language of the bilingual or polyglot adult aphasic in Israel. *British Journal of Disorders of Communication*, **10**, 61-69.

Geschwind, N. 1971. Current concepts: Aphasia. *New England Journal of Medicine*, **284**, 654-656.

Goodglass, H., & Kaplan, E. 1983. *Boston Diagnostic Aphasia Examination*, 2nd ed. Philadelphia: Lea and Febiger.

Hollingshead, A.B. 1977. *Four Factor Index of Social Status*. Unpublished paper, Department of Sociology, Yale University.

Paradis, M. 1993. Bilingual aphasia rehabilitation. In Paradis, M. (Ed.), *Foundations of Aphasia Rehabilitation* (pp. 413-419). New York: Pergamon Press.

Robey, R. 1994. The efficacy of treatment for aphasic persons: A meta-analysis. *Brain and Language*, **47**, 582-608.

Whurr, R., Lorch, M.P., & Nye, C. 1992. A meta-analysis of studies carried out between 1946 and 1986 concerned with the efficacy of speech and language therapy treatment for aphasic patients. *European Journal of Disorders of Communication*, **27**, 1-17.

Youssef, N.H. 1992. *The Demographics of Immigration: A Socio-Demographic Profile of the Foreign-Born Population in New York State*. New York: Center for Migration Studies.

4 Assessment of bilinguality in aphasia: issues and examples from multicultural Hawaii

Nina Dronkers, Yumi Yamasaki,
G. Webster Ross and Lon White

Cases of bilingual aphasia offer valuable information concerning the neural mechanisms of language. One of the most interesting aspects of bilingual aphasia is the occasional finding of differential impairment between a bilingual's two languages. Cases have been reported of "differential recovery" in which the patient does not regain his languages to the same extent. Paradis (1977, 1989) provides comprehensive reviews of such cases. These cases contribute to speculation that multiple languages might, at least in some instances, be represented by separate brain mechanisms.

Another pattern of differential impairment, that of "differential aphasia", has been described by Albert and Obler (1978) and Silverberg and Gordon (1979) . In these cases, language assessment resulted in a different type of aphasia for each language. In the Albert and Obler case, a left posterior temporal tumor caused an expressive aphasia in English, a receptive aphasia in Hebrew, and a mixed (expressive and receptive) aphasia in Hungarian and in French. Silverberg and Gordon's first case suffered a non-fluent aphasia in Spanish, but was fluent in Hebrew. Their second patient experienced a global aphasia in Hebrew, but only a mild word-finding difficulty in Russian. These cases again lead to speculation that multiple languages may rely on different circuitry or processes and raise important issues regarding the localization of language ability in the brain.

Given the importance of these issues, it is critical to define the many parameters that could influence the assessment of bilingual aphasia. For instance, it might generally be assumed that, premorbidly, the patient was truly bilingual. In most cases, this assumption is a hard one to meet. Very few individuals are ever completely bilingual. Many people use each of their languages in different contexts and find it difficult to switch languages across contexts. Many acquired their languages at different times in their lives or in a different manner, thus shaping the way in which the languages may be used or accessed.

Second, the assessment of bilingual aphasia assumes that both patient and examiner speak the same languages and the same dialects of those languages. Numerous researchers have addressed this issue with regard to the evaluation and education of school children who speak languages and dialects that differ from the language of instruction. Sato (1989) has discussed the consequences of this problem with particular regard to the situation in Hawaii in which Hawaiian Creole English is often spoken in place of standard English. Paradis and Libben (1987) have warned against trivializing these issues in the assessment of bilingual aphasia and have called for detailed interviews and standardized testing to compensate for these potential problems.

The present paper provides examples for the importance of these issues in the assessment of bilingual aphasia. Specifically, we will review twelve cases of multilingual aphasia in Japanese-Americans living in the state of Hawaii. In particular, we will discuss two cases of differential language impairment between the two languages tested: standard Japanese and standard English. Explanations for this differential impairment will be discussed in relation to the two assumptions of binguality described above, placed against the backdrop of a fascinating multicultural environment.

In the beginning, there was an island   (Bickerton, 1977, p. 72)

Before proceeding with the descriptions of the patients and their language deficits, it is important to understand the context in which these assessments took place. Though mostly known for their magnificent valleys, volcanos, sunsets and ocean views, the islands of Hawaii are also the meeting place for many different ethnic groups. The original inhabitants were presumably the Polynesians who settled the islands as early as the eighth centrury A.D. Since the arrival of Captain James Cook in the eighteenth century, travelers from numerous different countries and societies began immigrating to Hawaii. The Japanese began arriving in greater numbers around the late 1880s when a change in U.S. tariff laws allowed the Hawaiian plantations to significantly increase their exportation of sugar. This resulted in the immigration of many different groups of people, who came to Hawaii in the capacity of indentured laborers. Thus, the integration of Chinese, Japanese, Filipinos, Koreans, Portuguese, Puerto Ricans, and other ethnic groups began in earnest. Soon, these immigrants outnumbered the original inhabitants by a significant number. (See Takaki, 1983, and Lind, 1980, for a review.)

As on other colonialized islands, these immigrants found themselves in need of a common language with which to communicate not only with each other, but with the overlords of the plantations, as well. This led to the development of a " pidgin", a vernacular incorporating features of all the contributing languages, but which never replaced the speaker's native language   (Bickerton, 1981) . The pidgin spoken by given individuals was heavily influenced by their own native languages to the extent that their ethnicity could easily be determined by their speech alone. An example of this can be seen below in the speech of a Japanese immigrant interviewed for the Nonstandard Hawaiian English Project (Bickerton and Odo, 1976, cited in Sato, 1985).

> *Verbatim Transcription*: samtaim gud rod get, samtaim, olsem ben get, enguru get, no? enikain sem. olsem hyumen life, olsem. gud rodu get, enguru get, mauntin get - no?

> *Direct Translation*: sometimes-good-road-get, sometimes, all same-bend-get, angle get, no? any kind-same. all same-human-life, all same. good-road-get, angle-get, mountain-get - no?

> *Standard English Translation*: Sometimes there's a good road, sometimes there's something like a bend, an angle, right? Everything's like that. Human life is the same. There are good roads, there are angles, there are mountains – right?

This pidgin thus became the primary means of communication between the laborers from different countries as well as with the plantation bosses. Still, at home, and in the plantation camps, which were generally ethnically segregated, these individuals spoke the language of their homeland. (Another complicating factor is that the pidgin itself could differ from camp to camp or from island to island, depending on how many different ethnic groups came to that plantation to work.)

The children of these immigrants are generally credited with the relatively quick creolization of Hawaiian Pidgin English. A creole is a pidgin that becomes the native language of its speakers. It carries features from the original pidgin and borrows heavily from the colonial language, as well as the languages that contributed to it. Unlike pidgin, there is no clear influence of any one language on the creole, as in the example below.

> *Verbatim Transcription*: luk nau, a bin go si Toni abaut go spansa da kidz, ae, da baeskitbawl tim, da wan ai ste koch fo - ai tel, ... ai no si wai yu gaiz no kaen spansa da kidz.
>
> *Direct Translation:* look-now, I-been-go-see-Tony-about-go-sponsor-the-kids, eh, the-basketball-team, the-one-I-stay-coach-for - I-tell, ... I-no-see-why-you- guys-no-can-sponsor-the-kids.
>
> *Standard English Translation*: Look now, I went to see Tony about [their] sponsoring the kids, eh, the basketball team that I'm coaching – I said, ... I don't see why you can't sponsor the kids

These children and their subsequent generations of children developed Hawaiian Creole English as their native language once the influence of the immigrant language began to wear off. They spoke Hawaiian Creole English with their friends from other camps, in the playground at school, and, later, at work. But, in addition to the creole, the children of the original immigrants also spoke their parents' language at home, and were thus bilingual during their acquisition of language. When they reached school age, they were also taught Standard English in the classroom, since at that time, Hawaiian Creole English was considered "bad English" and was actively discouraged. Most children of Japanese parents also attended Japanese language school, in which they were taught to read and write Japanese.

Assessing Bilinguality

Twelve patients with this sociolinguistic background came to our attention by way of their participation in the Honolulu Heart Program (HHP), a prospective epidemiologic study of cardiovascular disease and stroke among Japanese-American men. All HHP participants were born between 1900 and 1919 and were residents of the island of Oahu during the study's inception in 1965. Of the original 8,006 participants, approximately 4,200 were still living at the time when the fourth full examination of the entire cohort began, in 1991. Over the last 29 years of the study, extensive information on cultural and medical characteristics of the participants has been gathered in order to study risk factors of cardiovascular disease and stroke. With the fourth exam, an aging component was also added to study dementia and other age-related diseases.

From this fairly homogeneous group of patients, twelve patients who had suffered a thromboembolic infarct or haemorrhage resulting in speech or language impairment and who were considered bilingual on the basis of their responses to previous questionnaires were selected. They ranged in age from 73 to 90 years, were between one and 12 years post onset of their stroke, and had achieved between eight and 14 years of education. Patients were also screened for major medical problems that might have contributed to their aphasia.

All of the patients in this study were the children of Japanese immigrants to Hawaii around the turn of the century. All were born into Japanese-speaking households in the Hawaiian islands, either Oahu, Maui, Kauai, or the big island of Hawaii. All learned Hawaiian Creole English (known in the islands as "Pidgin English") with their friends and others in the community and, with one exception (Patient MI), acquired Standard English in public school. This language background thus made them trilingual. All were married to women who also spoke the same three languages and almost all had visited Japan at some point in their lives. Thus, these patients represent (1) a comparatively large series of multilingual aphasic patients, (2) patients with equally long and well-documented medical histories, (3) a series of patients speaking the same languages and with similar cultural backgrounds, and (4) bilingual speakers of languages that are structurally very different (Japanese and English).

All patients were first interviewed in standard English by a native standard English speaker (ND) to establish their language histories and to obtain a conversational sample in that language. They were then administered the Western Aphasia Battery (WAB), the Motor Speech Evaluation, if appropriate, and two other experimental measures as part of a pilot study on bilingual aphasia in this cohort (Dronkers, Ross, Yamasaki, & White, in preparation). Once the English evaluation was completed, the patient was given a break, after which testing resumed, this time in Japanese, also by a native speaker (YY) speaking Yamaguchi dialect. The conversation protocol, the Japanese translation of the WAB and the experimental measures were thus administered twice, once in each standard language. Formal testing in Hawaiian Creole English was not possible due to a number of linguistic and social issues. All testing was completed within one 2 1/2 hour visit.

The Western Aphasia Battery classifies patients into aphasia types on the basis of four scores: fluency (as measured by responses to six questions and a picture description of a picnic scene), auditory comprehension (measuring yes/no responses to questions and comprehension of single words and sentences), repetition (of 20 sentences increasing in complexity), and naming (of 20 objects, of the names of as many animals as possible, and naming by completing sentences and responding to questions). Table 1 lists the twelve study patients and their WAB classifications by these criteria in English and in Japanese.

In general, a pattern of parallel recovery between the two languages was found, in which testing revealed similar deficits on both evaluations. Four patients were globally aphasic in both English and Japanese. Three were anomic in both languages. One classified with a Wernicke's aphasia in both Japanese and English, and two were found to be within normal limits in both languages. These two patients reported that they currently did not speak as well as they had before the stroke, but their deficits were mild enough so as not to be detected by the WAB, a battery designed to assess more severe deficits.

There were two exceptions to the overall pattern of parallel recovery. One patient was found to have a conduction aphasia in English, and an anomic aphasia in Japanese. The second was diagnosed with a Wernicke's aphasia in English but a Broca's aphasia in Japanese. This latter case demonstrated a particularly striking dissociation, since Wernicke's aphasia is considered a fluent aphasia, and Broca's a nonfluent one. These two cases will be discussed in more detail.

Table 1. Aphasia type in each language for each study patient

Patient	Aphasia Type in English	Aphasia Type in Japanese
Parallel Aphasia		
TI	Global	Global
YO	Global	Global
CS	Global	Global
HY	Global	Global
HO	Anomic	Anomic
RY	Anomic	Anomic
JK	Anomic	Anomic
GM	Wernicke's	Wernicke's
ST	WNL	WNL
SY	WNL	WNL
Differential Aphasia		
MI	Conduction	Anomic
SM	Wernicke's	Broca's

Patient MI: Conduction and Anomic Aphasia

Patient MI was born on the island of Maui but was sent to Japan for his education. When he was 15, he returned to Hawaii where he worked on the plantations and subsequently as a driver for a warehouse, learning Hawaiian Creole English on the job. His first language remained Japanese which he spoke at home with his wife and family. He never attended public school in the United States, and apparently was never truly competent in standard English, a fact not apparent to us at the time of testing. Since his stroke at age 72, he complained of word finding difficulty in both HCE and Japanese. He was tested for the present study two years after his stroke.

Table 2. Western Aphasia Battery Summary Scores for Patient MI

WAB Subtest	Score in English	Score in Japanese
Fluency	6	6
Auditory Comprehension	8.9	8.8
Repetition	6.6	9.2
Naming	7.4	6.6
Aphasia Type	*Conduction*	*Anomic*

maximum score possible for each subtest = 10

WAB summary scores for Patient MI can be found in Table 2. His scores for fluency and auditory comprehension were comparable for both languages. Naming were slightly better in English than in Japanese. His repetition scores, however, were markedly different, with English suffering the most on these tasks. Below are some examples of the types of errors made by this patient on the WAB repetition subtest.

> Examiner: The telephone is ringing.
> Patient MI: Telephone is ringing.
> Examiner: No ifs, ands, or buts.
> Patient MI: No if, and, or but.

Errors consisted largely of omissions of articles and plural -s endings for all the words of the sentence. This pattern was rather different than that usually seen in conduction aphasia. These patients will more typically omit the last words of longer sentences rather than make consistent errors throughout. The constructions produced by MI on repetition were more like those heard in Hawaiian Creole English and led us to suspect that our scoring of his responses was biased by the rules of standard English. In other words, MI may have scored lower on the repetition subtests because he produced repetitions which were correct for HCE but not for standard English.

To compensate for this, we sought to administer the same tests to normal, non-aphasic individuals who shared the same language background and bilinguality as our aphasic patients, but who had not suffered any neurologic impairment. Honolulu Heart Study files were examined to find six non-aphasic participants who matched the study patients on degree of multilinguality reported, age and country of acquisition of their languages, educational environment, and use of English and Japanese during their lifetimes. These participants were contacted and administered the same battery of tests in standard English and Japanese as was given to the 12 aphasic patients. The results from these control subjects were then examined and items missed by the majority were omitted from the patients' protocols. This yielded a WAB score for each aphasic patient which adjusted for the differences between HCE and standard English.

Table 3. Adjusted Western Aphasia Battery Summary Scores for Patient MI

WAB Subtest	Score in English	Score in Japanese
Fluency	6	6
Auditory Comprehension	9.1	8.8
Repetition	8.1	9.2
Naming	7.4	6.6
Aphasia Type	*Anomic*	*Anomic*

maximum score possible for each subtest = 10

Table 3 shows these adjusted WAB summary scores for Patient MI. Adjustment resulted in little change for the fluency, auditory comprehension and naming measures. A substantial improvement could be seen for repetition in English with an increase from 6.6 to 8.1. This higher score now placed the patient above the WAB cutoff of 6.9 for conduction aphasia and now categorized him with an anomic aphasia in both languages. Thus, the grammatical differences between HCE and standard English were enough to cause an erroneous diagnosis of aphasia type in this particular patient.

Patient SM: Wernicke's and Broca's Aphasia

Our second patient with differential aphasia was born on the island of Oahu to Japanese parents. He completed junior high school and also attended Japanese language school. He claimed to have spoken Japanese well and could read and write it fairly well, even before his stroke at age 74, though he had never been in the habit of doing so. He worked as a fisherman for 28 years and spoke Hawaiian Creole English with his co-workers. His wife, now deceased, also spoke English and Japanese, but he currently resided with his daughter and her family who spoke English.

Patient SM's performance resulted in a Wernicke's aphasia in Japanese and a Broca's aphasia in English. Table 4 reviews his scores on the Western Aphasia Battery in both languages. The most apparent difference between English and Japanese lay in those tasks which involve production, i.e., fluency, repetition and naming. His lack of responses caused him to receive lower scores in Japanese than in English on these tasks. On the other hand, his auditory comprehension scores were quite comparable indicating similar competency between languages at least on tasks that did not involve speaking. Adjustment of scores, as was done for the previous patient, did not affect SM's performance since it was the production of his Japanese, not his English, which was compromised.

Table 4. Western Aphasia Battery Summary Scores for Patient SM

WAB Subtest	Score in English	Score in Japanese
Fluency	8	4
Auditory Comprehension	4.3	4.8
Repetition	6.2	2.0
Naming	4.6	.2
Aphasia Type	*Wernicke's*	*Broca's*

maximum score possible for each subtest = 10

Patient SM's description of the WAB picture is a good example of his production in English. Here he is asked to describe a scene in which a couple is having a picnic in front of their house by the water. This sample yielded him a fluency rating of 8 on the WAB. This score, in combination with his performance in auditory comprehension, repetition and naming categorized him with a fluent Wernicke's aphasia.

> Patient SM: "I guess a girl, lady and a man, eh? I guess sitting down and, ah, in different chair, and dis a flag, eh? Well, dat's all I can tell."
> Examiner: "Can you tell what that is?"
> Patient SM: "Well, a bird 'n a lady."
> Examiner: "And what's that person doing?"
> Patient SM: "Well, ah, just lookin', dat's all."

Examiner: "Can you tell what this is over here?"
Patient SM: "Well, dat's a ship."
Examiner: "How about this over here?"
Patient SM: "Dat's a tree and, a ... house."

In Japanese, however, Patient SM produced only a few isolated words, switched frequently to English, and would not respond to further attempts at eliciting more Japanese. This resulted in a fluency rating of 4 on the WAB, indicating a telegraphic style using only single words and automatic phrases. The classification parameters of the WAB places all patients with fluency ratings of 0 to 4 in the category of nonfluent aphasias. In this case, SM's comprehension, repetition and naming scores yielded a diagnosis of Broca's aphasia.

Whether Patient SM simply chose not to speak more Japanese, or, was in fact, disabled by the aphasia, is impossible to tell. The fact that his comprehension scores were so similar would imply that he was far more competent in Japanese than his production scores indicated. Test scores are often influenced by attentional and motivational factors, and this seemed to be the case here. Thus, this examination is a good example of the difficulty in assessing the bilinguality of an individual, particularly when the aphasia itself prevents an adequate determination of the patient's premorbid language skills.

Conclusions

The linguistic and social issues surrounding the assessment of bilingual aphasia in this patient group proved to be exceedingly complex. First, the issue of bilinguality is complicated by the widespread use of Hawaiian Creole English (HCE) in Hawaii, making the assessment of standard English somewhat difficult. Our patients occasionally made what would be considered errors in standard English, but would be correct in HCE. Thus, the degree of bilinguality must be qualified by the level of premorbid proficiency for all languages previously learned, especially those which bear some resemblance to each other and which are susceptible to frequent switching between languages

Second, we learned to be extremely cautious in assuming that patients were equally competent in all languages premorbidly. We attempted to solve this problem by reviewing the questionnaires completed by these patients during the early years of their participation in the Honolulu Heart Program. Even so, language use changes throughout one's lifetime. Language proficiency in childhood may not be maintained in later ages, nor is it the case that the language used during one's working years will necessarily be carried ten or twenty years into retirement.

Third, the assessment of language competency is a sensitive one in Hawaii, particularly for English. Hawaiian Creole English has long carried the stigma of being "bad English" instead of, in fact, a language with its own rules and vocabulary. Making inquiries to an HCE speaker about one's proficiency in English brought looks of confusion and in some cases embarrassment, depending on whether the patients understood us to mean "school English" or "pidgin English". Some patients reported never speaking standard English at home, while others considered it essential to adopt standard English as their native language. In general, patients conveyed that they used whichever language was necessary (Hawaiian Creole English, standard English, or Japanese) to get their message across.

In sum, the assessment of aphasia in these 12 bilingual Japanese-Americans has generally supported the theory that injury to the brain affects all the patients' languages equally. However, the finding of differential impairment between languages in at least two patients causes us to reexamine not only the issue of multiple language processing in the brain, but the linguistic and social issues surrounding the evaluation of these languages, as well.

Acknowledgement

This work was supported by a grant from the Dean's Fund at the School of Medicine University of California, Davis.

References

Albert, M. L., & Obler, L. 1978. *The Bilingual Brain: Neuropsychological and Neurolinguistic Aspects of Bilingualism*. New York: Academic Press

Bickerton, D. 1977. *The tongues of islands*. Islands, pp. 68-77.

Bickerton, D. 1981. *The Roots of Language*. Ann Arbor, Michigan: Karoma.

Bickerton, D., & Odo, C. 1976. Change and variation in Hawaiian English. I: General phonology and pidgin syntax No. (Final report on National Science Foundation Project No. GS-39748).

Dronkers, N. F., Ross, G. W., Yamasaki, Y., & White, L. (in preparation). Bilingual aphasia in Japanese-Americans residing in Hawaii: A report of 12 cases.

Lind, A. W. 1980. *Hawaii's people* (Fourth Edition ed.). Honolulu: The University Press of Hawaii.

Paradis, M. 1977. Bilingualism and aphasia. In H. Whitaker & H. A. Whitaker (eds.), *Studies in Neurolinguistics*, vol. 2 (pp. 65-121). New York: Academic Press.

Paradis, M. 1989. Bilingual and polyglot aphasia. In F. Boller & J. Grafman (eds.), *Handbook of Neuropsychology* (pp. 117-140). Amsterdam: Elsevier.

Paradis, M., & Libben, G. 1987. *The assessment of bilingual aphasia*. Hillsdale, NJ.: Lawrence Erlbaum.

Sato, C. 1989. A nonstandard approach to standard English. *TESOL Quarterly*, **23**, 259-282.

Sato, C. J. 1985. Linguistic inequality in Hawaii: The post-creole dilemma. In N. Wolfson & J. Manes (eds.), *Language of Inequality*. Berlin: Mouton.

Silverberg, R., & Gordon, H. W. 1979. Differential aphasia in two bilingual individuals. *Neurology*, **29**, 51-55.

Takaki, R. 1983. Pau Hana: *Plantation Life and Labor in Hawaii*, 1835-1920. Honolulu: University of Hawaii Press.

II. Case studies

5   Acquired aphasia in a bilingual child

Franco Fabbro and Michel Paradis

Neurolinguistic data on acquired aphasia in children

General characteristics

Acquired aphasia in childhood refers to language disorders due to cerebral lesions which have occurred after language acquisition, generally from age 2 to 15 (Hécaen, 1976; Basso, 1992). Acquired childhood aphasia is generally reported to present typical characteristics, which can be observed in almost every young patient: Mutism immediately post-onset with absence of spontaneous speech (Bernhardt, 1885; Guttmann, 1942), extremely rare logorrhea, generally observed in children aged over 10 with lesions due to encephalitis or severe cranial trauma with consequent epilepsy (Pötzl, 1926; Alajouanine & Lhermitte, 1965; Van Hout & Lyon, 1986). Severe auditory comprehension deficits are very rare. In patients who have already learned to write, disorders of writing and of written comprehension have been reported with some frequency (Branco-Lefèvre, 1950).

The most commonly reported symptoms (Satz & Bullard-Bates, 1981; Ozanne & Murdoch, 1992) are simplified syntax with telegraphic style in oral speech (Guttmann, 1942), word-finding difficulties and impoverished lexicon (Alajouanine & Lhermitte, 1965), articulatory disorders (Guttmann, 1942), reading disorders (Alajouanine & Lhermitte, 1965), transient symptoms with good recovery (Bernhardt, 1885; Lenneberg, 1967) and acalculia as a very frequently associated symptom (Hécaen, 1976). Further symptoms observed in older aphasic children are disorders of grammar, anomias, and phonemic, verbal and semantic paraphasias. Naming disorders are frequent and persistent. Phonemic paraphasias are more frequent than semantic paraphasias. Three cases of Wernicke's aphasia in children have been described (Van Dongen, Loonen & Van Dongen, 1985; Van Hout & Lyon, 1986).

Table 1. Frequency of different aphasic symptoms in 15 cases of childhood aphasia due to left hemisphere lesions (Hécaen, 1976)

	Number of cases	%	Evolution
Mutism	9	60	from 5 days to 3 months
Articulatory disorders	12	80	persistent in 4 cases
Auditory verbal comprehension dis.	6	40	persistent in 1 case
Naming disorders	7	46	persistent in 3 cases
Paraphasia	1	7	transient
Reading disorders	9	60	persistent in 3 cases
Writing disorders	13	86	persistent in 7 cases
Acalculia	11	73	frequently persistent

These are transient symptoms and recovery is generally rapid and satisfactory. However, simplified syntax, reduced lexicon, slightly disrupted articulation, written language impairments and acalculia tend to persist. Table 1 shows the frequency of different aphasic symptoms according to Hécaen (1976).

It has been recently observed that comprehension disorders associated with lesions to the left temporal lobe are less frequent in aphasic children than in adults. However, comprehension deficits, albeit differing in severity and in prognosis have been observed (Van Hout, Evard & Lyon, 1985; Vargha-Khadem, Gorman & Waters, 1985; Cooper & Flowers, 1987). For a recent overview of childhood aphasia incidence, symptoms and recovery, see Satz and Lewis (1993).

Evolution and recovery of acquired childhood aphasia

Although aphasic children show rapid and satisfactory recovery of language from the clinical point of view, recent studies suggest that recovery is hardly ever complete in children. "Although the recovery is certainly more striking than in the adult, it is important to stress the persistence, at times permanent, of mild verbal deficits, particularly in writing and arithmetic" (Hécaen 1976). Even in those cases where recovery is reported to occur, serious cognitive and academic difficulties often remain and the majority of children with acquired childhood aphasia, even after apparent recovery, have difficulty in following a normal progression through school (Lees & Neville, 1990; Ozanne & Murdoch, 1992).

Acquired aphasia in bilingual children

Only one case of acquired aphasia in a bilingual child has been described so far (Bouquet, Tuvo & Paci, 1981). This was the case of a bilingual Italian-Croatian 4-year-old boy who spoke Italian with his parents and Croatian with his grandmother and his cousins. In a car accident he suffered injury to the temporo-parietal areas of his left hemisphere. After a period of mutism for about one month immediately after the accident, he started recovering Italian first, and only after three months did he begin to speak Croatian. Six months later he could speak Italian fluently, whereas in Croatian he spoke correctly but, as his mother said, not naturally, as if he had to translate from Italian into Croatian what he was going to say. Three years after the lesion, the child was diagnosed as having recovered both languages completely.

The present chapter describes another recent case of acquired aphasia in a bilingual child. In 1993, a young Friulian-Italian bilingual aphasic patient, K.B., who had been followed since 1987 was tested with the Friulian (Paradis & Fabbro, 1993) and the Italian (Paradis & Canzanella, 1990) versions of the *Bilingual Aphasia Test* (BAT). In addition, the BAT results were compared with those obtained with two other unilingual tests, the Italian version of the *Aachener Aphasie-Test* (Luzzati, Willmes & De Bleser, 1992) and an Italian battery of tests for the evaluation of language disorders in children (Ferrari, De Renzi, Faglioni, Barbieri, 1981).

The Friulian Language

Friulian is a Rhaeto-Romance language spoken by over half a million people in north-eastern Italy in areas bordering on Austria and Slovenia. The structural distance between Friulian and Italian may be roughly compared to that between Catalan and Spanish. Friulians also understand, speak and write Italian, the official language used for instruction in the schools.

Table 2. Friulian and Italian phoneme inventories

Friulian						
consonants	bilabial	labio-dental	dental/alveolar	palato-alveolar	palatal	velar
stops	p b		t d		k' g'	k g
fricatives		f v	s z	ʃ		
affricates			ts dz	tʃ dʒ		
nasals	m		n		ɲ	
laterals			l			
rhotics			r			
glides						

vowels	lax			tense		
	front	central	back	front	central	back
high	i		u	ī		ū
mid-high	e		o	c̄		ō
mid-low	ɛ		ɔ	ɛ̄		ɔ̄
low		a			ā	

Italian						
consonants	bilabial	labio-dental	dental/alveolar	palato-alveolar	palatal	velar
stops	p b		t d			k g
fricatives		f v	s z			
affricates			ts dz	tʃ dʒ		
nasals	m		n			
laterals			l		ʎ	
rhotics			r			
glides	w				j	

vowels	front	central	back			
high	i		u			
mid-high	e		o			
mid-low	ɛ		ɔ			
low		a				

At the phonological level, Friulian and Italian differ in two main aspects (Table 2). Friulian has palatal consonants which do not exist in Italian. Unlike Italian, Friulian has short and long vowels that contrast phonemically (e.g., *lat* = milk; *lât* = gone). At the lexical level, there are many significant differences between the two languages. Table 3 shows the words used on the naming and translation tasks in the Friulian and Italian versions of the BAT.

Table 3. Translation equivalents from the Friulian/Italian BAT (Part C)

Friulian	Italian	Friulian	Italian	Friulian	Italian
428. morâr	albero	438. curtis	coltello	448. rasôr	rasoio
429. nêf	neve	439. puarte	porta	449. mûr	muro
430. balcon	finestra	440. orele	orecchio	450. cuel	collo
431. martiel	martello	441. savalon	sabbia	451. spongje	burro
432. pès	pesce	442. valîs	valigia	452. cjapiel	cappello
433. lat	latte	443. amôr	amore	453. tristerie	cattiveria
434. cjaval	cavallo	444. bruteçe	bruttezza	454. contentece	gioia
435. cjamese	camicia	445. coragjo	coraggio	455. pore	paura
436. rose	fiore	446. onestât	onestá	456. matetât	pazzia
437. cjadrê	sedia	447. rason	ragione	457. bieleçe	bellezza

At the syntactic level, a substantial difference is that in Italian subject pronouns are optional and most often omitted, whereas in Friulian, not only are they always obligatory, but in most contexts nouns and pronouns must be coupled with a reinforcing (pleonastic) pronoun, as in the following examples:

Friulian:	Noaltris	*o*	sin	boins fruz	
Italian:	Noi		siamo	bravi ragazzi	(We are good boys)

Friulian:	Checo	*al*	nete	le machine	
Italian:	Francesco		pulisce	l'auto	(Frank washes the car)

For a comprehensive description of the Friulian language, see Nazzi Matalon (1977) and Haiman & Benincà (1992).

In addition to speakers living in Friuli, about 500,000 people living in Argentina are of Friulian origin. In many of these families, Friulian is still spoken as mother tongue along with Spanish. In Canada, there are tens of thousands of Friulian immigrants, most of them based around Toronto, who speak Friulian besides English. Substantial Friulian communities also live in France, Germany, and Australia.

Neurolinguistic evaluation of K.B.

Clinical history

K.B., a right-handed girl, was born on 27 December, 1978. Friulian is K.B.'s native language. Her parents, grandparents and sister speak Friulian at home. At the age of 3, K.B. was sent to kindergarden, where Italian was the official language and where she started to learn that language. At 6 she was enrolled in elementary school, where she learned to read and write in Italian.

At the age of 7 years and 4 months, while attending the second class of elementary school, she suddenly had an episode of loss of consciousness lasting about 30 minutes. When she recovered consciousness, she could not speak and presented a right hemiplegia. She was diagnosed as having suffered from an idiopathic childhood hemiplegia (Bickerstaff, 1972).

At the time of her admission at the hospital, the patient presented an aphasia with inability to speak, but good comprehension of oral speech commands both in Friulian and in Italian. A CT-scan performed a few days later showed an ischemic lesion in the left temporo-frontal lobe and in the left basal ganglia. Site and extent of lesion are shown in the CT-scan performed 19 months after the stroke (Figures 1 and 2).

After one week of complete mutism, K.B. started producing monosyllables, after two weeks she produced some words in Italian with phonemic paraphasias. One month after her accident she started producing simple sentences in Italian (L2), speaking very slowly. Even though addressed in Friulian by her parents, she answered in Italian (with several phonemic paraphasias).

For one month she only spoke Italian and only after two months did she start speaking Friulian too. Speech was slow and exhibited telegraphic style in both languages; at times she omitted words and did not conjugate verbs appropriately.

Soon afterwards she began a program of speech therapy in Italian which lasted for about 1.5 years. She learned to write with her left hand.

Since then, K.B. has been followed neurologically and neurolinguistically. The girl went back to school and was individually followed by a special teacher, thus succeeding in completing elementary school (5 years in total) and 3 years of junior high school. In June 1993 she successfully completed the first year at a vocational training school (catering services).

At present, only with careful investigations can one detect slight deficits in oral speech. Her mother, who speaks in Friulian with her, still has the impression that she speaks somewhat telegraphically. Even though the girl improved dramatically, she still has severe disorders in writing and arithmetic. From a neurological point of view K.B. only presents minimal difficulties in the fine movements of the right hand and slight pyramidal signs of the right leg (Babinski sign, slight hypertonia).

Neuropsychological assessment

K.B. has preserved intelligence. She has no problems of apraxia, agnosia, verbal memory or temporal orientation. A dichotic listening test and a verbal-manual interference test were compatible with a right-hemisphere superiority for verbal functions (Table 4).

Neurolinguistic assessment

a) Results on Ferrari, De Renzi, Faglioni and Barbieri's (1981) test are provided in Table 5. In April 1989 at the age of 11, K.B. already presented a normal clinical situation according to this battery of tests for detecting children's language

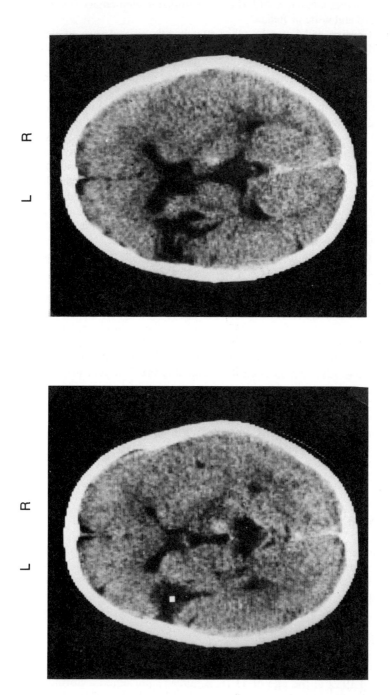

Figure 1. CT scans of patient K.B. showing an ischemic lesion to the left fronto-temporal lobe and to the left basal ganglia (performed on 10 December 1987).

L   R

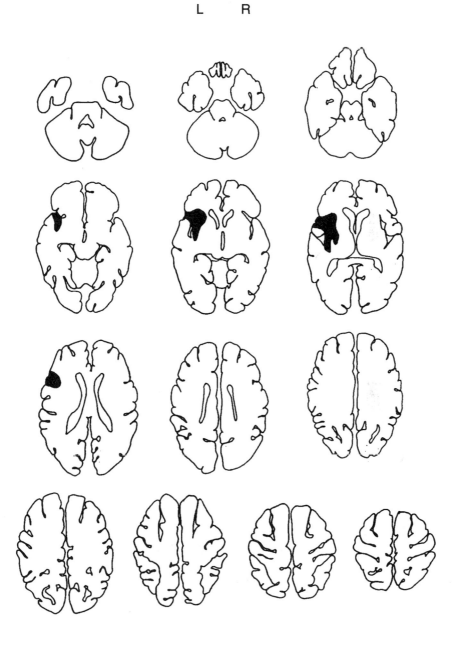

Figure 2. The templates following Damasio & Damasio (1989: 203) show the extent of the lesion. They represent an elaboration of CT scan data.

Table 4. Neuropsychological assessment

Patient: K.B. (born 27 December 1978)
Onset of disease: 5 March 1986

April 1987:
Wechsler Intelligence Scale for Children (WISC) in L2
        Verbal IQ = 108
        Performance IQ = 106
        Total IQ = 107
Dichotic listening test in L2 (Kimura 1963)
        Right ear = 20 digits/60
        Left ear = 41 digits/60
Verbal-manual interference in L2 (Sussman et al. 1982)
        Right hand = 10%
        Left hand = 20%

April 1993:
        Left-hand preference (Briggs & Nebes, 1975): -22
        Temporal orientation (Benton et al., 1983): 100/100
        Digit span (Benton et al., 1983) : 5
        Constructive apraxia (De Renzi, 1982): 22/22
        Ideomotor apraxia (Benton et al., 1983): 20/20
        Bucco-facial apraxia (Benton et al., 1983): 18/20
        Left-right orientation (Benton et al., 1983): 19/20
        Identification of objects, faces, colors (Bisiach et al., 1982): correct
        Digital agnosia (Benton et al., 1983): 24/24

Table 5. A battery for detecting children language disorders
(Ferrari, De Renzi, Faglioni & Barbieri, 1981)

Date of test administration: April 24th, 1989 (age 10 years and 4 months)

Test administered in Italian (L2)

	Correct items	Evaluation
Visual naming	13/20	> 5° normal
Spontaneous speech	6/10	> 5° normal
Sentence repetition	14/14	> 5° normal
Token Test	35/36	> 5° normal

disorders, which was administered in Italian. However, she still had serious problems, as revealed by her school records (especially in writing and mathematics).

b) Results on the Italian version of the *Aachener Aphasie-Test* (Luzzati, Willmes & De Bleser, 1992) obtained in April 1993 are provided in Table 6. Although in some parts of the test there were slight to minimal deficits, the automatic classification system yielded the final result of only 6.9% aphasic performance.

Table 6. Aachener Aphasie-Test AAT (Italian Version)
(Luzzati, Willmes & De Bleser, 1992)

Date of test administration: April 13th, 1993 (age 14 years and 4 months)

Test in Italian L2

	Evaluation	
Spontaneous Speech		
Communicative behavior	5/5	
Articulation and prosody	4/5	
Automatic speech	5/5	
Semantic structure	5/5	
Phonemic structure	5/5	
Syntactic structure	4/5	
	Raw Score	Degree of Deficit
Token Test	48/50	minimal
Repetition	140/150	slight-minimal
Written language	88/90	slight-minimal
Naming	119/120	minimal
Comprehension	100/120	slight-minimal

ALLOC Classification
(non-parametric program for discriminative analysis)

Aphasia = 6.9%
Non aphasia = 93.1%

---

c) Results obtained from the patient's spontaneous speech for the *Bilingual Aphasia Test* in Friulian are provided in Table 7, and in Italian in Table 8. Morphosyntactic errors are analyzed in Table 9.

In both languages K.B. presents *agrammatic features*: omission of free grammatical morphemes in obligatory contexts are more frequent in L1 than in L2 (Friulian = 16.51%; Italian = 0.8%) and they are mainly related to the omission of obligatory pronouns (31 errors out of 36).

The patient produced some *phonemic and semantic paraphasias* in both languages. This deficit is in agreement with the clinical observations by Van Hout et al. (1985) and Cooper and Flowers (1987), who found these deficits to be persistent in acquired childhood aphasias.

Table 7. Analysis of 3.5 minutes of Friulian spontaneous speech

Number of utterances	73
Total number of words	449
Mean length of utterance	6.15
Mean length of the 5 longest utterances	9.6
Number of different words	128
Type/token ratio	0.61
Number of neologisms	Ø
Number of phonemic paraphasias resulting in nonwords	6
Number of phonemic paraphasias resulting in words	3
Number of semantic paraphasias	3
Number of verbal paraphasias (unrelated words)	Ø

Morphosyntactic errors and percent in obligatory contexts	Number	Percent
Omission of free grammatical morphemes	36	16.51
Omission of full verbs	1	1.6
Substitution of inflectional morphemes	2	1.1
Substitution of free grammatical morphemes	2	0.9
Addition of grammatical morphemes in inappropriate contexts	Ø	Ø

Number of word-order errors	Ø
Number of verbs per utterance	0.8
Number of subordinate clauses	6
Number of intraphrasal pauses	20
Number of circumlocutions	Ø
Number of stereotypic phrases	2
Evidence of word finding difficulties	20

Detection of foreign accent (0: none; 5: very strong)	Ø
Number of inappropriate foreign words	5
Number of semantically deviant sentences	Ø
The discourse is cohesive	Yes
The discourse is pragmatically sound	Yes

Echolalia	Number	Percent
Partial or total repetitions of the examiner's questions	Ø	Ø
Self-repetitions	1	1.2
Words in echoed utterances	Ø	Ø
Words in self-repetitions	2	0.3
Total number of utterances repeated	1	1.2
Total number of words repeated	2	0.3

Table 8. Analysis of 5.5 minutes of Italian spontaneous speech

Number of utterances	81
Total number of words	532
Mean length of utterance	6.56
Mean length of the 5 longest utterances	12.6
Number of different words	126
Type/token ratio	0.45
Number of neologisms	Ø
Number of phonemic paraphasias resulting in nonwords	10
Number of phonemic paraphasias resulting in words	2
Number of semantic paraphasias	3
Number of verbal paraphasias (unrelated words)	Ø

Morphosyntactic errors and percent in obligatory contexts	Number	Percent
Omission of free grammatical morphemes	2	0.8
Omission of full verbs	Ø	Ø
Substitution of inflectional morphemes	2	0.7
Substitution of free grammatical morphemes	4	1.6
Addition of grammatical morphemes in inappropriate contexts	4	1.6

Number of word-order errors	Ø
Number of verbs per utterance	0.95
Number of subordinate clauses	3
Number of intraphrasal pauses	40
Number of circumlocutions	Ø
Number of stereotypic phrases	20
Evidence of word finding difficulties	40

Detection of foreign accent (0: none; 5: very strong)	Ø
Number of inappropriate foreign words	4
Number of semantically deviant sentences	Ø
The discourse is cohesive	Yes
The discourse is pragmatically sound	Yes

Echolalia	Number	Percent
Partial or total repetitions of the examiner's questions	1	1.3
Self-repetitions	11	15.0
Words in echoed utterances	3	0.6
Words in self-repetitions	28	6.2
Total number of utterances repeated	12	16.4
Total number of words repeated	31	6.9

Table 9.   Morphosyntactic errors and percentage of errors in obligatory contexts

Omission of free grammatical morphemes

	L1	16.5%	**L2**	0.8%
Prepositions	Ø	Ø	Ø	Ø
Conjunctions	Ø	Ø	Ø	Ø
Articles	1	4.3%	2	3.8%
Obligatory pronouns	31	43.6%	Ø	Ø
Auxilary verbs	4	15.4%	Ø	Ø
Omission of full verbs	1	1.6%	Ø	Ø

Substitution of inflectional morphemes

	L1	1.1%	**L2**	0.7%
Verbs	2	3.2%	1	1.0%
Adjectives	Ø	Ø	1	1.5%
Nouns	Ø	Ø	Ø	Ø

Substitution of free grammatical morphemes

	L1	0.9%	**L2**	1.6%
Prepositions	Ø	Ø	2	4.0%
Conjunctions	Ø	Ø	Ø	Ø
Articles	Ø	Ø	1	1.9%
Obligatory pronouns	2	2.8%	1	1.8%
Auxilary verbs	Ø	Ø	Ø	Ø

Addition of grammatical morphemes in inappropriate context

	L1	Ø	**L2**	1.6%
Prepositions	Ø	Ø	Ø	Ø
Conjunctions	Ø	Ø	Ø	Ø
Articles	Ø	Ø	1	1.9%
Obligatory pronouns	Ø	Ø	3	5.4%
Auxilary verbs	Ø	Ø	Ø	Ø

K.B. also demonstrates *word-finding difficulty*, especially in L2 (L1 = 20; L2 = 40). This kind of impairment has been often observed in children with acquired aphasia and tends to persist (Hécaen 1983).

Sporadic perseverations and echolalias occurred in spontaneous speech in L2.

Results obtained by Linguistic levels for various language skills are provided for Italian in Table 10 and for Friulian in Table 11. Results obtained in both directions (i.e., from L1 → L2 and from L2 → L1) on the recognition of lexical translation equivalents in a list of words in the other language, translation of words, translation of sentences, and grammaticality judgements on sentences erroneously incorporating a morphosyntactic feature of the other language, are given in Table 12.

Table 10. Bilingual Aphasia Test scores in Friulian

Scores by linguistic level and skill

Compre	Repet	Jdgmt	LexAcc	Propos	Readg	Writg		
17/18	28/30	0/0	3/3	3/3	10/10	0/0	Phonlgy	61/64
0/0	0/0	0/0	15/23	15/23	0/0	0/0	Mrphlgy	30/46
105/117	5/7	10/10	3/3	16/18	16/20	5/5	Lexicon	160/180
60/63	28/30	27/30	47/56	3/3	19/20	15/15	Syntax	199/217
11/11	0/0	10/10	29/33	3/3	6/6	0/0	Smntics	59/63
Compre	Repet	Jdgmt	LexAcc	Propos	Readg	Writg		
193/209	61/67	47/50	97/118	40/50	51/56	20/20		

Decimal scores by linguistic level and skill

Compre	Repet	Jdgmt	LexAcc	Propos	Readg	Writg		
0.944	0.933	N/A	1.000	1.000	1.000	N/A	Phonlgy	0.953
N/A	N/A	N/A	0.652	0.652	N/A	N/A	Mrphlgy	0.652
0.897	0.714	1.000	1.000	0.888	0.800	1.000	Lexicon	0.888
0.952	0.933	0.900	0.839	1.000	0.950	1.000	Syntax	0.917
1.000	N/A	1.000	0.878	1.000	1.000	N/A	Smntics	0.936
Compre	Repet	Jdgmt	LexAcc	Propos	Readg	Writg		
0.923	0.910	0.940	0.822	0.800	0.910	1.000		

Table 11. Bilingual Aphasia Test scores in Italian

Scores by linguistic level and skill

Compre	Repet	Jdgmt	LexAcc	Propos	Readg	Writg		
16/18	30/30	0/0	3/3	3/3	9/10	0/0	Phonlgy	61/64
0/0	0/0	0/0	16/23	16/23	0/0	0/0	Mrphlgy	32/46
106/117	7/7	10/10	3/3	18/18	20/20	5/5	Lexicon	169/180
60/63	30/30	30/30	51/56	3/3	18/20	15/15	Syntax	207/217
9/11	0/0	8/10	29/33	3/3	6/6	0/0	Smntics	55/63
Compre	Repet	Jdgmt	LexAcc	Propos	Readg	Writg		
191/209	67/67	48/50	102/118	43/50	53/56	20/20		

Decimal scores by linguistic level and skill

Compre	Repet	Jdgmt	LexAcc	Propos	Readg	Writg		
0.888	1.000	N/A	1.000	1.000	0.900	N/A	Phonlgy	0.953
N/A	N/A	N/A	0.695	0.695	N/A	N/A	Mrphlgy	0.695
0.905	1.000	1.000	1.000	1.000	1.000	1.000	Lexicon	0.938
0.952	1.000	1.000	0.910	1.000	0.900	1.000	Syntax	0.953
0.818	N/A	0.800	0.878	1.000	1.000	N/A	Smntics	0.873
Compre	Repet	Jdgmt	LexAcc	Propos	Readg	Writg		
0.913	1.000	0.960	0.864	0.860	0.946	1.000		

Table 12. Bilingual Aphasia Test, Part C

Scores by section

Word recognition L1 → L2	5/5	1.000
Word recognition L2 → L1	5/5	1.000
Translation of concrete words L1 → L2	4/5	0.800
Translation of abstract words L1 → L2	4/5	0.800
Translation of concrete words L2 → L1	4/5	0.800
Translation of abstract words L2 → L1	3/5	0.600
Translation of sentences L1 → L2	2/6	0.333
Translation of sentences L2 → L1	0/6	0.000
Grammaticality Judgments L1	14/14	1.000
Grammaticality Judgments L2	14/14	1.000

Scores by linguistic level and skill

		L1 → L2				L2 → L1	
2/6	14/14	Mrphosyntax	16/20	0/6	14/14	Mrphosyntax	14/20
13/15	0/0	Lexicon	13/15	12/15	0/0	Lexicon	12/15
		Translation	15/21			Translation	12/21
		Gram. judgm	14/14			Gram. judgm	14/14

Decimal scores

		L1 → L2				L2 → L1	
0.333	1.000	Mrphosyntax	0.800	0.000	1.000	Mrphosyntax	0.700
0.866	n/a	Lexicon	0.866	0.800	n/a	Lexicon	0.800
		Translation	0.714			Translation	0.571
		Gram. jdgmnt	1.000			Gram.jdgmnt	1.000

This analysis revealed that both languages showed a parallel recovery, with a slight superiority of L2 over L1 (average correct responses in L2= 93.47%; L1 = 90.07%, t-test p =.06). The most disrupted linguistic level is morphology (L1 = 65.2%; L2 = 69.5%). Mental arithmetic was disrupted in both languages.

TRANSLATION TASKS

Translation of concrete words is good, whereas translation of abstract words and sentences is extremely poor and is worse from L2 into L1 than from L1 into L2. Grammaticality judgements are good in both languages.

SPONTANEOUS WRITING

A neurolinguistic analysis of 37 compositions, which the patient had written in class at the age of 13 (third grade of secondary school), was performed and revealed a significant amount of aphasic mistakes, such as agrammatic and paragrammatic errors, phonemic, semantic and verbal paraphasias, neologisms and spelling mistakes (Table 13).

Table 13. Spontaneous writing in Italian (L2)

Analysis of 37 compositions written in class during the 3rd grade of secondary school (Patient's age 13 years)

	Total	Mean
Number of sentences	1116	30.1
Total number of words	5975	168.5
Mean length of sentence	5.3	-
Number of different words	-	64.9
Type/token ratio	-	0.78
Number of neologisms	9	0.24
Number of literal paraphasias → non-words	60	1.62
Number of literal paraphasias → words	8	0.21
Number of semantic paraphasias	9	0.24
Number of verbal paraphasias	4	0.10
Number of spelling mistakes	118	3.19
Number of perseverations	4	0.10
Number of paragrammatisms	96	2.59
Number of missing obligatory gramm. morphemes	88	2.37
Number of word-order errors	6	0.16
Number of verbs per sentence	-	0.97
Number of subordinate clauses	365	9.86
Number of circumlocutions	-	-
Number of stereotypic phrases	5	0.13
Number of semantically deviant sentences	4	0.10
The text is cohesive	yes	
The text is pragmatically sound	yes	

Conclusions

Four main conclusions can be drawn from our analysis of K.B.

1. The BAT offered the possibility to test the patient's two languages with equivalent instruments. One of these languages is Friulian, for which there is no other test battery. It also provides a more discriminating analysis of linguistic disorders than the *Aachener Aphasie-Test* or Ferrari's (1981) battery, as ascertained in a study by De Luca, Fabbro, Vorano & Lovati (1994).

2. Most probably, even though from a clinical point of view language recovery in children may appear complete, it might hardly ever be so (Ozanne and Murdoch 1992). For example, K.B. still presents difficulties in morphology, in writing and in mental arithmetic, which were detrimental to her school achievement.

3. Generally speaking, in the case of a bilingual child, as for adults, there might be apparent differential deficits due to structural differences between the two languages. In K.B. omissions of free grammatical morphemes were more frequent in L1 (Friulian), because in Friulian personal pronouns are always obligatory (Nazzi Matalon 1977; Haiman and Benincà 1992), whereas in Italian, her L2, they can be omitted, and also because very often in Friulian these pronouns are doubled

(redundant personal pronouns). This shows how the same aphasic deficit may be more evident in one language than (or even not present) in another.

4. The fact that K.B. performed generally better on linguistic skills in L2 than in L1 may be due to the explicit learning of L2 in the school environment. The components of explicit metalinguistic knowledge, being subserved by declarative memory, are likely to be more resistant to aphasic disorders than components of implicit linguistic competence that rely on procedural memory (Paradis 1994). It may also be due to a more frequent use of L2 than L1 in a wider variety of situations. Or it may be an artefact of the structural differences between the two languages (Paradis, 1988).

References

Alajouanine, T., & Lhermitte F. 1965. Acquired aphasia in children. *Brain,* **88**, 653-662.

Basso, A. 1992. Aphasia in left-handers and children. *Journal of Neurolinguistics*, **7** , 347-361.

Benton, A.L., Hamsher, K., Varney, N.R., & Spreen, O. 1983. *Contributions to neuropsychological assessment. A clinical manual.* New York: Oxford University Press.

Bernhardt, M. 1885. Über die spastische Cerebralparalyse im Kindesalter (Hemiplegia spastica infantilis), nebst einem Exkurs über Aphasie bei Kindern. *Archiv für pathologische Anatomie und Physiologie und für klinische Medizin*, **102**, 26-80.

Bickerstaff, E.R. 1972. Cerebrovascular disease in infancy and childhood. In Vinken P.J. and Bruyn G.W. (Eds.) *Handbook of Clinical Neurology, Vascular Diseases of the Nervous System, Part II.* Amsterdam: North Holland.

Bisiach, E., Cappa, S., & Vallar, G. 1983. *Guida all'esame neuropsicologico.* Milano: Cortina.

Branco-Lefèvre, A.F. 1950. Contribuição para o estudo da psicopatologia da afasia en criancas. *Archivos Neuro-Psyquiatria* (San Paulo), **8**, 345-393.

Briggs, G.C. & Nebes, R.D. 1975. Patterns of hand preference in a student population. *Cortex*, **11**, 230-238.

Bouquet, F., Tuvo F., & Paci M. 1981. Afasia traumatica in un bambino bilingue nel 5° anno di vita. *Neuropsichiatria Infantile*, **235-236**, 159-169.

Cooper, J.A., & Flowers C.R. 1987. Children with a history of acquired apahsia: Residual language and academic impairments. *Journal of Speech and Hearing Disorders*, **52**, 251-262.

Cross, J.A. and Ozanne A.E. 1992. Acquired childhood aphasia: Assessment and treatment. In Murdoch B.E. (Ed.) *Acquired Neurological Speech/Language Disorders in Childhood*, London: Taylor and Francis.

De Luca, G., Fabbro, F., Vorano, L., & Lovati, L. 1994. Valutazione con il Bilingual Aphasia Test (BAT) della rieducazione dell'afasico multilingue. Paper presented at the 4th Meeting, Disturbi cognitivi, comportamentali e della comunicazione nelle lesioni cerebrali acquisite, Ospedale di Medicina Fisica e Riabilitazione "Gervasutta", Udine, Italy, 1 July.

De Renzi, E. 1982. Disorders of space exploration and cognition. Baffins Lane: Wiley & Sons.

Ferrari, E., De Renzi E., Faglioni P., & Barbieri E. 1981. Standardizzazione di una batteria per la valutazione dei disturbi del linguaggio nell'età scolare. *Neuropsichiatria Infantile*, **235-236**, 145-158.

Guttmann, E. 1942. Aphasia in children. *Brain*, **65**, 205-219.

Haiman, J., & Benincà, P. 1992. *The Rhaeto-Romance Languages*. London: Routledge.

Hécaen, H. 1976. Acquired aphasia in children and the ontogenesis of hemispheric functional specialization. *Brain and Language*, **3**, 114-134.

Hécaen, H. 1983. Acquired aphasia in children: Revisited. *Neuropsychologia*, **21**, 581-587.

Kimura, D. 1963. Speech lateralization in young children as determined by an auditory test. *Journal of Comparative Physiological Psychology*, **56**, 899-902.

Lees, J.A. & Neville, B.G.R. 1990. Acquired aphasia in childhood: Case studies of five children. *Aphasiology*, **5**, 463-478.

Lenneberg, E. 1967. *Biogical Foundations of Language*. New York: Wiley.

Luzzati, C., Willmes, K., & De Bleser, R. 1992. *Aachener Aphasie-Test, Versione Italiana*. Firenze: Organizzazioni Speciali.

Nazzi Matalon, Z. 1977. *Marilenghe. Gramatiche Furlane*. Gurize: Istitût di Studis Furlans.

Ozanne, A.E., & Murdoch B.E. 1992. Acquired childhood aphasia: Neuropathology, linguistic characteristics and prognosis. In B.E. Murdoch (Ed.), *Acquired Neurological Speech/Language Disorders in Childhood*, London: Taylor and Francis.

Paradis, M. 1988. Recent developments in the study of agrammatism: Their import for the assessment of bilingual aphasia. *Journal of Neurolinguistics*, **3**, 127-160.

Paradis, M. 1994. Neurolinguistic aspects of implicit and explicit memory: Implications for bilingualism and SLA. In N. Ellis (Ed.) *Implicit and Explicit Learning of Languages* (Pp. 393-419). London: Academic Press.

Paradis, M. & Canzanella, M. 1990. *Test per l'afasia in un bilingue*. Hillsdale, NJ.: Lawrence Erlbaum Associates.

Paradis, M. & Fabbro, F. 1993. *Test pe afasie in tun bilingue*. Hillsdale, NJ.: Lawrence Erlbaum Associates.

Pötzl, T. 1926. Über sensorische Aphasie im Kindesalter. *Hals-, Nasen-Ohrenklinik*, **14**, 109-118.

Satz, P. & Bullard-Bates, C. 1981. Acquired aphasia in Children. In M. Taylor-Sarno (Ed.) *Acquired Aphasia*, New York: Academic Press.

Satz, O. & Lewis, R. 1993. Acquired aphasia in children. In G. Blanken, J. Dittmann, H. Grimm, J. Marshall & C.-W. Wallesch (eds.), *Linguistic disorders and pathologies* (Pp. 646-659). Berlin: Walter de Gruyter.

Sussman, H.M., Franklin, P., & Simon, T. 1982. Bilingual speech: bilateral control? *Brain and Language*, **15**, 125-142.

Van Dongen, H.R., Loonen M.C.B., & Van Dongen, K.J. 1985. Anatomical basis of acquired fluent aphasia in children. *Annals of Neurology*, **17**, 306-309.

Van Hout, A., Evrard P., & Lyon G. 1985. On the positive semiology of acquired aphasia in children. *Developmental Medicine and Child Neurology*, **27**, 231-241.

Van Hout, A. & Lyon G. 1986. Wernicke's aphasia in a 10-year-old boy. *Brain and Language*, **29**, 268-286.

Vargha-Khadem, F., Gorman, A.M. & Waters G.V. 1985. Aphasia and handedness in relation to hemispheric side, age and injury and severity of cerebral lesion during childhood. *Brain*, **108**, 677-696.

6 Oral and written naming in a multilingual aphasic patient

Nicole Stadie, Luise Springer, Ria de Bleser and Frauke Bürk

Introduction

Multilingual aphasias have been studied in the cognitive literature predominantly in order to discover the structure of the normal multilingual language system (e.g., Albert & Obler, 1978). Issues concerning the nature of this system are whether it is unitary, supporting representational elements of all the languages of the multilingual speaker (Chen & Leung, 1989), or whether there are multiple, language-specific systems (Potter, So,Von Eckardt & Feldman, 1984). A mixed approach is taken by de Groot (1992).

In psycholinguistic studies on lexical and conceptual representations in normal bilinguals, several experimental tasks are used to address these issues, for example, the measurement of reaction times in word translation compared to picture naming (Chen & Leung, 1989; Kroll & Curley, 1988; Potter,et al., 1984), the analysis of errors in word translation (de Groot, 1993), semantic priming within and between languages (Chen & Ng, 1989; Kirsner, Smith, Lockhart, King, & Jain, 1984; Schwanenflugel & Rey, 1986) and interlingual word associations (Taylor, 1976). In these studies, an influence has been found of variables which may differ across target languages such as word frequency (de Groot,1993), level of concreteness (Jin & Fischler, 1987), and context availability for concrete and abstract words (Schwanenflugel, Harnishfeger & Stowe, 1988). The presence or absence of phonemic/graphemic similarity of items across languages, i.e., of cognates versus noncognates, has also been found to play a role in bilingual lexical processing and has thus been taken into consideration especially in current connectionist models.

de Groot and Nas (1991), for example, propose that there is a unitary system for the cognate items of two languages but not for the noncognates. Whereas cognates such as Dutch *vader*: English *father* are linked to a single, language-unspecific semantic (conceptual) representation, noncognates such as Dutch *oom*: English *uncle* have separate, language-specific conceptual nodes. Cognate words are thus in an association network with semantically related words of both languages, whereas noncognates are linked only to conceptual representations of the same language. This is evidenced by the presence of interlingual semantic priming effects for cognates but not for noncognates.

If we assume that cognate items share one single semantic representation and that their lexical nodes are directly connected with each other, then the lexical system receives more activation during naming than in the case of noncognates. For multilingual aphasia, this would predict that the naming of cognate items will be more successful than the naming of noncognates in all languages. A further difference would be expected with respect to semantic errors. If cognates rely on a single semantic system, coordinate responses should occur intra- as well as inter-lingually, whereas only intralingual coordinate responses would be expected for an item which has no cognate in a non-target language.

The aims of the present study were (i) to examine patient S.H.'s oral and written naming in his native German language and two foreign languages, (ii) to analyse the quality of interlingual errors with respect to language typology, and (iii) to determine the influence of phonemic/graphemic similarity on the patient's naming in the various languages.

Subject

The patient, S.H., a native German, is a 76 year-old righthanded male professor of theology and classical philology. He suffered a left-hemispheric haemorrhage on October 1, 1992 without hemiplegia but with a severe aphasia. The CT-scan taken 1.5 months post onset showed a cortico-subcortical temporo-parietal lesion. Initially, S.H.'s aphasia in German was clinically diagnosed with the AAT (Aachen Aphasia Test, Huber, Poeck, Weniger & Willmes, 1984) as a severe Wernicke jargon aphasia. His spontaneous speech was fluent, paragrammatic, with frequent phonemic and semantic paraphasias and neologisms. S.H. was severely impaired in tasks of repetition, reading, writing, naming and comprehension.

At the time of the multilingual examination four months post onset, spontaneous communication had substantially improved. Speech was still fluent and paragrammatic with severe word finding problems but semantic paraphasias and neologisms had become rare. Phonemic paraphasias still occurred frequently as well as "conduite d'approche". There were also significant improvements on all AAT subtests. Single case assessment in German with a battery of tests (Stadie, Cholewa, De Bleser & Tabatabaie, 1994) based on a logogen-type information processing model for single words (Patterson, 1988) showed modality-specific impairments of the non-lexical routes in writing to dictation and repetition but not in reading, whereas lexical processing of monomorphemic words was well-preserved in all modalities. In particular, in writing to dictation, the patient was severely impaired in writing legal nonwords (18/40 correct responses) whereas he could write words with irregular (18/20 correct responses) as well as regular phoneme-grapheme correspondence (20/20 correct responses). Thus, S.H.'s writing of German words was obviously lexically based. Results of intelligence tests (LPS 50+, Sturm, Willmes & Horn, 1993) as well as memory tests (Wechsler-Memory-Scale, Böcher, 1968) showed average to above average performance.

In addition to German, his native language, S.H. had premorbid competence in spoken and written English, which he had first acquired in school. He continued to use it regularly in professional life for letter correspondence and at meetings as well as during a 10-months residence in Israel.

S.H. could also speak, read and write French, which he had learned when he was a prisoner of war in France for two years. S.H. rated his premorbid knowledge of French higher than that of English, but he was unable to produce spontaneous speech in either of these languages after the vascular accident. He also reported some premorbid passive knowledge of modern Hebrew and Danish. In addition, being a classical philologist and a theologian, S.H. had studied several classical languages including Latin, Greek, Hebrew, Aramaic, Phoenician, and ancient Egyptian. S.H.'s self-rating of his premorbid language competences is given in table 1.

Given his good to excellent premorbid active knowledge of French and English, these languages were selected for the cross-language naming study reported below.

Table 1. S.H.'s self-rating of his premorbid language competence

Modalities	Speaking	Comprehension		Writing
		Auditory	Reading	
Modern languages:				
German	perfect	perfect	perfect	perfect
French	good	excellent	excellent	good
English	moderate	excellent	excellent	moderate
Modern Hebrew	poor	good	good	poor
Danish	poor	good	poor	poor
Classical languages:				
Latin			excellent	good
Greek			excellent	good
Hebrew			excellent	good
Others			good	good

Cross-language naming study

Materials and methods

S.H.'s confrontation naming was examined in German, English and French with 257 line drawings (Snodgrass & Vanderwart, 1980) over a period of six weeks starting four months post onset. From the originally 260 pictures, three items (sandwich, baseball bat, American football) were omitted for cultural reasons. The published drawings were enlarged (x 3 = approx. 1.5" x 1.5") and mounted on plain white cards. They were presented individually for naming in two conditions, namely, oral and written naming. The oral naming and written naming tasks were blocked and counterbalanced for the different languages and modalities and performed in 30 sessions, each containing approximately 50 items. Oral responses were tape recorded and written responses were given by the patient on individual cards that were then removed.

Each language was examined by a different person who was a near-native speaker of the particular language. Responses were scored by four raters as correct or incorrect. Correct responses were either immediately correct, following a semantic or phonological approach, or selfcorrections. For the incorrect responses, a distinction was made between intralingual, interlingual and "other" errors. An error was classified as interlingual, for example, when the patient approached the target by means of a word or a circumlocution in another language. An intralingual error consisted of a substitution or circumlocution in the target language. "Other" errors consisted of no responses or stereotypes, substitutions of names of objects visually related to the target, or nonclassifiable errors which could not unambiguously be assigned to any of the previous categories. Responses and error types were stored for

Table 2. Categories used for rating responses in oral and written naming and examples of S.H.'s responses: (G)=German, (F)=French, (E)=English.

	Categories	Target item	S.H.'s responses
1.1	correct		
1.2	with semantic approach	Socke (G) porte (F) ear (E)	Strumpf, Socke fenètre, porte eye, ear
1.3	with phonemic approach	Pullover (G) cheveux (F) flag (E)	Po Pullover chevais, cheveux flap, flag
	I. intralingual errors		
2	phonemic paraphasia	Pistole (G) ancre (F) cloud (E)	pi.lo.ste,pi.lo.pi.lote acre clown...clows
3.1	semantic paraphasia: superordinate	Heuschrecke (G) orange (F) boot (E)	Insekt fruit shoe
3.2	semantic paraphasia: coordinate	Kappe (G) nuage (F) acordeon (E)	Mütze ciel harmonica
3.3	semantic paraphasia: subordinate, part/whole	Griff (G) oiseau (F) vase (E)	Tür canard flower
3.4	semantic neologism	Schloß (G)	Sicherschlüssel
4.1	appropriate circumlocution	Bollerwagen (G) rouleau à patisserie (F) prawn (E)	Wagen, ein kleiner rouleau pour gateau cildren for car
4.2	inappropriate circumlocution	- - tambour (F) roler skate (E)	- - situation militaire rolling wheel
	II. interlingual errors		
5.1.1	(Partial) translation from german	cerf-volant (F) whistle (E)	dracon pipe
5.1.2	correct German name instead of target name	éléphant (F) cake (E)	Elefant lage..cage.. Kuchen
5.1.3	incorrect German name instead of target name	robe (F) peach (E)	Rock Aprikose
5.2.1	sucessful approach via non- target language	Flasche (G) porc (F) bell (E)	the bottle, Flasche porcco, porc clock, cloche, bell
5.3.1	unsuccessful approach via non-target language	crocodile (E) chameau (F)	Krokodil, crewedow Kamel, taureau
5.3.1	correct name instead of target name	drapeau (F) bicicle (E)	flag biciclette
5.3.2	incorrect name instead of target name	needle (E)	aigle
	III others		
6	no response, stereotype		
7	visual error	Nagelfeile (G) limes à ongles (F) door opener (E)	Dolch couteau bell
8	non-classifiable		
9.1	first part of compound word	Tennisschläger (G)	Tennis
9.2	second part of compound word	rocking chair (E)	...chair

computer analyses of naming in each language and each modality with respect to stimulus characteristics such as familiarity, visual complexity or semantic category of the items (Snodgrass & Vanderwart, 1980). Table 2 gives the response categories used by the raters and examples of S.H.'s responses.

A classification of the stimuli was made with respect to the presence or absence of phonemic/graphemic similarity of the target name in all three languages or in any pair of languages. There were 38 items which were phonologically/ graphemically similar in all three languages, 46 items which were similar in German and English, 25 in English and French, and 13 in German and French. They were compared to the same number of phonemically and graphemically dissimilar items for each set in each modality.

Table 3a gives examples of names which are similar in German, English, and French, table 3b of French-German similarity, table 3c illustrates English-German similarity, and table 3d gives examples of items which are similar in English and French but not in German.

Results

There were no effects of familiarity nor of visual complexity in S.H.'s oral or written naming in any of the three languages and naming impairments were not restricted to specific semantic categories. Furthermore, the patient's responses in written naming showed that his writing reflected access to the graphemic output lexicon of the various languages. He was able to write orthographically irregular words and his responses obeyed the orthographic conventions of the target language. This is in line with his severe impairment in writing non-words to dictation and the absence of regularity effects for words in the German LeMo battery.

Table 4 summarizes the general results and the category of errors for oral and written naming of all 257 items in German, English and French. Correct responses in the patient's native German (G) language were significantly more frequent than in English (E) and French (F) both in oral (O) and written (W) naming (Fisher's exact test, two-tailed, Siegel 1968, GO/EO: p = .000; GO/FO: p = .000; GW/EW: p = .000; GW/FW: p = .000). There was no significant difference for correct oral naming responses between English and French but written naming was significantly better in English than in French (p = .006). However, within any single language, oral and written naming performance did not significantly differ, and correct and incorrect responses for a particular item were consistent across modalities in all languages (p = .01, exact McNemar-test, 1947, two-tailed). Thus, responses in oral and written naming could be treated together for subsequent analyses.

Intralingual errors (i.e., responses within the target language) were more frequent for the native German language than for the other languages. The percentage of "other" errors, in particular of the subtype "no response" was much more frequent in the patient's nonnative languages. Furthermore, semantic paraphasias were more frequent in the mother tongue than in the foreign languages, while circumlocutions occurred almost exclusively in the nonnative languages.

There was also a qualitative difference in the subtypes of semantic errors. Table 5 gives the specification of semantic errors for each language (oral and written naming taken together).

Table 3a.   Examples of phonemic/graphemic similar and dissimilar items for German, English and French words. INr.= Item Number corresponding to the pictures of Snodgrass & Vanderwart (1980)

	phonemic/graphemic similar				phonemic/graphemic dissimilar		
INr.	**German**	**English**	**French**	**INr.**	**German**	**English**	**French**
3	Krokodil	crocodile	crocodile	8	Pfeil	arrow	flèche
4	Anker	anchor	ancre	17	Scheune	barn	grange
16	Banane	banana	banane	18	Faß	barrel	tonneau
38	Bürste	brush	brosse	20	Korb	basket	panier
45	Kanone	cannon	canon	26	Gürtel	belt	ceinture
69	Krone	crown	couronne	28	Vogel	bird	oiseau
92	Flöte	flute	flûte	60	Uhr	watch	horloge
117	Harfe	harpe	harpe	62	Wolke	clouds	nuage
132	Lampe	lamp	lampe	78	Kleid	skirt	robe
174	Pfeife	pipe	pipe	105	Brille	glasses	lunettes
233	Tiger	tiger	tigre	121	Pferd	horse	cheval
236	Tomate	tomato	tomate	129	Drachen	dracon	cerf-volant
243	Trompete	trumpet	trompette	130	Messer	knife	couteau

Table 3b.   Examples of phonemic/graphemic similar and dissimilar items for German and French words. INr.= Item Number corresponding to the pictures of Snodgrass & Vanderwart (1980)

	phonemic/graphemic similar			phonemic/graphemic dissimilar	
INr.	**French**	**German**	**INr.**	**German**	**French**
25	cloche	Glocke	18	Faß	tonneau
66	maïs	Mais	20	Korb	panier
70	tasse	Tasse	21	Bär	ours
74	poupée	Puppe	22	Bett	lit
79	commode	Kommode	28	Vogel	oiseau
112	pistolet	Pistole	29	Bluse	chemisier
135	citron	Zitrone	30	Buch	livre
161	pinceau	Pinsel	31	Stiefel	botte
164	paon	Pfau	33	Schleife	noeud
170	paprika	Paprika	36	Brot	pain
173	ananas	Ananas	41	Knopf	bouton
232	cravate	Krawatte	44	Kerze	bougie
142	homard	Hummer	53	Stuhl	chaise

Table 3c. Examples of phonemic/graphemic similar and dissimilar items for German and English words. INr.= Item Number corresponding to the pictures of Snodgrass & Vanderwart (1980)

	phonemic/graphemic similar			phonemic/graphemic dissimilar	
INr.	**Deutsch**	**English**	INr.	**German**	**English**
6	Apfel	apple	73	Hund	dog
7	Arm	arm	87	Zaun	fence
21	Bär	bear	128	Schlüssel	key
22	Bett	bed	130	Messer	knife
30	Buch	book	148	Berg	mountain
36	Brot	bread	150	Pilz	mushroom
88	Finger	finger	157	Zwiebel	oignon
89	Fisch	fish	162	Hose	trousers
104	Glas	glass	172	Schwein	pig
113	Haar	hair	175	Krug	pot
115	Hand	hand	178	Tasche	bag
122	Haus	house	215	Löffel	spoon
146	Mond	moon	241	Baum	tree

Table 3d. Examples of phonemic/graphemic similar and dissimilar items for English and French words. INr.= Item Number corresponding to the pictures of Snodgrass & Vanderwart (1980)

	phonemic/graphemic similar			phonemic/graphemic dissimilar	
INr.	**English**	**French**	INr.	**English**	**French**
11	asparagus	asperge	89	fish	poisson
32	bottle	bouteille	90	flag	drapeau
41	button	bouton	98	fox	renard
52	chain	chaîne	104	glass	verre
53	chair	chaise	113	hair	cheveux
56	scissors	ciseau	121	horse	cheval
82	eagle	aigle	146	moon	lune
91	flower	fleur	187	ring	bague
140	lion	lion	202	sheep	mouton
148	mountain	montagne	215	spoon	cuillère
157	oignon	oignon	241	tree	arbre
159	ostrich	autruche	255	whistle	sifflet
226	table	table	250	watch	montre

Table 4. Categorization of oral and written naming responses in German, English and French

Response	oral naming			written naming			oral and written naming		
	German n=257	English n=257	French n=257	German n=257	English n=257	French n=257	German n=514	English n=514	French n=514
correct	202 78,6%	85 33,1%	73 28,4%	198 77,0%	87 33,9%	58 22,6%	400 77,8%	172 33,4%	131 25,4%
incorrect	55 21,4%	172 67,0%	184 71,6%	59 23,0%	170 66,1%	199 77,4%	114 22,1%	342 66,5%	383 74,5%
intralingual errors Σ	34 61,8%	55 32,0%	65 35,3%	42 71,2%	64 37,6%	105 52,8%	76 66,6%	97 28,3%	170 44,3%
phonemic errors	9 16,7%	13 7,5%	25 13,5%	12 20,3%	17 10,0%	38 19,1%	21 18,4%	30 8,7%	63 16,4%
semantic errors	24 43,6%	29 16,8%	26 14,1%	30 50,8%	32 19,0%%	28 14,0%	54 47,3%	61 17,8%	54 14,0%
cirumlocution	1 1,8%	13 7,5%	14 7,6%	-	15 8,9%	39 19,6%	1 0,8%	28 8,1%	53 13,8%
interlingual errors Σ	6 10,9%	51 29,7%	31 16,8%	-	26 15,3%	24 12,1%	6 5,2%	77 22,5%	55 14,3%
approach via non-target language	6 10,9%	9 5,2%	4 2,2%	-	2 1,2%	4 2,0%	6 5,2%	11 3,2%	8 2,0%
partial transl. from german	-	13 .7,5%	10 5,4%	-	7 4,1%	4 2,0%	-	20 5,8%	14 3,6%
german instead of target name	-	24 14,0%	7 3,8%	-	10 5,9%	5 2,5%	-	34 9,9%	12 3,1%
non-german but non-target language name	-	5 2,9%	10 5,4%	-	7 4,1%	11 5,5%	-	12 3,5%	21 5,4%
other errors Σ	15 27,3%	66 38,45	88 47,8%	17 28,8%	80 47,1%	70 35,2%	32 28,0%	146 42,6%	158 41,2
no response/ stereotypes	5 9,1%	47 27,3%	74 40,2%	6 10,2%	61 35,9%	54 27,1%	11 9,6	108 31,5%	128 33,4%
visual error	3 5,5%	4 2,3%	2 1,1%	3 5,1%	3 1,7%	-	6 5,2%	7 2,0%	2 0,5%
non-classifiable errors	7 12,7%	15 8,7%	12 6,5%	8 13,6%	16 9,4%	16 8,0%	15 13,1%	31 9,0%	28 7,3%

Table 5. S.H.: Specification of semantic paraphasias in oral and written naming for each language

oral & written naming	German (n=514)	English (n=514)	French (n=514)
semantic errors Σ	54	61	54
superordinate	8 15%	28 46%	16 30%
coordinate	38 70%	25 41%	33 61%
subordinate; part/whole	7 13%	6 10%	5 9%
neologism	1 2%	2 3%	-

The majority of semantic errors were coordinate names in German (70% of semantic errors), with a small proportion of superordinate (15 %) and subordinate names (13%). In French, there were 61% coordinates, 30% superordinates and 9 % subordinates. However, in English, coordinate (41%) and superordinate names (46%) were almost equally represented, and there were only 10% of subordinate errors.

Interlingual errors (i.e., responses from the non-target language) were restricted almost completely to naming responses in the nonnative languages, although they were significantly less frequent than intralingual errors (English: $p = .0009$; French: $p = .000$).

In order to examine the role of the native German language in the production of interlingual errors in English and French naming, errors with and without German as (part of) the response were compared.

Table 6. S.H.: Pairwise comparison (Fisher's exact test, Siegel, 1968) of the amount of interlingual errors with and without German responses

interlingual errors for **English** responses (oral and written) (n=77)	
interlingual error with German	interlingual error no German
54	23
.0000	

interlingual errors for **French** responses (oral and written) (n=55)	
interlingual error with German	interlingual error no German
26	24
.8483	

Code switching from the target language to German occured significantly more often in English (p = .000) than in French, where there was no significant difference between the two groups of interlingual errors.

A further analysis was made of the responses produced to targets classified as either phonemically/graphemically similar or dissimilar in two or three languages (see table 3a-d for examples). Again, there were no significant differences between oral and written naming for the different classes of stimuli, so that responses in both modalities could be conflated.

Table 7 compares the number of correct responses in each language to phonemically/graphemically similar and dissimilar items. There were no significant differences between the similar and dissimilar conditions for naming in the native and active language, German. In other words, it was irrelevant whether phonological/ graphemic features were shared with a foreign name. However, the production of a foreign name benefited significantly from a neighbor in another language,and the difference of correct responses in the similar versus dissimilar conditions was highly significant (p = .0001 for English, p = .0202 for French).

Table 7. Pairwise comparison (Fisher's exact test, Siegel, 1968) between S.H.'s amount of correct responses to phonemic/ graphemic similar items in the German naming task (G,E,F; G,E;G,F), English namig task (G,E,F; E,G;E,F) and French naming task (G,E,F; F,G;F,E)

German (n=194)	
phonemic/graphemic similarity	phonemic/graphemic dissimilarity
161 83,0%	148 76,2%
.1300	

English (n=218)	
phonemic/graphemic similarity	phonemic/graphemic dissimilarity
112 51,4%	71 32,5%
.0001	

French (n=152)	
phonemic/graphemic similarity	phonemic/graphemic dissimilarity
44 29,%	26 17,1%
.0202	

Discussion

We presented the results on multilingual picture naming of a highly educated German patient whose spontaneous speech production in his native language was fluent and paragrammatic but who was unable to communicate spontaneously in any of the nonnative languages he mastered premorbidly. The results of oral and written picture naming in German, English and French showed some interesting patterns. There was no difference between oral and written picture naming in any of the languages, but German naming was generally much better preserved. Qualitative analyses of the semantic errors showed that substitutions of a name coordinate to the target were predominant in German, whereas in the nonnative languages, semantic errors were not restricted to coordinates but involved superordinate concepts as well as circumlocutions. Also in contrast to German, naming in the nonnative languages was characterized by a large amount of omissions. Furthermore, there was a large proportion of interference errors in English and French. Such interlingual errors hardly occurred in German naming.

An interpretation of the patterns of performance of our patient is possible within a spreading-activation account. This class of models generally assumes that retrieval takes place in a lexical network consisting of semantic, word, and phonemic nodes (e.g. Dell, 1988). Each node possesses an activation level that reflects the extent to which it is participating in the processing, and each activated node sends activation to other nodes through weighted connections. The weight or strength of a connection determines the amount of activation that is sent per unit time. The connection pattern reflects the composition of lexical units. Figure 1 shows the evolution of feedforward and feedback priming activation processes leading up to the selection of a targeted lexical node. Semantic and lexical nodes appearing more than once in the figure are actually the same nodes at different time steps.

Conceptual processes send activation to a semantic representation (first order priming). The activation from this primed semantic representation (an array of nodes or features) spreads forward through the lexical network and primes a target lexical node. Other lexical nodes that are semantically related or semantically and (by chance) phonemically related to the targeted node also receive some weak priming from this feedforward activation. Activation from the target lexical node spreads to the phonemic network and primes its corresponding phonemic nodes or features. The activation level of the lexical node is stabilized by feedback from activated phonemic nodes, which prime other lexical nodes sharing phonemic features with the target. When retrieval is enacted, the lexical node with the highest activation level receives a jolt of activation and a response is initiated. In normal circumstances, it is likely that the target lexical node will be the most activated at the moment of selection, but word substitutions that are semantically, phonemically, or multiply related to the target can occur as a consequence of a mishap. If a competitor node's activation is raised by feed-forward semantic priming or feedback phonemic priming to a level higher than the target node when selection occurs, that competitor node will be selected to guide phonemic output processing.

Assuming that English and French of S.H. are dormant (see his inability to produce spontaneous speech in these languages versus the fluent paragrammatic speech output in German) whereas his active language is his native German, it may be expected that in word production tasks, German words will reach activation

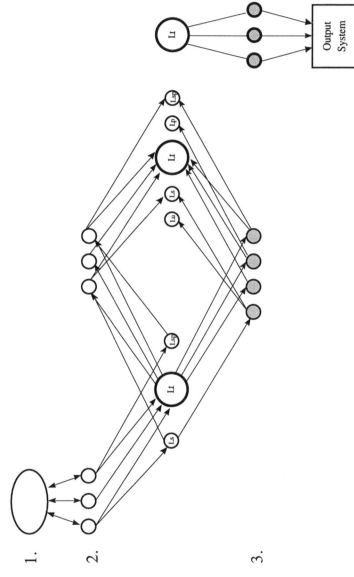

Figure 1. Spreading activation model for language output (Dell, 1988).
1. conceptual system; 2. semantic network; 3. phonological network; Lu= untreated lexical node, Lt= targeted lexical node, Ls= lexical nodes that share semantic features, Lp= phonologically related lexical nodes, Lsp= phonologically and semantically related lexical nodes.

thresholds more easily than words in English or French. This explains the better naming in German than in the other languages. Analyses of the incorrect responses in German showed the substitution of either phonemically or semantically closely related associates. The last category includes predominantly coordinate names rather than superordinates, which indicate inadequate activation of lexical nodes rather than a semantic impairment (Shallice, 1988). The absence of interlanguage errors in German shows that words of the dormant languages are apparently not, or not sufficiently, strongly coactivated with the target since they do not occur as substitutes in cases of failure in German naming.

If English or French is selected, naming is severely impaired and, in contrast to German, there are many omissions and circumlocutions, suggesting that no phonological node is found. Some intralingual errors also occur in naming in the nonnative languages, so that phonemically or semantically related forms of the target language are substituted. However, in contrast to German, superordinates rather than coordinates occurred predominantly within the category of semantic errors. A further study is necessary to determine whether semantic paraphasias in these languages would also be coordinate responses in the case of cognate items, as some connectionist models predict.

Another category of errors, especially in English, are interlingual responses, in which substitutions of the activated German name occur. The rarity of interlingual errors in French might reflect an inhibition on the part of the patient, a highly trained philologist, to substitute German if French, a Romance language, is selected.

Lexical activation was significantly more successful in English and French if the target name shared phonemic/graphemic features with the name in another language. In the framework of spreading activation, this facilitatory effect can be easily understood since there is more activation in the system: the semantic node will primarily activate the corresponding lexical node of the selected language but will also coactivate those of the other languages. The same will hold for feedforward and feedbackward activation of the phonological nodes.

In general, the unitary model of multilingual lexical processing does not explain the naming pattern of this patient. According to this model, naming would be qualitatively similar in all languages, and interlanguage errors should also occur in the native language. Models with multiple, language-specific systems cannot interpret the data either, since they would not predict interlanguage responses for any language. The general pattern of multilingual naming of our patient is better interpretable within a mixed model, which proposes that identical items in different languages (e.g. cognate words) are represented in a single system, but that nonidentical elements would be treated in different systems.

Acknowledgement

The authors wish to acknowledge Christiane Plaum for her assistance in the examination of the patient and the evaluation of the responses.

References

Albert, M. & Obler, L. (1978). *The Bilingual Brain*. New York: Academic Press, 1978.

Böcher, W. (1968). Erfahrungen mit dem Gedächtnistest (Wechsler Memory Scale). bei einer deutschen Versuchsgruppe von 200 normalen Versuchspersonen. *Diagnostica*, **9**, 56-68.

Chen, H.-C. & Leung, Y.-S. (1989). Patterns of lexical processing in a nonnative language. *Journal of Experimental Psychology: Learning, Memory and Cognition*, **15**, 316-325.

Chen, H.-C. & Ng, M.-L. (1989). Semantic facilitation and translation priming effects in Chinese-English bilinguals. *Memory and Cognition*, **17**, 454-462.

Dell, G. (1988). The retrieval of phonological form in production: Tests of predictions from a connectionist model. *Journal of Memory and Language*, **27**, 124-142.

de Groot, A. M. B. de (1992). Bilingual lexical representation: A closer look at conceptual representations. In R. Rost & L. Katz (Eds.). *Orthography, Phonology, Morphology, and Meaning*. Amsterdam: Elsevier.

de Groot, A.M.B. de & Nas, G.L.J. (1991). Lexical representations of cognates and noncognates in compound bilinguals. *Journal of Memory and Language*, **30**, 90-123.

de Groot, A.M.B. de (1993). Determinants in word translation. *Journal of Experimental Psychology: Learning, Memory and Cognition*,

Huber, W., Poeck, K., Weniger, D. & Willmes, K. (1984). The Aachen Aphasia Test. In F. C. Rose (Ed.)., *Progress in Aphasiology*, New York: Raven Press.

Jin, Y.-S. & Fishler, I. (1987). Effects of concreteness on cross-language priming of lexical decision. Paper presented at the Southeastern Psychological Association Meeting, Atlanta, Georgia.

Kirsner, K.; Smith, M. C.; Lockhart, R. S.; King, M. L. & Jain, M. (1984). The bilingual lexicon: Language-specific units in an integrated network. *Journal of Verbal Learning and Verbal Behavior*, **23**, 291-300.

Kroll, J.F. & Curley, J. (1988). Lexical memory in novice bilinguals: The role of concepts in retrieving second language words. In M. Gruneberg, P. Morris & R. Sykes (Eds.). *Practical Aspects of Memory, Vol. 2*. London: J. Wiley & Sons.

McNemar, Q. (1947) Note on the sampling error of the difference between correlated proportions or percentages. *Psychometrica*, **12**, 153-157.

Patterson, K.E. (1988). Acquired disorders of spelling. In G. Denes; C. Semenza & P. Bissiachi (eds.). *Perspectives on Cognitive Neuropsychology*. Londion: LEA:

Potter, M.C., So, K.-F., Von Eckardt,B. & Feldman, L.B. (1984). Lexical and conceptual representation in beginning and proficient bilinguals. *Journal of Verbal Learning and Verbal Behavior*, **23**, 23-38.

Schwanenflugel, E. J. & Rey, M. (1986). Interlingual semantic facilitation: Evidence for a common representational system in the bilingual lexicon. *Journal of Memory and Language*, **25**, 605-618.

Schwanenflugel, P.J., Harnishfeger, K.K. & Stowe, R.W. (1988). Context availability and lexical decisions for abstract and concrete words. *Journal of Memory and Language*, **27**, 499-520.

Shallice, T. (1988). *From Neuropsychology to Mental Structure*. Cambridge: University Press.

Siegel, S. (1956) *Nonparametric Statistics for the Behavioral Sciences*. New York: McGraw Hill.

Snodgrass, J.G. & Vanderwart, M.A. (1980). Standardized set of 260 pictures: Norms for name agreement, familiarity and visual complexity. *Journal of Experimental Learning and Verbal Behaviour*, **23**, 39-66.

Stadie, N., Cholewa, J., De Bleser, R. & Tabatabaie, S. (1994). Das neurolinguistische Expertensystem LeMo I. Theoretischer Rahmen und Konstruktionsmerkmale des Testteils LEXIKON. *Neurolinguistik,* **1**, 1-27.

Sturm, W., Willmes, K. & Horn, W. (1993). *Leistungsprüfsystem für 50 bis 90jährige (LPS 50+). Handanweisung.* Göttingen: Hogrefe.

Taylor, I. (1976). Similarity between French and English words–A factor to be considered in bilingual language behavior? *Journal of Psycholinguistic Research,* **5**, 85-94.

7   Impaired and preserved picture naming in two bilingual patients with brain damage

Helgard Kremin and Maria De Agostini

Introduction

Surveys of the literature on aphasia in bilinguals and polyglots have shown that patients who spoke two or more languages may show differential language impairments after their cerebral accident. This statement also holds for the function of naming (Paradis, Goldblum & Abidi, 1982; Paradis & Goldblum, 1989). In this chapter, we report on another case with differential picture naming in three languages. We also present a patient who shows the unusual pattern of preserved bilingual picture naming in spite of severely impaired semantic comprehension. According to Paradis (1989), "so far, no cases of preserved production without comprehension (save for pure word deafness or rare cases of echolalia) have been reported" (p.132).

Naming in the framework of models of word recognition and word production

The main assumption of recent picture confrontation models within the information processing framework is that there is a sequence of stages involved in picture naming (Morton, 1985; Riddoch & Humphreys, 1987; Lesser, 1989, among others). The crucial common argument in these models is that once a picture is "recognized", at the level of visual structural descriptive analysis, its corresponding semantic representation is accessed, in a semantic information store, which then addresses entries in the output lexicon. Therefore, an impaired semantic system should result in naming impairment.

In contrast, Kremin (1986), on the basis of two case studies exhibiting the pattern of spared naming in spite of grossly impaired semantic comprehension, favours a dual pathway model. In this view (and analogous to the two lexical pathways of retrieving phonology and meaning for the reading of words), "normal", rapid and automatic naming of familiar pictures is achieved by a pathway bypassing semantic treatment. Such a "direct" pathway for picture naming which bypasses the semantic system has indeed been considered a theoretical possibility by Warren & Morton (1982) but was abandoned, among other reasons, because of lack of neuropsychological data.

Differentially impaired picture naming in a trilingual patient

Clinical case description

VED, a 35 year-old right-handed woman, was hospitalized for epilectic seizures

101

which started when she was 18. Some months later a tumor (astrocytoma) in the right temporal lobe was surgically removed.

The Wada Test which was practised with bilateral injection before the intervention had shown that the patient's left hemisphere was dominant for language. However, EEG examinations had shown anomalies, apparently independent, in both temporal regions. One can thus not exclude that this patient had two different lesions: a tumor in the right hemisphere and another lesion, of unknown etiology, in the left hemisphere.

Neuropsychological examination (Boller & Hécaen, 1979) was conducted twice in Italian. The patient's performances were identical before and after the intervention. Repetition, reading and writing was flawless. Oral and written comprehension was preserved for isolated words, sentences and the execution of verbal commands. Digit span was 6 foreward. The patient complained about hesitations and word-finding difficulties in spontaneous speech. Standard testing of naming revealed that the patient had modality independent naming difficulties (60% correct naming for visual and tactile presentation of real objects; 50% correct naming of line drawings). She was thus diagnosed as exhibiting the syndrome of pure amnestic aphasia.

Acquisition of, and exposure to, three different languages

The patient was born in northern Italy, in a village of the province of Bergamo with its own dialect, the Bergamasc. The patient used this native language with her family in an otherwise Italian surrounding. When she was eight years old her family moved to the German speaking part of Switzerland. The patient's schooling (10 years) was thus almost entirely in German. At the age of 20 the patient decided to go back to Italy and to take advantage of her knowledge of Italian and German as a secretary. She continued to speak her local dialect with friends and family.

Formal investigation of Naming

DIFFERENTIALLY DISTURBED NAMING IN THREE LANGUAGES

From the studies on bilinguism, no firm hypothesis can be derived as regards the preservation/perturbation of the various languages to which an individual patient was exposed (see Paradis, 1989). We therefore systematically studied the patient's oral naming of the *same* pictures (DO 80 - Deloche, Metz-Lutz, Kremin, Hannequin, Ferrand, Perrier, Dordain, Quint, Cardebat, Lota, Van Der Linden, Larroque, Bunel, Pichard & Naud, 1990) in the three languages the patient had acquired. Table 1 represents her naming performances.

Table 1. Patient VED: Production of target word for same pictures in three different languages (% correct)

Bergamasc	Italian	German
80% (64/80)	65% (52/80)	26% (21/80)

The results show that the patient's picture naming in her native language, Bergamasc, which she used during her whole life with her family, is best preserved. As regards the other two languages, Italian which is the language she has been most exposed to, from early childhood on, is better preserved than German, in spite of the fact that the latter was the only language used in school and in the geographical surroundings during twelve years (age 8 to 20) and in spite of the fact that the patient continued to use German in her professional life.

APROPOS THE SYNDROME OF AMNESTIC APHASIA

Amnestic aphasia is an early (Pitres, 1898) and apparently well defined clinical syndrome of language impairment. According to recent psycholinguistic investigations anomic patients typically name action pictures better than object pictures whereas agrammatic patients show the reverse pattern (Miceli, Silveri, Villa & Caramazza, 1984; Zingeser & Berndt, 1988). It was also suggested that patients with pure amnestic aphasia benefit from contextual cues. Thus the patient described by Zingeser & Berndt (1988) was better at noun retrieval in sentence completion as compared to picture naming and naming from a verbal definition. We verified these assumptions by testing VED in Italian.

THE EFFECT OF GRAMMATICAL CLASS ON PICTURE NAMING

We used two sets of pictures, 30 object pictures and 30 action pictures, from our experimental battery. Note that this material was originally constructed for French: target nouns and verbs were pairwise matched for (relatively high) frequency.

The results show that VED named object and action pictures equally well (97% vs 93% respectively). The patient thus did not show the 'selective' deficit of verb retrieval observed with many other anomic patients.

In fact, the initial assumption of Miceli and colleagues that anomics show better object than action naming (and agrammatic aphasics the reverse dissociation) is not necessarily confirmed by the reported data. On the one hand, Basso, Razzano, Faglioni, & Zanobio (1990) reported that an impairment of action picture naming is not necessarily associated with anomia since two patients of their series exhibited the reverse pattern with action pictures>object pictures. On the other hand, Kremin (1994a) described a patient who suffered from a truly selective deficit of action picture naming in the context of fluent aphasia. Taken together these findings substantiate the claim that there is no *causal* relationship between selective impairments on object vs. action picture naming and precise type(s) of aphasia (see also Kremin & Basso, 1993, for a more detailed review).

THE EFFECT OF CONTEXT ON THE PRODUCTION OF THE TARGET WORD

We studied VED's noun production (in Italian) with production tasks similar to those of Zingeser & Berndt (1988), that is, (i) picture naming, (ii) naming from verbal definitions (e.g., What is the name of the animal that usually protects the house?), and (iii) sentence completion (e.g., The animal which barks is a ...), with and without simultaneous picture presentation.

The results show that VED had similar difficulties of noun retrieval in all oral production tasks. She named 84% (21/25) of the object pictures as compared to 80% (20/25) of the verbal definitions. As regards sentence completion the patient retrieved 70% (28/40) of the target nouns without picture presentation as compared to 77.5%

(31/40) with simultaneous picture presentation; naming the corresponding object pictures resulted in 70% (28/40) correct productions.

These results suggest that the facilitating effect of sentence completion which Zingeser and Berndt observed with their case of pure anomia is not *causally* related to the syndrome of amnestic aphasia. Rather, the dissociation they described seems to document an individual pattern of their patient HY.

FUNCTIONAL LOCALISATION OF THE PATIENT'S NAMING DEFICIT

The fact that VED flawlessly recognized the corresponding target word of unnamed pictures indicates that in her case the disruption of name retrieval occured at a post-semantic stage (Gainotti, Silveri, Villa & Miceli, 1986).

In all three languages the patient's naming errors were similar. They consisted of numerous frank omissions and semantic paraphasias *together* with adequate comments (see appendix). Such an error pattern was described in other patients with post-semantic naming disturbances (Le Dorze & Nespoulous, 1989; Caramazza & Hillis, 1990).

However, retrieval of the lexical form is probably not a unitary process. Kempen & Huijbers (1983) distinguish two main stages: from the semantic system the information is first sent to lexicalization "Level 1" —which activates a dictionary of "abstract" pre-phonological lexical items which are syntactically specified— and then to lexicalization "Level 2" where the corresponding phono- logical form is activated. Indeed, the naming impairment of some patients seems to reflect a disruption between Level 1 and Level 2.

Following Goodglass, Kaplan, Weintraub, & Ackerman's (1976) line of reasoning it may be argued that the patients' tacit knowledge of the unnamed target word discriminates between different types of naming impairments. In the case of post-semantic naming disturbances, attainment of the pre-phonological Level 1 would thus imply correct gender assigment and, probably, also some global knowledge as regards the 'physical' form of the target word, for example whether it is "long" or "short". If the information attains Level 2 the patient would also show some degree of phonological knowledge about the unnamed word such as its initial phoneme/letter, its length in terms of number of syllabes and/or recognition of some parts of the target word in a multiple choice. Indeed, Henaff Gonon Bruckert, & Michel (1989) presented a case who correctly produced the grammatical gender of unnamed target words (and correctly commented upon their meaning).

In order to test VED's tacit knowledge we chose 50 drawings from the Boston Naming Test (Kaplan, Goodglass & Weintraub, 1983) of which half the (Italian) names are of masculine and half of feminine grammatical gender. In instances of incorrect picture naming or absence of response, we tested the patient's lexical knowledge at Level 1 by asking her to indicate (a) the length of the target word (short/long) and (b) its grammatical gender. Knowledge at level Level 2 referred to (c) the number of syllables and (d) the initial phoneme and/or letter of the target word. (This test series was only administered in Italian.)

The results show that the patient named only 14/50 (28%) pictures correctly. With regard to the 36 incorrectly named pictures we observed the following performance: (a) length of target word: 32/36 nil responses, 4/36 incorrect responses; (b) gender assignment: 26/36 nil responses, 2/36 incorrect and 8/36 correct responses; (c) number of syllables: 36/36 nil responses; (d) initial phoneme/letter: 36/36 nil responses.

Such performance documents that the patient has no tacit knowledge at all of lexical/phonological caracteristics of the nouns corresponding to unnamed object pictures. VED's post-semantic naming disturbance is thus best described as a disconnection between the semantic system and both levels of lexicalization, Level 1 and Level 2.

This case newly documents that the clinical term "anomia" or "amnestic aphasia" applies to a heterogeneous group of patients with aphasic language impairment. It furnishes further experimental evidence for our claim (Kremin & Basso, 1993) that there is no causal relationship between impairments on object and/or action picture naming and precise type(s) of aphasia. Aphasia syndromes are mostly the result of the pattern of vascularization of the brain whereas the dissociation between different word classes is a principle of language organization.

Preserved naming in a bilingual patient in spite of severely disturbed semantic comprehension

As already mentioned, standard models of naming do not allow for the constellation of preserved picture naming in spite of impaired semantic comprehension. The theoretical possibility of naming by direct visuophonological connections bypassing semantic comprehension has been discussed but explicitly rejected (Warren & Morton, 1982).

The theoretical position according to which naming is necessarily mediated by semantic treatment is challenged by the description of some patients who name pictures without comprehension (Kremin, 1986; Shuren, Geldmacher & Heilman, 1993; David, Fluchaire, Brennen, & Pellat, 1994; Kremin, Beauchamp, & Perrier, 1994; Kremin, 1994b). We present another case with this rare constellation in which oral naming was preserved in both languages used by the subject.

Case description

C.O., a 55-year-old woman, was hospitalized for more formal exploration of a frontal syndrome (onset of Pick's disease). She was born in Italy and went to France at the age of 21. She has used both languages in her daily life ever since.

Preserved bilingual naming in spite of impaired picture comprehension

We systematically tested the patient's oral naming of the same pictures (DO 80, Deloche et al., 1990) in both of the patient's languages. As in a former study (Kremin et al., 1994) we administered the *Pyramid and Palm Tree Test* (PPTT, Howard & Patterson, 1992) in order to study semantic picture comprehension. In this picture judgement task the patient has to match, for example, a picture of a KENNEL to a picture of a CAT and a DOG. If subjects have impairments in semantic processing, they produce errors in this task. According to Howard and Patterson (1992), normal performance with the series of picture triads is three errors or less.

In addition, we adminstered a French test of written synonym comprehension where the patient had to recognize whether a pair of words (n = 40) has the same meaning (e.g. *couteau* = *canif*; *couteau/carafe*; *religion* = *croyance*; *religion/ roulement*).

The results (table 2) show that C.O. has normal naming but impaired comprehension of pictures and of words.

Table 2. Patient C.O.: Oral naming and semantic
comprehension of pictures and words

French: Picture naming	Italian: Picture naming	PPTT: Picture comprehension	Written word comprehension
97% (78/80)	95% (76/80)	69% (36/52)	67% (27/40)

In French (78/80) and in Italian (76/80), the patient's oral naming of pictures stayed within the normal range. However, on the PPTT she showed severely disturbed picture comprehension with only 36/52 items correct. The compre- hension of written synonyms (which were read flawlessly by the patient) was also severely disturbed since she correctly judged only 27/40 word pairs. In fact C.O. consistently recognized only 6 concrete and 1 abstract item. Nevertheless the function of naming was preserved in this bilingual patient who suffered from severe comprehension disturbances in the frame of a degenerating illness.

Conclusion

We studied the naming performances of two patients who used more than one language. One patient (who suffered from the clinical syndrome of pure anomia) showed differential impairment in her three languages. Picture naming in her native language, Bergamasc, an Italian dialect rather dissimilar from Italian, was better preserved than her naming in Italian. German, a language she was exposed to during her schooling and which she used in her professional life, was still more severely impaired. It could thus be argued that the patient's naming impairment reflects the order of acquisition of these three languages: the language learned first being best preserved. But the naming impairment also parallels the patient's linguistic 'familiarity' in terms of amount of exposure to and practice of the different languages.

In contrast, the second patient (who suffered from a degenerative brain disease) showed equally preserved picture naming in Italian and French, in spite of a severe disturbance at the level of semantic analysis. Her case adds bilingual evidence to the unusual pattern of normal naming without comprehension.

Acknowledgements

We are thankful to Prof. Bruno Dubois, Clinique des maladies du système nerveux, La Salpêtrière, for calling Patient CO. to our attention.

Part of this study was undertaken while the authors were participating in the EC Project BMH1-CT 92-0218, European Standardized Computerized Assessment of

Brain-Damaged Patients (ESCAPE), (Project Leader: G. Deloche, Paris), a Biomed 1 subprogramme supported by the Commission of the European Communities, January 1993-December 1995.

References

Basso, A., Razzano, C., Faglioni, P., & Zanobio, E. 1990. Confrontation naming, picture description and action naming in aphasic patients. *Aphasiology,* **4**, 185-195.

Boller, F., & Hécaen, H. 1979. L'évaluation des fonctions neuropsychologiques: Examen standard de l'Unité de Recherches Neuropsychologiques et Neurolinguistiques (U. 111) I.N.S.E.R.M. *Revue de Psychologie Appliquée,* **29**, 247-266.

Caramazza, A., & Hillis, A.E. 1990. Where do semantic errors come from? *Cortex,* **26**, 95-122.

David, D., Fluchaire, I., Brennen, T., & Pellat, J. 1994. Dénommer sans connaissances sémantiques? a propos d'un cas de démnence d'Alzheimer. In M. Poncet, B. Michel & A Nieoullon (eds) *Actualités sur la maladie d'Alzheimer et les syndromes apparentés* (pp. 223-224). Marseille: Solal.

Deloche, G., Metz-Lutz, M.N., Kremin, H., Hannequin, D., Ferrand, I., Perrier, D., Dordain, M., Quint, S., Cardebat, D., Lota, A.M., Van Der Linden, M., Larroque, C., Bunel, G., Pichard, B., & Naud, E. 1990. *Test de Dénomination orale de 80 images: DO 80*. Réalisation de l'atelier "Dénomination" du Réseau de Recherche Clinique I.N.S.E.R.M. 1986-1989 sous la coordination de G. Deloche.

Gainotti, G., Silveri, M.C., Villa, G., & Miceli, G. 1986. Anomia with and without lexical comprehension. *Brain and Language*, **29**, 18-33.

Goodglass, H., Kaplan, E., Weintraub, S., & Ackerman, N. 1976. The "Tip-of-the-tongue" phenomenon in aphasia. *Cortex*, **12**, 145-153.

Henaff Gonon, M.A., Bruckert, R., & Michel, F. 1989. Lexicalization in an anomic patient. *Neuropsychologia*, **27**, 391-407.

Howard, D., & Patterson, K.E. 1992. *The Pyramid and Palm Tree Test*. Bury-St-Edmunds: Themes Valley Test Company.

Kaplan, E., Goodglass, H., & Weintraub, S. 1983. *The Boston Naming Test*. Philadelphia: Lea & Febiger.

Kempen, G., & Huijbers, P. 1983. The lexicalization process in sentence production and naming: Indirect election of words. *Cognition*, **14**, 185-209.

Kremin, H. 1986. Spared naming without comprehension. *Journal of Neurolinguistics,* **2**, 131-150.

Kremin, H. 1994a. Selective impairments of action naming: arguments and a case study. *Linguistische Berichte,* Sonderheft **6**, 62-82. (Special Issue "Linguistics and Cognitive Neuroscience. Theoretical and Empirical Studies on Language Disorders" edited by D. Hillert).

Kremin, H. 1994b. Naming and Reading without Comprehension. *17th Annual European Conference of the International Neuropsychological Society*, Angers, France, June 22-25, 1994.

Kremin, H., & Basso, A. 1993. The Mental Lexicon: nouns and verbs. In F.J. Stachowiak, R. De Bleser, G. Deloche, R. Kaschel, H. Kremin, P. North, L. Pizzamiglio, I. Robertson, & B. Wilson (eds.), *Developments in the Assessment and Rehabilitation of Brain-Damaged Patients: Perspectives from a European Concerted Action* (Pp.233-242).

Tübingen: Narr Verlag.

Kremin, H., Beauchamp, D., & Perrier, D. 1994. Naming without picture comprehension? Apropos the oral naming and semantic comprehension of pictures by patients with Alzheimer disease. *Aphasiology, 8*, 291-294.

Kremin, H., & De Agostini. 1993. A propos d'aphasie amnésique pure: étude d'un sujet trilingue. *Revue de Neuropsychologie, 3*, 118-119.

Le Dorze, G., & Nespoulous, J.L. 1989. Anomia in moderate aphasia: problems in accessing the lexical representation. *Brain and Language, 37*, 381-400.

Lesser, R. 1989. Some issues in the neuropsychological rehabilitation of anomia. In X. Seron & G. Deloche (Eds.) *Cognitive Approaches in Neuropsychological Rehabilitation* (pp. 65-104). Hillsdale: Lawrence Erlbaum Associates.

Miceli, G., Silveri, M.C., Villa, G., & Caramazza, A. 1984. On the basis for the agrammatic's difficulty in producing main verbs. *Cortex, 20*, 207-220.

Morton, J. 1985. Naming. In S. Newman and R. Epstein (eds) *Current perspectives in dysphasia* (pp. 217-230). Edinburgh: Churchill Livington.

Paradis, M. 1989. Bilingual and polyglot aphasia. In F. Boller and J. Grafman (Eds.), *Handbook of Neuropsychology, Vol. 2* (Pp. 117-140). Amsterdam: Elsevier Science Publishers.

Paradis, M., & Goldblum, M.C. 1989. Selective crossed aphasia followed by reciprocal antagonism in a trilingual patient. *Brain and Language, 36*, 62-75.

Paradis, M., Goldblum, M.C., & Abidi, R. 1982. Alternate antagonism with paradoxical translation behavior in two bilingual aphasic patients. *Brain and Language, 15*, 55-69.

Pitres, A. 1898. *L'Aphasie amnésique et ses variétés cliniques*. Paris: Félix Alcan.

Riddoch, M.J., & Humphreys, G.W. 1987. Picture Naming. in G.W. Humphreys and M.J. Riddoch (eds) *Visual Object Processing: A Cognitive Neuropsychological Approach*. Hillsdale: Lawrence Erlbaum Associates.

Shuren, J., Geldmacher, D., & Heilman, K.M. 1993. Nonoptic aphasia: aphasia with preserved confrontation naming in Alzheimer's disease. *Neurology, 43*, 1900-1907.

Warren, C., & Morton, J. 1982. The effects of priming on picture recognition. *British Journal of Psychology, 73*, 117-129.

Zingeser, L.B., & Berndt, R.S. 1988. Grammatical class and context effects in a case of pure anomia: implications for models of language production. *Cognitive Neuropsychology, 5*, 473-516.

Appendix

VED's oral naming of the same 80 pictures in Italian and in German:

AEREO: +

FLUGZEUG: ...... +

POSACENERE: +

ASCHENBECHER: ... für Zigaretten

LUMACA: la ...

SCHNECKE: ...... nein

CORDA: +

SEIL (zum Springen): ...... nein

STIVALE: è più alto... +

STIEFEL: ...... +

CAPPELLO: +

HUT: ....

CARRIOLA: carretta

SCHUBKARREN: ...... nein

CROCE: +

KREUZ: +

POLTRONA: +

SESSEL: kein Stuhl

CONIGLIO: topo quello che mangia ... non il gallo

HASE/KANINCHEN: ...... nein

TELEFONO: +

TELEFON: +

MANO: +

HAND: +

BANDIERA: +

FAHNE: ...... nein

GALLO: gallina

HAHN: ein Huhn, nein...

INNAFFIATOIO: per annaffiare

GIESSKANNE: ....

ZEBRA: in Africa ... veloce...

ZEBRA: ......

MARTELLO: +

HAMMER: ......

ROSA: fiore ... +

ROSE: +

ABETE/PINO: per Natale...

TANNENBAUM: zu Weihnachten...

PAVONE: stupendo

PFAU: ......

ELICOTTERO: ......

HELICOPTER: ......

FRECCIA: la indice... +

PFEIL: ......

SEDIA: +

STUHL: +

ELEFANTE: +

ELEFANT: +

FISARMONICA: per suonare

AKKORDEON: ...... nein

LUCCHETTO: ......

SCHLOSS: ......

PIEDE: +

FUSS: +

TARTARUGA: animale lento ...

SCHILDKRÖTE: ......

SECCHIO: bidet

EIMER: ein Kessel

CANNONE: +

KANONE: nein

MUCCA: +

KUH: ... gibt Milch

TAMBURO: per suonare la batteria

TROMMEL: ....

PETTINE: +

KAMM: ......

ZOCCOLO: una scarpa ... +

HOLZSCHUH: ......

PENTOLA: +

TOPF: ein......

SCRIVANIA: tavolino

SCHREIBTISCH: ......

ASPIRAPOLVERE: per pulire

STAUBSAUGER: zum Saubermachen

RETE/GRIGLIA: +

GITTER/ZAUN: ......

FRAGOLA: frutto, non è l'uva

ERDBEERE: ......

LEONE: +

LÖWE: das ist nicht schwierig ......

ASCIA: per rompere la legna

AXT: ... nein

OMBRELLO: quando piove serve per ......

REGENSCHIRM: bei Regen braucht man einen ......

CAVALLO: +

PFERD: ... sehr einfach ......

PIPA: +

PFEIFE: damit raucht man
SERPENTE: ......
SCHLANGE: ... nein
CAMPANA: +
GLOCKE: ......
MESTOLO: ......
SUPPENKELLE: nein
ANITRA: oca
ENTE: ...nein
BABBO-NATALE: +
WEIHNACHTSMANN: ...
GATTO: +
KATZE: +
SCOPA: +
BESEN: ......
BOTTIGLIA: +
FLASCHE: ......
COMO'/CASSETTONE: non è un armadio
KOMMODE: ......
STELLA: +
STERN: ...... +
ORSO: +
BÄR: ... es gibt weisse und braune...
TRENO: +
ZUG/EISENBAHN: ... nein
SCOIATTOLO: ......
EICHHÖRNCHEN: ......
CANDELA: +
KERZE:... wenn das Licht ausgeht braucht man
    eine ......
SGABELLO: +
SCHEMEL: Sessel... Stuhl...
MASCHERA: ......
MASKE: nein
FUNGO: +
PILZ: ......
COLTELLO: +

MESSER: ... man isst mit Gabel und...
CANGURO: ......
KÄNGERU: nein
PANCHINA: +
BANK: ...+
FARFALLA: +
SCHMETTERLING: ein... nein
GIRAFFA: +
GIRAFFE:... nein
BILANCIA: pesa
WAAGE: ......
CANE: +
HUND: sehr einfach!...... +
FORCHETTA: pirù (Bergamasc)
GABEL: +
BASTONE: .....
(SPAZIER)STOCK: nein
PERA: +
BIRNE: +
SOLE: +
SONNE: +
GALLINA: +
HUHN: +
CUORE: +
HERZ: +
RINOCERONTE: ......
RHINOZEROS: ... nein
FORBICI: +
SCHERE: ......
PESCE: +
FISCH: ......
SPAZZOLA: +
BÜRSTE: ... für die Haare....
LIMONE: +
ZITRONE: +
LETTO: +
BETT: +

8 Patterns of language deficits in two Korean-Japanese bilingual aphasic patients —A clinical report

Sumiko Sasanuma and Hea Suk Park

Introduction

Korean and Japanese are known to be structurally similar in many respects (Kuno 1973). Japanese is an SOV language and so is Korean. The basic word order of transitive sentences in both language is that of Subject-Object-Verb, with the very rigid verb-final constraint (verbs must appear in the sentence-final position). As a corollary, some additional characteristics such as left-branching and postpositional characteristics are also shared by the two languages. Furthermore, the writing systems of the two languages share unique characteristics of making use of two distinctive scripts in combination: kanji (logographic/morphographic symbols of Chinese origin) and Kana (phonetic symbols for syllables or moras) in Japanese, and Kanji and Hangul (phonetic symbols for phonemes or phonetic features; see Sampson, 1985, for a detailed discussion on this point) in Korean. In brain damaged patients various types of dissociations between Kanji and Kana processing as well as between Kanji and Hangul have been reported to emerge (Sasanuma 1980, 1985, 1986, 1994; Paradis, Hagiwara & Hildebrandt, 1985; Park, Sasanuma, Sunwoo, Rah & Shin, 1992). This similarity between Korean and Japanese for several aspects of language structure, particularly for the syntactic rule system, will be expected to affect the processes of acquisition as well as loss and recovery of the two languages. It will be expected to exert a facilitatory effect on the acquisition of the second language even if the acquisition takes place later (as opposed to early) in life, or in separate (as opposed to the same) contexts. In the case of aphasia due to brain insult, on the other hand, the pattern of deficits and the recovery of the two structurally similar languages may tend to be parallel rather than differential (Paradis 1989). There may also be positive transfer of the therapeutic benefits from the treated to the non-treated language as a function of the similarity between the two languages (Paradis 1993).

Few preceding studies exist on Korean-Japanese or Japanese-Korean bilingual aphasic patients, against which to test these hypotheses. We have had the opportunity of investigating two Korean-Japanese aphasic patients in the use of two equivalent tests of aphasia, one in Korean and the other in Japanese.

Method

Tests

Two parallel tests of aphasia described below were used as the major component of the testing materials.

1. Aphasia test in Japanese. The *Test for Differential Diagnosis of Aphasia* (TDDA) (Sasanuma, Itoh, Watamori, Fukusako & Monoi, 1978), one of the comprehensive tests of aphasia currently in use in Japan, was used for evaluating the aphasic deficits in Japanese in the two bilingual patients. The TDDA can be thought of as a hybrid of the *Minnesota Test for Differential Diagnosis of Aphasia* (Schuell 1965) and the *Boston Diagnostic Aphasia Examination* (Goodglass and Kaplan 1972, 1983). Needless to say, the nature and type of specific subtests in the TDDA are uniquely Japanese, reflecting the Japanese language structure. An example is the inclusion in the battery of subtests for processing words written in Kana and Kanji, because the relative performance on Kana and Kanji words provides important information for the diagnosis and treatment of Japanese aphasic patients (Sasanuma 1986). The TDDA comprises five domains corresponding to four major modalities of language (auditory and reading comprehension, and spoken and written production) as well as arithmetic function, from 5 to 13 subtests in each domain, with a total of 47 subtests.

2. Aphasia test in Korean. *The Korean Aphasia Test Battery*, which is essentially the Korean version of the TDDA (Park et al., 1992), was used to evaluate the Korean language deficits in the two bilingual aphasic patients. This battery has been given to more than a hundred Korean aphasic patients and their control subjects thus far as part of the standardization procedure and has proved to be a reliable as well as valid test of aphasia for the target population (Park et al., in preparation). In constructing the battery, special care was taken that the two tests should be equivalent in terms of the overall test organization and the level of linguistic complexity for each task. The subtests for Kana processing were replaced by those for Hangul processing, while those for kanji were retained with necessary modifications in the choice of individual items. Table 1 is a summary of the nature and types of the tasks under the four language modalities in the two equivalent tests of aphasia in Korean and Japanese.

Subjects and the Overall Study Plan

Two Korean born Korean-Japanese bilingual patients with stroke-induced aphasia served as the subjects. The language evaluation using the two equivalent tests of aphasia described above was given to Case 1 at 3 months post onset. Case 2 was evaluated initially at 2.5 months post onset, received systematic language therapy for the following 3 months, and was evaluated again at 5.5 months post onset using the same two tests.

Case 1

CASE HISTORY

The first patient is a 62-year-old, right-handed ex-government official born in a small city near Seoul. He was brought up in a unilingual Korean-speaking environment until age 6 when he was enrolled in a Japanese primary school where Japanese was the exclusive language used due to the occupation by the Japanese army. The exclusive use of Japanese in his school life continued for a total of 9 years (from 1936 to 1945) until the third year of the middle school, when World War II came to an end. After the

Table 1. The nature and types of the tasks under the four language modalities in the two equivalent tests of aphasia in Korean and Japanese

Auditory Modality:
  Auditory recognition of high- and low-frequency words
  Auditory retention span for words
  Digit pointing span forward
  Auditory comprehension of simple sentences
  Following spoken commands
  Comprehension of spoken narratives

Reading Modality:
  Kana/Hangul and pronunciation matching
  Oral reading of Kana/Hangul and Kanji words
  Reading comprehension of Kana/Hangul and Kanji words
  Reading comprehension of simple sentences
  Following written commands
  Comprehension of written narratives

Oral Production Modality:
  Serial speech (Count from 1 to 20)
  Repetition of syllables/moras
  Repetition of words and sentences
  Confrontation naming of high- and low-frequency words
  Word fluency (syllable-based and category based)
  Spontaneous production of sentences and narratives

Writing Modality:
  Serial writing (write from 1 to 10)
  Writing single Kana/Hangul characters to dictation
  Written confrontation naming of Kana/Hangul- and Kanji-words
  Writing Kana/Hangul- and Kanji-words to dictation
  Writing sentences to dictation
  Spontaneous writing of sentences and narratives

war he completed his high school and college education in Korea (in a Korean unilingual environment), and worked for an agency of the national government until 1990 when he quit the office and established a new Korean-Japanese trading company. All through these intervening years his command of Japanese, both spoken and written, appeared to be excellent. He tried to keep up the level of competence he had acquired during his 9 years of attendance in the Japanese school through his ingenuity and effort (by regularly reading Japanese journals/novels, making several visits to Japan each year as part of his official activities, etc.).

In November 1992, he suffered a cerebral infarction in the left middle cerebral artery region, leaving him with mild anomic aphasia, and was referred to the Speech Pathology Section of the Rehabilitation Center, Yonsei University College of Medicine. Neurological findings were unremarkable with no paralysis or paresis of his extremities nor praxic or gnosic disabilities.

LANGUAGE EVALUATION

The two equivalent tests of aphasia were given to him 3 months post onset, when the patient was judged to have reached the stage of neurological stability, and yet had not been exposed extensively to various forms of systematic or unsystematic environmental linguistic stimulation inherent in his daily living.

FINDINGS

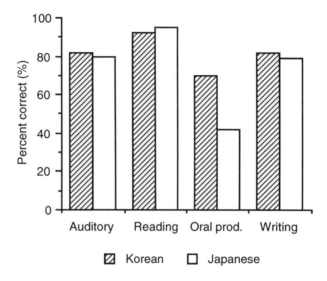

Figure 1. Results of the initial evaluation for Case 1 on four language modalities in Korean and Japanese

Figure 1 summarizes the test results in terms of the percentage of correct responses in each of the four language modalities. Overall patterns of impairment across the four modalities in the two languages are essentially similar to each other, with relative preservation of auditory comprehension, reading, and writing abilities, against substantial impairment in oral production. The degree of impairment in the latter modality, however, is clearly greater in Japanese than in Korean, while the levels of performance in the three preserved modalities for the two languages are almost identical. His oral production in both languages was fluent and grammatical but with occasional anomia for nouns as well as verbs, which was more marked in Japanese than in Korean, as was demonstrated in poorer test scores in Japanese than in Korean in confrontation naming of both high- and low-frequency words, and production of simple sentences and paragraphs. The degree of preservation in the remaining three modalities, on the other hand, was quite high or near functional in both languages. A few errors that he committed in the writing modality in Japanese comprised omission or addition of diacritical marks for some Kana characters, that would reflect voicing confusions, probably because the Korean phonology has no underlying voicing contrasts.

The fact that his residence is too far to commute to the Speech/Language Pathology Section as an outpatient precluded the opportunity for further observation of the recovery process of aphasia in this patient.

Case 2

CASE HISTORY

The second patient is a 29-year-old right-handed owner of a small trading company in Seoul. He was born in July 1964 to a Korean mother and a Chinese father, who had come to Korea at the age of 16 and married the patient's mother. Since the major language spoken at home was Korean (his father rarely using Chinese at home and his mother never speaking any languages other than Korean), it will be safe to assume that he was brought up in a unilingual Korean-speaking environment as a child. His first exposure to Japanese was in 1982 at the age of 18 when he came to Japan to have his college education at Kansai University, where he majored in business administration. After four years of college life, he had a job in a Japanese-Korean trading company and continued to stay in Japan for five more years until 1991 when he returned to Seoul and established a trading company of his own. During the 9 years spent in Japan, he acquired an excellent command of Japanese, both spoken and written. Upon return to Korea, he made full use of his bilingual competence in the business transactions, suggesting that his premorbid proficiency in the two languages was almost equal.

In November 1993, he suffered a left intra-cerebral haemorrhage at the subcortical region of the frontoparietal lobe, confirmed by CT-scan, followed by removal of a large hematoma. He was left with moderate nonfluent aphasia plus right hemiplegia which was more marked on his upper extremity.

INITIAL LANGUAGE EVALUATION

The patient was given the two equivalent tests of aphasia in Korean and Japanese at 2.5 months post onset. Figure 2 summarizes the overall results in terms of the four language modalities. It can be seen that the pattern as well as the degree of impairment of the two languages are similar to each other as a whole, although a closer look discloses that the performance levels in the oral production and writing modalities are somewhat worse in Japanese than in Korean. His spontaneous speech in both languages was mildly nonfluent and short-phrased with many instances of phoneme substitutions and distortions due to verbal apraxia. In oral production of Japanese words and sentences, he often exhibited a failure to keep the voicing distinction as well as the animate-inanimate distinction for "to be" verbs (ir-u for animate existence and ar-u for inanimate existence) in simple sentences. The fact that these distinctions do not exist in Korean may partially explain the emergence of these errors. Of interest was selective impairment in processing Hangul in Korean and Kana in Japanese relative to Kanji processing in both languages, particularly in writing. This pattern of deficits seems to be analogous to "deep agraphia" in alphabetic scripts (Coltheart, Patterson & Marshall, 1980), and appears to reflect a common underlying impairment in phonological processing of written codes (Sasanuma and Fujimura 1972; Sasanuma 1980, 1986; among others).

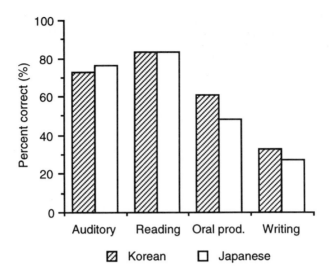

Figure 2. Results of the initial evaluation for Case 2 on four
language modalities in Korean and Japanese

Language Therapy

On the basis of this initial evaluation as well as to comply with his and his family's request, the patient was enrolled in a systematic language therapy programme in Korean for a period of three months, three 45-minutes sessions per week, for the total of 36 sessions. The major therapeutic approach adopted was the stimulation approach developed by Schuell, Jenkins & Pabon (1964) and expanded by Chapey and her colleagues (1981, 1986), which consisted essentially of intensive, controlled stimulation of impaired processes. Some specific tasks focused on selected areas (e.g., writing in Hangul, which was particularly impaired in this patient) were also incorporated. The stimulus words which appear in the language tests were carefully eliminated from the therapy materials. The therapy was terminated at the end of three months due to his discharge from the University Hospital.

Post-Therapy Language Evaluation

Figure 3 gives a summary of the patient's performance on the Korean and Japanese aphasia tests administered a week after the termination of the 3-month therapy in Korean. The upper layers on the four modalities represent the gains over the initial evaluation.

A glance at Figure 3 indicates that the pattern of post-therapy performance across the four modalities is essentially similar to that of his pre-therapy performance but with sizable improvement in the four modalities in both languages. A closer look, however, discloses that the gains on the expressive modalities, particularly the writing modality which was most impaired in this patient, are much greater in Korean, the treated

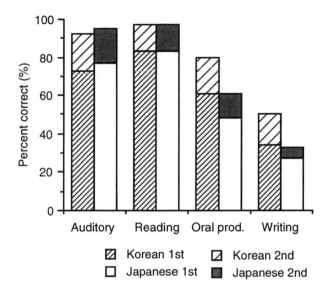

Figure 3. Results of the post-therapy evaluation for Case 2 against his initial, pre-therapy performance on four language modalities in Korean and Japanese

language, than in Japanese, the untreated language. In fact, improvement is almost negligible in the writing modality in Japanese.

How about the nature and content of improvement in each modality? In the two receptive modalities, auditory and reading comprehension, the major gains in both languages were obtained on those tasks with relatively high cognitive demands, e.g., comprehension of long complex sentences and following two- or more-step commands.

In the oral output modality, improvement was seen in confrontation naming of mainly low-frequency words, sentence and narrative production, and word fluency in both languages, but somewhat to a lesser degree in Japanese. There was a considerable improvement in keeping the voicing distinction as well as animate-inanimate "to-be" distinction in Japanese, but some sporadic errors were still observed at the post-treatment evaluation. Of interest was the emergence of so called involuntary mixing of the two languages in the sentence and narrative production tasks in Japanese. That is to say, the Japanese case particle [ga], the nominative marker, was replaced by the corresponding Korean particle [i] on several occasions, which would reflect the similarity of the syntactic structures of the two languages. Involuntary mixing has been viewed as a failure to exercise full control over a relatively intact system (Green 1986). Since this mixing was not observed in his initial testing, it would appear that a certain degree of recovery of the relatively intact language may be a prerequisite for mixing to take place. Of further note, this mixing in Case 2 was unidirectional in the sense that corresponding mixing was not observed in the Korean subtests, reflecting a somewhat greater recovery rate in oral production in Korean relative to Japanese at the time of post-therapy testing. It might thus be the case that intensive therapy over the past 13 weeks only in Korean led to the use of practiced Korean particles in unpracticed Japanese sentences.

Another observation of interest was the dissociation in performance in Case 2 between the two types of word fluency tests in Korean: syllable- (Hangul) based and category-based fluency tests. His scores on these two types of tasks at the pre-therapy evaluation were 0/min (Hangul) versus 5/min (category), and at the post-therapy evaluation they were 1/min (Hangul) versus 12/min (category), still maintaining a highly selective impairment in retrieving words with reference to word initial syllables, which was in sharp contrast to marked increase in retrieving words with reference to semantic categories ("animal" and "household objects"). Of further interest, a parallel but less dramatic pattern of dissociation was observed in the corresponding tasks in Japanese, with pre-therapy scores of 0/min (Kana) versus 2/min (category) and post-therapy scores of 2/min (Kana) versus 5/min (category). These findings appear to indicate that certain types (or severity) of phonological deficits, or impaired phonological processing/ manipulations (that are supposed to underlie the poor performance of the syllable-based word fluency task) would tend to be highly resistant to improvement, although incorporation of some specific training (which was not possible this time) may have changed the prognosis to some extent.

Finally, in the writing modality, the therapeutic intervention focused on Hangul processing (the most impaired aspect) brought about marked increase in the number of correctly written Hangul words. In Japanese, the untreated language, however, the increase in the correctly written Kana words was negligible, indicating essentially no transfer of therapeutic benefits from Hangul to Kana. Writing kanji words, on the other hand, showed moderate improvement in both languages. There was no change in the ability of the patient to write sentences and narratives in either language. His performance was practically nil at the time of pre-therapy evaluation, and this condition persisted until the end of the 3-month therapy period.

Discussion

From the history of the second language (Japanese) acquisition in Case 1 and Case 2, the two patients can safely be judged to be "coordinate" bilinguals who have acquired each language in a separate context (Lambert & Fillenbaum, 1959). This would result, according to these authors, in more neurologically separated neural structures underlying the two languages relative to "compound" bilinguals who have acquired both languages in the same context, and accordingly the patients would be likely to suffer more differential, rather than similar, patterns of aphasic deficits/recovery in the two languages. This prediction, however, did not materialize with either of our two patients. Paradis (1977, 1983) had already cast doubt on this hypothesis on the basis of his careful review of the data from all cases surveyed by Lambert and Fillenbaum (1959) as well as more recent cases reported by other authors (L'Hermitte, Hécaen, Dubois, Culioli & Tabouret-Keller, 1966; Hécaen, Mazaro, Ramier, Goldblum, & Merienne, 1971, among others) which revealed no particular relationship between the context of language acquisition and the pattern of aphasic deficits or recovery.

The structural distance between the two languages of bilingual patients constitutes another variable that may exert a crucial influence upon the pattern of loss and recovery (Ovcharova, Raichev & Geleva 1968, quoted by Paradis, 1989 and elaborated further in Paradis 1993). According to this hypothesis, structurally similar languages will tend to be impaired and recovered more equally than the structurally different languages which are more likely to be affected and recovered differentially. Furthermore, to the extent that the two languages are similar for any aspect of language structure (e.g., semantic/lexical, syntactic, morphological, phonological), positive transfer of the effects of therapy from the treated to the non-treated language may be expected (Paradis, 1993). There are multiple possible reasons proposed for this transfer to occur (Paradis, 1989). The one that appears to be most relevant to the present purpose states that the language substrata may be shared to a greater degree for the two languages that are structurally similar, while in cases where the two languages are less similar for some aspects of language structure, greater differential representation in the language area would be predicted (Paradis, 1989). According to this proposition, to the extent that the two languages are similar there will be a greater likelihood for an activation of a specific process of one language (aroused by therapeutic stimulation) to transfer to the corresponding process of another language with greater opportunities for similar improvement in both languages.

What we actually found in our two bilingual patients was that (1) Both patients showed essentially parallel patterns of aphasia in the two languages with roughly similar degrees of impairment in all major modalities (with some exceptions that will be discussed shortly) at the initial evaluations, 3 and 2.5 months post onset for Case 1 and Case 2, respectively; and (2) in Case 2, following a 3-month systematic language therapy which was given exclusively in Korean in a community where Korean was the only language in the environment, the amount as well as the content of the recovery in the two languages was virtually identical in the two receptive modalities (auditory and reading comprehension), and similar in the oral output modality. In writing, on the other hand, clearly greater improvement in the treated relative to the untreated language was observed.

The first finding is largely consonant with the structural distance hypothesis. The overall patterns of aphasia as well as the degree of impairment in most modalities was similar in the two languages for both patients, with the following exceptions. In Case 1 with anomic aphasia, the degree of impairment in the oral production modality was clearly greater in Japanese, the second language, relative to Korean, the native language. A possible explanation will have to do with his anomia, selective difficulty in the retrieval of lexical items, which is the major cause of his relatively poor performance on this modality. As pointed out before, the structural similarity between Korean and Japanese is most pronounced in the syntactic rule system, and much less in surface lexicon or phonology. It is probable, therefore, that the brain insult incurred by the patient might have exaggerated a small difference in his lexical processing competence that might have existed pre-onset between Korean and Japanese, i.e., somewhat weaker premorbid association with Japanese words relative to Korean words due to the limited exposure to the former.

Another exception will be seen in the performance of Case 2 at the time of initial evaluation. He showed somewhat greater deficit in Japanese relative to Korean in in his oral production ability again, while in all other modalities the difference in performance between the two languages, if any, was minimum. The nature of the deficit in Case 2, however, was phonological as well as apraxic, rather than anomic which characterized Case 1.

The second finding, regarding transfer of the therapeutic effects in Case 2, also offers support for the structural distance hypothesis. Almost complete positive transfer took place in the two relatively well preserved receptive modalities, auditory and visual (reading) comprehension. Since what was gained most through therapy in these modalities was comprehension of complex sentences, it would appear that the highly similar syntactic structures in the two languages constitute the most plausible variable that was responsible for facilitating the transfer. Additionally, comprehension of language in these receptive modalities is inherently related to the semantic system of respective languages, and we assume, along with Voinescu et al. (1977), that the overlap of these semantic systems, or "deep structures", among different languages, whether related or unrelated, should be extensive. To the extent that this assumption is valid, it would offer at least partial explanation for complete or near complete transfer of recovery in the receptive modalities even between unrelated languages. Watamori and Sasanuma (1976, 1978), in fact, found that their two English-Japanese bilingual patients, one with Broca's and the other with Wernicke's aphasia, showed almost simultaneous recovery of auditory comprehension in both languages, following intensive language therapy given exclusively in English in the Japanese environment.

Somewhat less complete transfer of therapeutic benefits from Korean to Japanese was observed in the oral production modality of Case 2. This is probably because whatever gains obtained through the therapeutic approach focused on the impaired "output phonology" in Korean in this patient would not easily be transferred to Japanese, since the phonological structure of the two languages show more differences than similarities (Sampson, 1985). Emergence of mixing at the sentence level in Japanese might have been another factor partially responsible for somewhat poorer overall oral production performance in Japanese relative to Korean.

In contrast to the sizable positive transfer observed in the three preceding modalities, the degree of transfer in the writing modality, which was the most severely impaired of all modalities in Case 2, was negligible if any. This can be explained in terms of interactions among several variables involved: the nature of improvement obtained in the treated language, the type of the therapeutic intervention that appeared to be responsible for that improvement, as well as the substantial difference between the writing systems for Hangul and Kana. The content of the major gains in the writing modality in Case 2 was marked increase in the number of correctly written Hangul words, which was promoted by specific therapy that helped him to acquire and develop some new maneuvers or strategies to compensate for his impaired process. That is to say, the improvement he obtained may reflect acquisition of compensatory strategies rather than the restitution of the impaired function (i.e., phonological processing) *per se*. This type of achievement will not transfer automatically to the non-treated language, probably because the specific type of compensatory strategies required will depend on language specific features.

Concluding remarks

To summarize, these findings taken together would appear to be in general support of the structural distance hypothesis (Paradis, 1993), demonstrating the predicted positive transfer of therapeutic benefits for various aspects of the two structurally related languages, Korean and Japanese. Our data have further shown, however, that this structural distance variable does interact with additional variables, such as types of aphasia (i.e., the overall patterns, the nature and the relative severity of deficits across different modalities), and specific methods of therapeutic intervention directed to specific aspects of language impaired, among others, modifying the relative degree of transfer in each target area.

Some evidence in the literature on bilingual patients who were speakers of structurally unrelated languages tends to complement our findings. One example is the study of the recovery process in a 69-year-old right-handed English-Japanese bilingual man with severe Broca's aphasia (Watamori and Sasanuma 1976, 1978). After receiving systematic language therapy in English for 12 months in a Japanese speaking community, he demonstrated only partial transfer from the treated to the non-treated language. The degree of improvement in the treated language was clearly greater than that in the non-treated language across all modalities except auditory comprehension (as pointed out above), and the largest difference in the amount of gains was observed in writing where the difference between the two writing systems of English and Japanese is particularly great. The second English-Japanese bilingual patient reported by the same authors (Watamori and Sasanuma, 1987) is a 52-year-old right-handed man with Wernicke's aphasia, who also showed, after 6 months of language therapy, only partial transfer from the treated (English) to the non-treated (Japanese) language. The difference in the degree of improvement was greatest in the reading and writing modalities.

These findings would strengthen our tentative conclusion that the structural distance of the languages in question constitutes a crucial variable which, with dynamic interactions with other variables already discussed, will affect the relative recovery rate of different aspects of language structure in each language involved.

Acknowledgements

This study was supported in part by the research grant, the Toyota Foundation. We are grateful to Dr. Ueon Woo Rah, Yonsei University college of Medicine, for neurological information on the two patients. We would also like to express our sincere gratitude to our subjects who were infinitely patient as well as cooperative in going through many hours of language tasks.

References

Chapey, R. 1981. *Language Intervention Strategies in Adult Aphasia.* Baltimore: Williams & Wilkins.
Chapey, R. 1986. *Language Intervention Strategies in Adult Aphasia.* 2nd Ed., Baltimore: Williams & Wilkins.
Coltheart, M., Patterson K., & Marshall J.C. (eds.) 1980. *Deep dyslexia.* London: Routledge and Kegan Paul.
Goodglass, H., & Kaplan, E. 1972. *The Assessment of Aphasia and Related Disorders.* Philadelphia: Lea & Febiger.
Goodglass, H., & Kaplan, E 1983. *The Assessment of Aphasia and Related Disorders.* 2nd Ed., Philadelphia: Lea & Febiger.
Green, D.W. 1986. Control, activation, and resource: A framework and a model for the control

of speech in bilinguals. *Brain and Language*, **27**, 210-223.

Hécaen, H., Mazaro, G., Ramier, A., Goldblum, M.C., & Merienne, L. 1971. Aphasie croisée chez un droitier bilingue. *Revue neurologique*, **124**, 319-323.

L'Hermitte, R., Hécaen, H., Dubois, J., Culioli, A., & Tabouret-Keller, A. 1966. Le problème de l'aphasie des polyglottes: Remarques sur quelques observations. *Neuropsychologia*, **4**, 315-329.

Kuno, S. 1973. Typological Characteristics of Japanese. In S. Kuno. *The Structure of the Japanese Language* (pp. 3-34). Cambridge: The MIT Press.

Lambert, W.E., & Fillenbaum, S. 1959. A pilot study of aphasia among bilinguals. *Canadian Journal of Psychology*, **13**, 28-34.

Ovcharova, P., Raichev R., Geleva T. 1968. Afaziia u Poligloti. *Nevrologiia, Psikhiatriia i Nevrokhirurgiia*, **7**, 183-190.

Paradis, M. 1977. Bilingualism and aphasia. In H. & H.A. Whitaker (eds.) *Studies in Neurolinguistics*, vol. 3, (pp.65-121). New York: Academic Press.

Paradis, M. (ed.) 1983. *Readings on Aphasia in Bilinguals and Polyglots*. Montreal: Marcel Didier. (Lambert and Fillenbaum's cases, pp. 626-635).

Paradis, M. 1989. Bilingual and polyglot aphasia. In F. Boller and J. Grafman (eds.), *Handbook of Neuropsychology*, vol. 2, (pp.117-140). Amsterdam: Elsevier Science.

Paradis, M. 1993. Bilingual aphasia rehabilitation. In M. Paradis (ed.), *Foundations of Aphasia Rehabilitation* (pp.413-419). Oxford: Pergamon Press.

Paradis, M., Hagiwara, H. & Hildebrandt, N. 1985. *Neurolinguistic Aspects of the Japanese Writing System*, New York: Academic Press.

Park, H.S., Sasanuma, S., Sunwoo ,I.N., Rah, U.W., & Shin J.S. 1992. The Preliminary Clinical Application of the Tentative Korean Aphasia Test Battery Form (1). *Korean Neuropsychology*, **10**, 350-357.

Sampson, G. 1985. *Writing Systems: A Linguistic Introduction.* (pp. 120-144). London: Hutchinson.

Sasanuma, S. & Fujimura, O. 1971. Selective impairment of phonetic and non-phonetic transcription of words in Japanese aphasic patients: Kana vs. kanji in visual recognition and writing. *Cortex*, **7**, 1-18.

Sasanuma, S. 1980. Acquired dyslexia in Japanese. In M. Coltheart, K. Patterson, and J.C. Marshall (eds.) *Deep Dyslexia* (pp.48-90.) London: Routledge and Kegan Paul.

Sasanuma, S. 1986. Universal and language-specific symptomatology and treatment of aphasia. *Folia Phoniatrica*, **38**, 121-175.

Sasanuma, S. 1994. Neuropsychology of reading: Universal and language-specific features of reading impairment. In P. Bertelson, P. Eelen, and G. d'Ydewalle (eds.), *International Perspectives on Psychological Science*, Vol.1 (pp. 105-125): Leading Themes, Hove: Lawrence Erlbaum Associates.

Sasanuma, S., Itoh, M., Watamori, T., Fukusako, Y. & Monoi, H. 1978. *Treatment of Aphasia*. Tokyo: Igaku-shoin (in Japanese).

Schuell, H. 1965. *Differential Diagnosis of Aphasia with the Minnesota Test*. Minneapolis: University of Minnesota Press.

Schuell, H., Jenkins, J., & Pabon, E. 1964. *Aphasia in Adults: Diagnosis, Prognosis and Treatment*. New York: Harper & Row.

Voinescu, I., Vish, E., Sirian, S., & Maretsis, M. 1977. Aphasia in a polyglot. *Brain and Language*, **4**, 165-176.

Watamori, T.S., & Sasanuma, S. 1976. The recovery process of a bilingual aphasic. *Journal of Communication Disorders*, **9**, 157-166.

Watamori, T.S., & Sasanuma, S. 1978. The recovery processes of two English-Japanese bilingual aphasics. *Brain and Language*, **6**, 127-140.

9 Breakdown of functional categories in three Farsi-English bilingual aphasic patients

Reza Nilipour and Michel Paradis

Introduction

New trends in aphasiological studies have resulted in making available more pathological data from languages structurally distant from those commonly investigated so far (Obler & Menn, 1988). One major outcome has been to achieve a better understanding of the nature of aphasia in general and of agrammatic aphasia in particular. The findings have allowed researchers to identify universal and language-specific effects on the surface manifestations of agrammatism and eventually to evaluate competing theoretical explanations (Menn & Obler, 1990; Paradis, 1988 for full discussion).

This chapter discusses the extent of verb phrase (VP) construction breakdown in each language of three Farsi-English bilingual aphasic patients. The patients to be discussed are native speakers of Farsi who had a good command of English premorbidly and whose university education was in English.

It will be shown that grammatical deficits in the same patient have different surface manifestations in Farsi and English. Farsi and English represent two structurally distant languages. Farsi is a morphologically rich language with free word order, whereas English has a relatively fixed word order and a much less complex verbal inflectional morphology.

It is suggested that the surface manifestations of the deficit in a bilingual patient may be a function of the specific structure of each language, since the nature of the possible errors is determined by the structure of the language system (Paradis, 1988). There are more opportunities for errors in VP constructions in Farsi than in English. Farsi thus appears more vulnerable.

A brief description of relevant aspects of Farsi grammar

Syntax

Farsi is basically considered an S-O-V language (i.e. the canonical word order in kernel sentences is subject + object + verb). However, except for some pragmatic constraints on the verb in the sentence final position, all constituents of the sentence can be moved leftward or rightward and the basic word order can be changed accordingly. In other words, the main constituents of the sentence can be reshuffled depending on the syntactic strategies or pragmatic aspects of the sentence. For example, sentence (1) represents the basic word order in standard Farsi, but sentences

(2) through (6) are also acceptable grammatical word order variations of the same sentence:

1. /man ketâb râ xândam/	"I studied the book" (canonical)
2. /man xândam ketâb râ/	"It is I who *studied* the book" (emphasis on subject and verb)
3. /ketâb râ man xândam/	"The book is what I studied"
4. /ketâb râ xândam man/	"The book is what I *studied*" (primary emphasis on object and secondary emphasis on verb)
5. /xândam man ketâb râ/	"Studying is what I did with the book"
6. /xândam ketâb râ man/	"Studying is what I did with the *book*" (primary emphasis on verb and secondary emphasis on object)

Every conjugated form of a verb carries not only "tense" but also "person" and "number" of the subject. The object of the verb is identified by a particle. The direct object by a postpositional particle (/râ/) and the indirect object by a prepositional particle (/be/). The conjugated form of the verb as well as the particles allow the leftward and rightward movements of the main constituents of the same sentence without any ambiguity or grammatical violation.

Focus is signaled by fronting the emphasized element. The first element in the sentence receives primary emphasis. The second element, if moved out of its canonical position, receives secondary emphasis and so on. Prosody may be substituted for change in word order to signal emphasis.

There are 16 possible acceptable word order variants of sentence (1):

1. /man ketâb râ be Ali dâdam/   ("I gave the book to Ali")
   I (the) book to   Ali gave-1st pers. sing

The following are some of the possible variants:

1.1 /ketâb râ man be Ali dâdam/	(It is the book that I studied)
1.2 /be Ali man ketâb râ dâdam/	(It is to Ali that I gave the book)
1.3 /dâdam man be Ali ketâb râ/	(It is giving to Ali that I did with the book)

Sentence (1) is the canonical word order pattern, but sentences (1.2), and (1.3) are grammatically acceptable sentences. These syntactic variations are basically governed by pragmatic and/or stylistic features of the sentence. It is because of this syntactic flexibility that Farsi may be considered a free word order language. This word order variability is made possible by a rich and regular morphology. The restrictions are basically on local word-order (i.e. within the boundaries of each major constituent; e.g. *ADJ + N, *AUX + V).

There is no gender in Farsi, hence no gender agreement. There is also no number agreement on adjectives in N + ADJ constructions. But there is subject-verb agreement with respect to number.

Morphology

Farsi is an inflectional language with a relatively regular morphology. The basic morphological patterns include inflectional as well as derivational bound morphemes which are attached to the base form of the word as a prefix or suffix.

INFLECTIONAL MORPHOLOGY

NOUN PHRASE

singular-plural:

Farsi words are made plural by adding the plural morpheme (/-hâ/ as unmarked morpheme for all nouns, /-ân/ as marked morpheme for some animate nouns) to the singular base form:

1. /ketâb/ → /ketâbhâ/
   "book"   "books"
2. /zan/ → /zanhâ/ or /zanân/
   "woman"   "women"   "women"
3. /deraxt/ → /deraxthâ/ or /deraxtân/
   "tree"   "trees"   "trees"

The plural marker is deleted when there is a number

4. /doderaxt/ → "two trees"
   "two tree"

Plural forms from Arabic:

There are also common alternative plural forms borrowed from Arabic. The two major groups are regular Arabic plurals and broken Arabic plurals.

   The regular Arabic plural is formed by adding an Arabic plural marker to the singular Arabic root.

Singular		Farsi plural	Arabic plural	
/kalame/	"word"	/kalamehâ/	/kalamât/	"words"
/taqsim/	"division"	/taqsimhâ/	/taqsimât/	"divisions"
/mostaxdem/	"employee"	/mostaxdemhâ/	/mostaxdemin/	"employees"
/majalle/	"journal"	/majallehâ/	/majallât/	"journals"
/mo ʔalem/	"teacher"	/mo ʔalemhâ/	/mo ʔalemin/	"teachers"

The broken plural is a phonological modification of the singular Arabic root whose form is usually determined idiosyncratically.

Singular		Farsi plural	Arabic plural	
/ketâb/	"book"	/ketâbhâ/	/kotob/	"books"
/sanad/	"document"	/sanadhâ/	/asnâd/	"documents"
/elm/	"science"	/elmhâ/	/olum/	"sciences"

/âlem/	"scientist"	/âlemân/	/olamâ/	"scientists"
/fe ʔl/	"verb"	/fe ʔlhâ/	/afʔâl/	"verbs"
/amir/	"general"	/amirân/	/omarâ/	"generals"
/qeyd/	"adverb"	/qeydhâ/	/qoyud/	"adverbs"

N + Adj / N + N

A noun can be preceded by an adjective or another noun. They are then connected to each other by a connective morpheme (izafe: /e/ = of). There is no agreement of any sort such as number, case or gender between a noun and its modifiers. Plural marker is attached to the head noun:

	N	ADJ		
1.	/ketâb-e book of	xub/ good	=	"a good book"
	/ketâbhâ-ye books of	xub good	=	"good books"
2.	/zan-e woman of	dânâ/ wise	=	"a wise woman"
	/zanhâ-ye	dânâ/	=	"wise women"
	/zanân-e	dânâ/	=	"wise women"
3.	/deraxt-e tree of	boland/ tall	=	"a tall tree"
	/deraxthâ-ye trees	boland/ of tall	=	"tall trees"
	/deraxtân-e trees of	boland/ tall	=	"tall trees"

N + N / N + pronoun

	N	N		
1.	/ketâb-e book of	reza/ Reza	=	"the book of Reza/Reza's book"
	/ketâbhâ-ye books of	reza/ Reza	=	"Reza's books"
2.	/zan-e wife of	man/ I	=	"my wife"
3.	/pesar-e son - of	to/ you	=	"your son"
	/pesarhâ-ye sons - of	to/ you	=	"your sons"
4.	/dar-e door of	xâne/ house	=	"the door of house"
	/darhâ-ye	xâne/	=	"the doors of the house"

DEFINITE / INDEFINITE

A definite noun is ordinarily unmarked while the indefinite noun is marked with a morpheme /i/.

1. /ketâbi/   "a book"
2. /medâdi/   "a pencil"
3. /u medâd râ be man dâd/   "s/he gave me the pencil"
    s/he pencil-particle to I gave
4. *u medâdi râ be man dâd*/   "s/he gave me a pencil"
    s/he pencil-a-particle to me gave

VERBS

Verbs are conjugated for "number," "person" and "tense" in Farsi. For every verb there is an infinitive form consisting of 3 parts, i.e. present tense stem, past tense marker and the infinitive morpheme:

1. /xordan/   →   /xor + d + an/   "to eat"
2. /paridan/   →   /par + id + an/   "to jump, to fly"
3. /busidan/   →   /bus + id + an/   "to kiss"

There are also some verbs that do not follow the regular pattern of present and past stems and undergo certain phonological processes.

Infinitive	Present stem	Past stem	
1. /âmadan/	/â-/	/âmad-/	"to come"
2. /bordan/	/bar/	/bord-/	"to take"
3. /didan/	/bin-/	/did/	"to see"
4. /foruxtan/	/foruš-/	/fruxt/	"to sell"

A typical verb conjugation is as follows.

Simple Present Tense

pronoun (optional)	prefix + verb stem + Ending (person & number)	
/(man)	mi-xor-am/	"I eat"
/(to)	mi-xor-i/	"you eat"
/(u)	mi-xor-ad/	"s/he eats"
/(mâ)	mi-xor-im/	"we eat"
/(šomâ)	mi-xor-id/	"you eat"
/(ânhâ)	mi-xor-and/	"they eat"

Simple Past Tense

/(man)	xor-d-am/	"I ate"
/(to)	xor-d-i/	"you ate"
/(u)	xor-d/	"s/he ate"
/(mâ)	xor-d-im/	"we ate"
/(šomâ)	xor-d-id/	"you ate"
/(ânhâ)	xor-d-and/	"they ate"

A verb ending represents "person" and "number" of the subject. Nominative pronoun as the subject of the verb may be deleted. Verb is the most highly inflected part of the sentence and is a polymorphemic word which carries both prefixes and suffixes.

1. */u nemidânad   če   bexorad/*   "He does not know what to eat"
   he not-mi-know-s what eat-s
2. */ânhâ pârsâl be dânešgâh naraftand* "They did not go to university last year"
   they last year to university not-go-ed-they
3. */ma hamiše ketâb mixaâmim/*   "We always study the book"
   we always book mi-study-1st pers. pl.

DERIVATIONAL MORPHOLOGY

Derivational morphemes are attached to verb stem, noun or adjective as suffixes to provide a new word class; e.g., present stem + â → Adj

1. *tavân + â → tavânâ*	"capable"
2. *tavân + mand → tavânmand*	"strong"
3. *tavân + gar → tavângar*	"rich"
4. *âmuz + ande → âmuzande*	
5. *rav + eš → raveš*	"method"/"way of doing things"

past stem + e → past participle

1. *xord + e → xorde*	"eaten"
2. *goft + e → gofte*	"said"

ADJ + i → N

1. *bad + i → badi*	"bad" → "badness"
2. *mardâne + i → mardânegi*	"man" → "manliness"

N + âne, N + i, V + i → ADJ

mard + âne → mardâne	"man" → "manly"/"relating to man"
cub + i → čubi	"wood" → "wooden"
sang + i → sangi	"stone" → "made of stone"
iran + i → irani	"Iran" → "Iranian"
xordan + i → xordani	"eat" → "edible"
didan + i → didani	"see" → "worth seeing"

Orthography

Farsi is written from right to left, except numbers which are written from left to right. The script is originally borrowed from Arabic. It consists of a total of 32 characters. They include Arabic characters (28) plus 4 additional characters (/p, č, ž, g/) representing 4 Farsi phonemes not found in Arabic.

The grapheme-phoneme correspondence is a rather complicated process even for native speakers of Farsi, due to the borrowed nature of the alphabet. Firstly, the number of phonemes in contemporary Standard Farsi is 29, consisting of 23 consonants and 6 vowels. One major problem is that in most cases there is no grapheme representation for the short vowels (e, a, o), though the long vowels (i, â, u) are represented by 3 of the 32 characters mentioned above. But in some contexts the short vowels are also represented by the same characters as the long vowels. These discrepancies can be a major source of ambiguity for a beginner or a non-Farsi speaker.

There is rarely a one-to-one correspondence between the consonants and the characters. This discrepancy is due to the major differences between Farsi and Arabic phonological systems. There are cases where one phoneme is represented by up to 4 different graphemes, especially in the case of borrowed words from Arabic with different graphemes but the same phonological representation in Farsi (e.g., /z/ = ذ ز ظ ض).

Case Studies

Cases 1 (T.B.) and 3 (A.S.) have been previously reported in Nilipour (1988) and Case 2 (P.A.) in Nilipour (1989). However, the patterns of breakdown of functional categories were not analyzed. Only the global patterns of recovery of these patients were described.

CASE 1 (T.B.)

ANAMNESIS

T.B. was a 26-year-old right-handed male native speaker of Farsi. His English background includes 6 years in high school at the rate of 3 hours per week and 4 years of English college education in Canada.

He was hospitalized for craniotomy and embolization as a result of a history of arteriovenous malformation (AVM) in 1982. He has undergone three craniotomies and embolization in the U.S. These were performed with resection of his AVM from the left temporo-parieto-occipital area.

A CT-scan in 1987 confirmed architectural damage and calcification of tissues of the left temporo-parieto-occipital cortex with signs of hypodensity of the right temporal lobe (See Nilipour, 1988 for further details).

Our systematic first assessment of the patient's aphasic deficits took place in October 1984. The patient was assessed with prepublication versions of the Bilingual Aphasia Test (BAT) in English (Paradis, Hummel & Libben, 1987), and Farsi (Paradis, Paribakht & Nilipour, 1987). Along with our initial assessments, several samples of the patient's spontaneous as well as descriptive speech in Farsi and English were collected during therapy and after therapy.

The BAT comprises 32 tasks, namely, five minutes of spontaneous speech; pointing; simple and complex commands; verbal auditory comprehension, syntactic auditory comprehension; recognition of semantic categories, synonyms and antonyms; grammaticality judgments and semantic acceptability; repetition of words and sentences; lexical decision; recitation of series, verbal fluency based on initial phoneme; naming; sentence construction; production of semantic and morphological opposites, derivational morphology; description of a series of six pictures depicting a story; mental arithmetic; listening comprehension of a paragraph; reading aloud words and sentences; reading words, sentences and a paragraph for comprehension; copying; dictation of words and sentences; spontaneaous writing. Scores are computed by linguistic level (phonological, morphological, syntactical, lexical, and semantic) and by skill (comprehension, repetition, judgment, lexical access, and propositionizing).

This approach allows one to detect task-specific or task-independent, modality-specific or modality-independent deficits at the level of the word, the sentence and the paragraph. One of the essential characteristics of the BAT is that its versions in different languages (60 so far) are not mere translations of the original, but linguistic equivalents, with each of the 32 tasks having its specific criterion of equivalence. A detailed account of the BAT, which gives, for each task, a specification of design considerations and cross-references with other tasks for purposes of diagnosis, a description of the stimuli, an explanation of the contribution of each task to the overall assessment, and criteria of cross-language equivalence, together with a discussion of the test's theoretical foundations within the framework of the neurolinguistics of bilingualism and a description of procedures for implementation and interpretation of results can be found in Paradis and Libben (1987).

Figure 1 shows T.B.'s overall performance in Farsi and Figure 2 his performance in English. Two years post-onset, the pattern of recovery was differential with Farsi better recovered than English. It must be noted that he was in an English language environment before and after the operation and that the first speech therapy program was provided for 4 months in English in the United States. Subsequently, he had received therapy in Farsi in Iran for about one year at the time of assessment.

The overall clinical picture of his aphasia symptoms were reduced fluent speech without articulatory difficulty, but with evidence of perseveration and word-finding difficulty. He had relatively good comprehension and repetition. Based on the initial assessment, the patient was diagnosed as having transcortical motor aphasia.

GRAMMATICAL VIOLATIONS

Violations in T.B.'s speech samples are varied and represent lexical access limita-tions as well as disruptions of VP. English violations are limited to occasional omissions of the main verb and only one example of subject-verb misagreement out of 40 utterances. No word order disruption was observed. Only two obligatory free morphemes were deleted, both indefinite articles. (He is Ø boy; he is Ø very bad bird.) Farsi sentences produced are syntactically varied and more complex. Violations are also varied and extensive. The violations in T.B.'s Farsi speech may be classified into 5 different groups, namely, obligatory morpheme deletion, subject-verb misagreement, verb deletion, verb substitution, tense substitution and lack of con-cordance.

Deletions of obligatory grammatical morphemes are restricted to pre-posed and post-posed particles /be/ and /râ/ and certain prepositions (e.g., /pesar be doxtar ne šun mide/ → /pesar Ø doxtar nešun mide/ ; /mardom do nafar râ bordan/ → /mardom do nafar Ø bordan/)

Subject-verb misagreement are due to singular subject with a plural verb, or plural subject with a singular verb (e.g., /ân nemitune xub budand/ singular subject, plural verb; /ânhâ parandehâ bud/ plural subject, singular verb; /setâ ba če mord/ plural subject, singular verb).

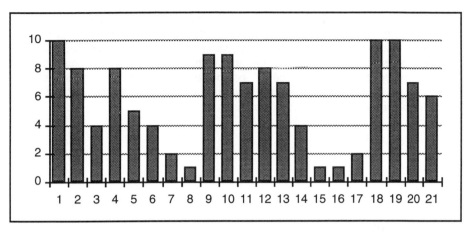

Figure 1. T.B.'s Farsi Profile on the BAT (November 1984).

1. Pointing; 2. Simple commands; 3. Semi-complex commands; 4. Verbal auditory discrimination; 5. Syntactic comprehension; 6. Semantic categories; 7. Synonyms; 8. Antonyms; 9. Grammaticality judgements; 10. Semantic acceptability; 11. Repetition (words); 12. Lexical decision; 13. Series; 14. Naming; 15. Derivational morphology; 16. Morphological opposites; 17. Listening comprehension; 18. Oral reading (words); 19. Copying; 20. Reading comprehension (words); 21. Reading comprehension (sentences).

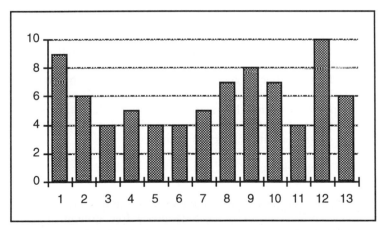

Figure 2. T.B.'s English Profile on the BAT (November 1984).

1. Pointing; 2. Simple commands; 3. Semi-complex commands; 4. Verbal auditory discrimination; 5. Syntactic comprehension; 6. Semantic categories; 7. Antonyms; 8. Grammaticality judgements; 9. Semantic acceptability; 10. Repetition (words); 11. Lexical decision; 12. Copying; 13. Reading comprehension (words).

Verb deletions are of two kinds: complete deletion of VP and deletion of either the nominal or verbal element of a compound verb (e.g., /un moqe? hanuz .../, /ba?dan ye doxtar .../, /doxter gofteš ke .../, /mire be xânum čiz../, /un taq xord .../).

Verb substitutions were either compound verbs with an empty nominal ("thing") or an onomatopoeic word followed by "be" or "become", and sometimes irrelevant choices (e.g., /badan ham čiz kardeš/, /hamin jur az ciz hast/, /qâr qâr rafteš čiz kone/, /in nemitunest aslan dast bokone/).

Case 2 (P.A.)

ANAMNESIS

P.A. was a 48-year-old right-handed female Farsi native speaker who had a bilingual high school education and a university education in English. She was hospitalized as a result of a CVA in 1983.

The clinical examination indicated a CVA syndrome in the left fronto-temporal area. The CT-scan showed infarction of the left fronto-temporal area due to thrombosis of the left middle cerebral artery. There was also extensive cerebral oedema.

The patient suffered from a right hemiplegia but was able to walk with a stick and to write with her left hand. She also exhibited central right facial hemiparesis. No hearing loss was observed and her visual field was normal.

The patient became aphasic and was evaluated 4 years post-onset using the Farsi (Paradis, Paribakht & Nilipour, 1987) and English (Paradis, Hummel & Libben, 1987) versions of the BAT.

P.A.'s performance in each language is represented in Figures 3 and 4. Her general performance is relatively the same in both languages and the final recovery pattern is parallel recovery. Her comprehension was preserved in both languages, but relatively impaired at the syntactic level. Her speech in Farsi was fluent and cohesive with no paraphasia or neologism. The patient's English production was limited, but with no dysfluency.

On the whole, the patient's general clinical picture may be characterized as exhibiting clearly impaired repetition (at the sentence level) and relatively well-preserved comprehension and fluent oral production. Her oral reading is also abnormal with relatively better comprehension. Based on the patient's clinical picture, she was diagnosed with conduction aphasia.

GRAMMATICAL VIOLATIONS

Grammatical violations appeared only in oral reading and to some extent in sentence repetition tasks. In English, there were abundant free grammatical morpheme omissions in obligatory contexts (36/37 in one task) and one case of subject-verb agreement violation (washes → wash, 1/10). Farsi violations were of a different nature. There were omissions of bound grammatical morphemes (12/18) and substitutions of grammatical particles (3/4); and verb tense substitutions (all sentences in the reading task, 10/10), producing the infinitive stem (i.e., the present tense stem + the past tense marker, but omitting the infinitive morpheme "an"), e.g.,

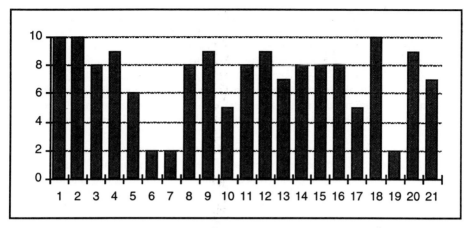

Figure 3. P.A.'s Farsi Profile on the BAT (2 March 1987)

1. Pointing; 2. Simple commands; 3. Semi-complex commands; 4. Verbal auditory discrimination; 5. Syntactic comprehension; 6. Synonyms; 7. Antonyms; 8. Repetition (words); 9. Lexical decision; 10. Repetition (sentences); 11. Series; 12. Naming; 13. Sentence comprehension; 14. Semantic opposites; 15. Listening comprehension; 16. Oral reading (words); 17. Reading comprehension (paragraph); 18. Copying; 19. Dictation (words); 20. Reading comprehension (words); 21. Reading comprehension (sentences).

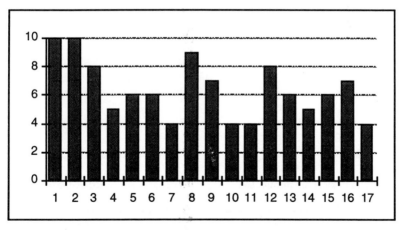

Figure 4. P.A.'s English Profile on the BAT (2 March 1987)

1. Pointing; 2. Simple commands; 3. Semi-complex commands; 4. Verbal auditory discrimination; 5. Syntactic comprehension; 6. Synonyms; 7. Antonyms; 8. Repetition (words); 9. Lexical decision; 10. Series; 11. Naming; 12. Listening comprehension; 13. Oral reading (words); 14. Reading comprehension (paragraph); 15. Copying; 16. Reading comprehension (words); 17. Reading comprehension (sentences).

midehad	→	*dâd*	(infinitive: *dâdan*)	"give"
mikonad	→	*kard*	(infinitive: *Kardan*)	"do"
nemikešad	→	*kešid*	(infinitive: *kešidan*)	"pull"
nemibusad	→	*busid*	(infinitive: *busidan*)	"kiss"

In Farsi VP was the most disrupted constituent with respect to both omission and substitution of grammatical morphemes. Interestingly, the past tense base form of the verb, the uninflected form of the verb and the third person singular past have the same form.

The patient was consistent in changing the verb inflectional paradigms and in omitting the negative morpheme in every sentence of the reading task. The sentences are selected for the variety of their syntactic structures. Omissions and substitutions in Farsi (Table 1) contrast with omissions only in English (Table 2), as prompted by the different structure of each language. Table 3 gives a comparison between the number of violations in reading sentences aloud in Farsi and in English.

Table 1. Patient P.A.'s violations in reading sentences aloud, Farsi version (Substitutions are indicated and omissions are marked by Ø)

377. /doxtar pesar râ hol midehad/ 　　　　　　　　　　dâd	(The girl pushes the boy)
378. /pedar be xodaš negâh mikonad/ 　　　　　Ø　　　　　　kard	(The father looks at self)
379. /sag râ gorbe gâz migirad/ 　　　　　　　　gereft	(The dog is bitten by the cat)
380. /in kâmiyun ast ke savâri râ kike šad/ 　　az　　Ø Ø　　　　kešai	(It is the truck that pulls the car)
381. /zan ân mard râ nemibusad/ 　　　　　　　busid	(The woman does not kiss the man)
382. /in sag ast ke gorbe gâzaš migirad/ 　　ân　　Ø Ø　　　　Ø gereft	(It is the dog that bites the cat)
383. /kâmiyun râ savân menikešad/ 　　　　　　　kešid	(The truck is not pulled by the car)
384. /ânhâ donbâle u midavand/ 　　Ø　　　david	(They are chasing him/her)
385. /xodaš râ ân zan mizanad/ 　　ânhâ Ø　　　busid	(The woman hits self)
386. /savaâri râ kamiyun memikešad/ 　　　　　　　kešid	(The car is not pulled by the truck)

Case 3 (A.S.)

ANAMNESIS

A.S. was a 49-year-old educated right-handed male native speaker of Farsi. Besides Farsi, he knew both German and English. He could read and write in all three

Table 2. Patient P.A.'s violations in reading sentences aloud, English version (Omissions are marked by Ø. Note the absence of substitutions)

377. The boy holds the girl. Ø Ø	(boy holds girl)
378. He washes himself Ø Ø	(wash himself)
379. The dog is bitten by the cat Ø Ø Ø Ø	(dog bitten cat)
380. It's the truck that pulls the car Ø Ø Ø	(truck that pulls car)
381. The boy does not push the girl Ø Ø Ø Ø	(boy push girl)
382. It is the dog that the cat bites Ø Ø Ø Ø Ø	(dog cat bites)
383. The truck is not pulled by the car Ø Ø Ø Ø Ø	(truck pulled car)
384. He holds her Ø Ø	(holds)
385. The girld is pushed by the boy Ø Ø Ø Ø	(girl pushed boy)
386. The woman is not kissed by the man Ø Ø Ø Ø Ø	(woman kissed man)

Table 3. Number of grammatical violations in reading aloud in Farsi and English for Patient P.A. (See description of the BAT section for reading sentences aloud in Paradis & Libben, 1987, pp. 124-125.)

Syntactic structures	Farsi	English
377. Standard word order, nouns as subject and object	1	2
378. Standard word order, pronominal reference	2	2
379. Passive in English, OSV in Farsi	1	4
380. Topicalised subject	4	4
381. Standard word order, negative	2	4
382. Negative passive in English, OSV in Farsi	2	5
383. Topicalised object	5	5
384. Standard word order, pronominal reference	2	2
385. Passive in English, OSV in Farsi	3	4
386. Negative passive in English, OSV in Farsi	2	5

languages, but Farsi and German were his dominant languages. He learned English in high school at the rate of three hours a week for 6 years. Then he learned German as a medical student in Germany for 16 years. He also spent one year in England as a medical researcher and had studied English for two years premorbidly. He was an experienced orthopedic surgeon.

A.S. became the victim of an explosion in 1985, which caused a left fronto-temporal trauma. Upon regaining consciousness, he was aphasic and was able to speak only a few words in Farsi, but after 16 days he switched to German. He comprehended both Farsi and German, but to everybody's surprise he spoke only in German, even to unilingual Farsi speaking visitors. This condition lasted for 3 weeks. He then switched back to Farsi. During that time, the patient was unable to speak English. Testing demonstrated his lack of understanding of English as well. A.S. regained the use of English only after he had maximally recovered both Farsi and German.

A CT-scan showed a left fronto-temporal lesion of about 2x2 cm. The patient suffered right lateral hemianopsia and right hemiparesis with emphasis on brachiofacial. There were no symptoms of apraxia or agnosia. He had good right-left recognition.

The patient was tested with equivalent versions of the BAT in Farsi (Paradis, Paribakht & Nilipour, 1987), German (Paradis & Lindner, 1987) and English (Paradis, Hummel & Libben, 1987). The general picture of the patient's residual capacities across languages based on the elicited responses is reported in detail in Nilipour and Ashayeri (1989).

English was poor overall. On no task did the patient score significantly better than in Farsi and German, but in many sections he scored considerably lower. Farsi and German were almost equally recovered. The initial recovery was a pattern of alternating antagonistic recovery, but the final overall recovery was differential, with Farsi better recovered than German, and English least.

Based on the patient's performance on tasks related to specific linguistic skills (comprehension, repetition, expression, judgment, reading and writing) compared to normal performance, his clinical symptomatic picture can be summarized as fluent speech, poor comprehension, relatively good repetition and impaired writing. Our trilingual patient was diagnosed as having transcortical sensory aphasia.

Several samples of his spontaneous and descriptive speech and writing have been collected for therapeutic and research purposes during the last phase of recovery.

GRAMMATICAL VIOLATIONS

Speech samples elicited from A.S. are varied and structurally more complex than T.B.'s. They come from both oral speech and writing. The sentences go beyond simple clause utterances and have a much higher MLU. There is also more variety in lexical verbs and tenses and a higher type/token ratio in the Farsi samples.

An analysis of the English data shows that the general structure of the English sentences is mostly intact. Word order disruptions and obligatory morpheme deletions are very rare. The acceptable utterances are varied with respect to length and structure. The remainder of the utterances can be grouped into two sets: (1) utterances with paraphasic or neologistic lexical items (e.g., I /mak/ speak more than before; they /kuk/ some verse for example); and (2) utterances with loose structure or uncontrolled lexical selection (e.g., they could many things at first we couldn't understand; I have like is difficult not like Germany; I have seen there by in the car; they couldn't more than they spoke all with them). Some intrusions of German and Farsi sentences in a conversation in Farsi or mixed utterances (e.g., "Aber I have not müde") were observed in his English descriptive and spontaneous speech.

Farsi utterances were more complex and varied than English ones. At the same time, there were more violations in Farsi at the level of the VP, both in his oral and written language. They may be classified into two groups: (1) subject-verb misagreement between first and second or third person, and (2) substitution of the complete main verb or of the nominal or verbal element of a compound verb.

Discussion

From the analysis of the language of three aphasic patients who were native speakers of Farsi and had a good command of English premorbidly, based on the results obtained on equivalent versions of the *Bilingual Aphasia Test,* including samples of spontaneous and descriptive speech, it becomes apparent that surface grammatical violations are conditioned, for a major part, by the specific structure of each language, in accordance with the corollary to Murphy's Law that states that only that which can go wrong will go wrong (Paradis, 1989). The type of possible error is determined by the structure of the system. Thus, surface manifestations of a same underlying deficit may differ in a bilingual patient's two languages because of the different opportunities for breakdown offered by each. Different constraints on the possible types of errors will result in different surface manifestations in each language.

To the extent that features identified as vulnerable are present, they will be susceptible to impairment. English, for instance, offers more opportunities for omission of free grammatical morphemes in obligatory contexts than Farsi. Hence, it is not surprising that bilingual Farsi-English aphasic patients drop more free standing grammatical morphemes, since there are far more obligatory contexts in that language. All articles were omitted in the English repetition task. Yet, there are no Farsi articles to be omitted. One could argue that in this case the tendency to omit articles in English was exacerbated by interference from Farsi, the patients' premorbidly dominant and subsequently best recovered language. But some of the free grammatical morphemes required in Farsi were also omitted.

The difference in omission of functional categories is one of degree, proportional to the number of obligatory contexts. Substitutions are restricted to Farsi inflectional morphemes, unless one assumes that the Ø morpheme was substituted in English wherever possible, an option not available in Farsi. Unlike English, Farsi offered many opportunities for omission or substitution of compound verb elements. Because of the structure of Farsi, most deletions and substitutions were related to VP, a constituent that is much less vulnerable in English.

Conclusion

All three patients examined did exhibit avoidance of problematic structures, syntactic simplification with a tendency to favor the canonical word order, omission of free grammatical morphemes, and substitution of inflectional morphemes in both languages, irrespective of the diagnosis (transcortical motor, conduction, and transcortical sensory aphasia). The differences in surface manifestations of their deficit were qualitatively similar but quantitatively diffent. The presence and frequency of various grammatical violations were consonant with the presence and frequency of vulnerable elements in the structure of each language. Their native language, which was also the language of the environment during recovery and that of therapy, was on the whole better preserved than their second language, to varying degrees in each patient, and with changes of dominance over time.

Acknowledgement

This research was funded by Grant 410-88-0821 and Grant 410-91-1864 of the Social Sciences and Humanities Research Council of Canada to Michel Paradis.

References

Menn, L. & Obler, L.K. 1990. *Agrammatism: a cross-language narrative sourcebook*. Amsterdam: John Benjamins.

Nilipour, R. 1988. Bilingual aphasia in Iran: apreliminary report. *Journal of Neurolinguistics*, **3**, 185-232.

Nilipour, R. 1989. Task-specific agrammatism in a Farsi-English bilingual patient. *Journal of Neurolinguistics*, **4**, 243-253.

Nilipour, R. & Ashayeri, H. 1989. Alternating antagonism between two languages with successive recovery of a third in a trilingual aphasic patient. *Brain and Language*, **36**, 23-48.

Obler, L.K. & Menn, L. 1988. Agrammatism: the current issues. *Journal of Neurolinguistics*, **4**, 63-76.

Paradis, M. 1988. Recent development in the study of agrammatism: their import for the assessment of bilingual aphasia. *Journal of Neurolinguistics*, **3**, 185-232.

Paradis, M. 1989. Linguistic parameters in the diagnosis of dyslexia in Japanese and Chinese. In P.G. Aaron & R. Malatesha Joshi (eds.), *Reading and writing disorders in different orthographic systems* (pp.231-266). Dordercht: Kluwer.

Paradis, M., Hummel, K., & Libben, G. 1987. *The bilingual aphasia test* (English version). Hillsdale, NJ.: Lawrence Erlbaum Associates.

Paradis, M. & Libben, G. 1987. *The assessment of bilingual aphasia*. Hillsdale, NJ.: Lawrence Erlbaum Associates.

Paradis, M., Lindner, O. 1987. *Aphasie Test in Deutsch für Zweisprachige*. Hillsdale, NJ.: Lawrence Erlbaum.

Paradis, M., Paribakht, T. & Nilipour, R. 1987. *Azomane zaban parishiye Farsi*. Hillsdale, NJ.: Lawrence Erlbaum Associates.

10 Differential impairments in four multilingual patients with subcortical lesions

Franco Fabbro and Michel Paradis

The present chapter aims at discussing recent data on the residual language of multilingual patients who became aphasic following subcortical lesions. First, the main linguistic functions of subcortical structures will be described, then recent advances in research on bilingual aphasics with subcortical lesions will be presented. These data result from our observations on 4 bilingual patients.

What is subcortical aphasia?

Subcortical aphasias are acquired language disorders due to lesions in the basal ganglia and/or in the thalamus of the dominant hemisphere. With the development of neuroimaging techniques, such as CT-scan and MRI, neurologists had the possibility to study subcortical aphasia and to ascertain the role that basal ganglia and the thalamus play in language processes. It was thus possible to find an explanation for aphasic symptoms in patients who did not have cortical lesions but merely subcortical lesions involving the basal ganglia, the thalamus and the white matter of the left hemisphere.

What characterizes subcortical aphasia?

Subcortical aphasias are generally nonfluent. Typically, patients with subcortical aphasia are reluctant to initiate speech and sometimes they may also reach levels of mutism; they answer questions only very briefly. Reduced speech initiation apparently results from the impairment of neural circuits accounting for motivation towards speech production, which include the limbic cortex, the basal ganglia, the thalamus, the supplementary motor area and Broca's area (Alexander, 1989; Wallesch & Papagno, 1988; Crosson, 1992).

Patients with subcortical aphasia quite often also show voice disorders (e.g., hypophonia), disrupted articulation often leading to mispronunciation, and a foreign accent syndrome. All these disorders suggest that left-hemispheric subcortical structures are involved in regulating the intensity and the quality of the voice (Graff-Redford, Cooper & Colsher, 1986; Blumstein, Alexander, Ryalls, Katz & Dworetzky, 1987; Gurd, Bessell, Bladon & Bamford, 1988).

Although subcortical aphasias manifest themselves as nonfluent aphasias, they nevertheless show particular symptoms which are typical of fluent aphasia, such as semantic and verbal paraphasias. In particular semantic paraphasias are possibly due to an alteration of the nervous circuits which monitor the semantic level of speech production. Subcortical structures, and precisely the cortico-thalamo-cortical loop and the cortico-striato-thalamo-cortical loop must thus be considered highly important for monitoring semantic aspects of language (Penfield & Roberts, 1959; Luria, 1977; Crosson, 1985; Wallesch & Papagno, 1988).

Several authors found that comprehension and repetition were generally well preserved. For example Wallesch and Papagno (1988) reported that language comprehension disturbances appear not to be a prominent feature of subcortical aphasia and that repetition was noted to be intact or only mildly disturbed in most cases. Démonet, Puel, Celsis & Cardebat (1991) observed an unusual syndrome subsequent to left subcortical lesions, which includes the following symptoms: reduction of spontaneous speech, verbal paraphasias and perseverations, frequent preservation of auditory comprehension and normal word repetition. On the other hand, Damasio, Damasio, Rizzo, Varney & Gersh (1982) suggest that comprehension deficits occur with lesions involving the anterior limb of the capsule wich carries projections from auditory cortex to the head of the caudate nucleus. Damage to this system produces paraphasias and aural comprehension deficits.

Patients with subcortical aphasia often show other specific disorders of speech production, such as perseverations and echolalia. Perseverations occur when patients repeat words or utterances that they themselves produced, whereas echolalia refers to the tendency to immediately repeat the last utterance produced by another person (e.g., the examiner). Both are due to impairments in the system accounting for the switching from one verbal element to the following within concatenated speech. Recent data show that basal ganglia are apparently determinant for the correct functioning of this switching mechanism (Gray, Feldon, Rawlins, Hemsley & Smith, 1991).

What characterizes subcortical aphasia in bilinguals?

Characteristic features of subcortical aphasia in bilinguals have not yet been reported. The main questions to be asked are the following:

1. Are there linguistic functions which are specific to the basal ganglia?
2. Do all languages known by the patient show the same degree of impairment, or are there differences between these languages?
3. Are there any translation impairments, and if so, in which direction?

Our data

The linguistic performance of four bilingual aphasic patients with localized vascular lesions confined mainly to left-hemisphere subcortical structures has been systematically analyzed and the results are reported below.

Case 1. E.M. is a 70-year-old right-handed woman; her first language (L1) is Venetan, her second language (L2) is Italian. She attended only 3 years of elementary school (in Italian). Prior to the lesion she had been speaking practically only Venetan (Veronese variant) both within her family and at work. She could perfectly understand and read Italian, though she hardly could speak it. In November 1990 she had a stroke which rendered her mute for about 15 days. After this period she began to speak

Italian, but was no longer able to speak in her native language. For this reason, after one year from the stroke she asked to be rehabilitated in Venetan. According to the *Aachener Aphasie Test* (AAT) (Luzzati, Willmes & De Bleser, 1992) administered in Italian, she presented a slight Broca's aphasia, while praxias, memory and intelligence were unimpaired. The neurological investigation revealed a slight motor and sensory right hemisyndrome. Magnetic Resonance Imagery (MRI) showed a localized ischemic lesion to the left putamen and to the body of the left caudate nucleus (Figure 1). Figures and Tables start on page 145. For further neurological and neuro-psychological data on this patient, see Aglioti and Fabbro (1993).

A description of the patient's spontaneous speech in Venetan is provided in Table 1 and in Italian in Table 2 (see Paradis & Libben, 1987). The data from the AAT are given in Table 3. The patient's morphosyntactic errors are analyzed in Table 4.

Case 2. C.B. is a 71-year old right-handed woman. Her first language is Friulian, her second language Italian, her third language (L3), English, which she learned at the age of 22, when she went to England and married an Englishman. She had 5 years of schooling in Italian. In 1983 she came back to Italy with her son, whereas her daughter stayed in London. In November 1993, 10 years after her return to Italy, she suffered an ischemic stroke. In April 1994 the AAT was administered in Italian and revealed 88% of Broca's aphasia and 12% of Wernicke's aphasia. She was also tested with the BAT in all three of her languages. In addition, the patient suffered from temporal disorientation and moderate depression; intelligence was only slightly impaired. She presented long delays in answering. The neurological investigation revealed a severe right hemiplegia of her arm and leg. MRI revealed an ischemic lesion to the head of the caudate nucleus, to a small portion of the putamen, and to the anterior portion of the internal capsule of the left hemisphere (Figures 2, 3 and 4).

Results of the patient's performance on the Friulian (Paradis & Fabbro, 1993), Italian (Paradis & Canzanella, 1990), and English (Paradis, Hummel & Libben, 1989) versions of the BAT are provided in Table 5. An analysis of her Friulian spontaneous speech is given in Table 6, of her Italian speech in Table 7, and of her English spontaneous speech in Table 8. An analysis of her morphosyntactic errors is provided in Table 9.

Part C of the BAT comprises four tasks in each direction: Recognition of the translation equivalent of 5 concrete words in a list of 10 words in the other language; Translation of 10 words (5 concrete and 5 abstract); Translation of 6 sentences, the first two containing one reversible morphosyntactic contrastive feature each, the next two containing two such features each, and the last two containing three contrastive features each. The last task is a grammaticality judgment task. Sentences are made ungrammatical by inappropriately incorporating a morphosyntactic feature of the other language. The structures of all sentences of Part C are identical across languages, and the interference errors in the grammaticality judgment task are mirror images of each other. Only the lexical items vary across languages (though within the same semantic category and frequency range). Each Part C is conceived for a specific pair of languages. The patient's scores on Part C of the BAT for Friulian/Italian are given in Table 10, for Friulian/English in Table 11, and for Italian/English in Table 12.

Case 3. El.M., a 56-year-old right-handed man. His first language is Friulian, his second language, Italian. He had received 11 years of schooling in Italian. In June

1991 he had a brain haemorrhage. In September 1993 he was administered the AAT in Italian, which revealed 100% of Broca's aphasia. The BAT was administered in both of his languages. Intelligence was preserved. His verbal memory span was 3. There were no apraxias. The patient was moderately depressed. Neurologically, he showed a severe right hemiplegia of the superior and inferior limbs, his right hemiface being only slightly hemiplegic, MRI revealed a wide subcortical lesion to the caudate nucleus, the putamen, the internal capsule, and to part of the globus pallidus and the thalamus (pulvinar) of the left hemisphere (Figures 5, 6 and 7).

Results of the patient's performance on the Friulian version of the BAT are provided in Table 13, and on the Italian version in Table 14. An analysis of his spontaneous speech in Friulian is given in Table 15, and in Italian in Table 16. An analysis of his morphosyntactic errors is provided in Table 17. The patient's scores on Part C of the BAT for Friulian/Italian are given in Table 18.

Case 4. O.R., a 63-year-old man. His first language is Friulian, his second language is Italian; he received 5 years of schooling in Italian. In January 1993 he had an ischemic stroke. Three months later he was tested with the AAT and the BAT. The AAT in his second language revealed 65% of Wernicke's aphasia and 35% of Broca's aphasia. The patient had preserved intelligence, praxis and memory. The neurological investigation detected a right hemiplegia. MRI revealed a lesion to the head and body of the left caudate nucleus, the left putamen, and portions of the cortex of the left insula (Figures 8, 9 and 10).

Results of the patient's performance on the Friulian version of the BAT are provided in Table 19, and on the Italian version in Table 20. An analysis of his spontaneous speech in Friulian is given in Table 21, and in Italian in Table 22. An analysis of his morphosyntactic errors is provided in Table 23. The patient's scores on Part C of the BAT for Friulian/Italian are given in Table 24.

Major aphasic symptoms observed in our bilingual aphasics with subcortical lesions (Table 25)

1. Two patients (C.B. and El.M.) had nonfluent aphasia in all languages, whereas E.M. was nonfluent in her L2 and unable to speak in her L1. In contrast, O.R. presented a fluent aphasia in all languages.

2. All patients presented agrammatic features with omissions of free grammatical morphemes within between 7.6% and 25% of all obligatory contexts.

3. All patients produced phonemic paraphasias in spontaneous speech. The 3 nonfluent patients produced semantic and verbal paraphasias, in spontaneous speech and/or in naming tasks. E.M., C.B. and O.R also produced neo- logisms.

4. All patients presented oral comprehension deficits, with an average of 61.4% correct answers, whereas repetition was significantly better, with a mean percentage of correct repetitions of 84.3% (t-test p <.01).

5. All patients exhibited perseverations and were echolalic.

6. Only E.M. presented severe mixing, producing 52% of words in L2 while trying

to speak in L1. Moreover, she could not translate words and sentences from L2 into L1, whereas the reverse was possible. The remaining 3 patients did not present relevant mixing problems. C.B. was not able to translate words from L3 into L1, although she understood fairly well the meaning of the words she was asked to translate.

Discussion

One of the major symptoms of subcortical aphasias are disorders of speech initiation, which may range from reduced spontaneous speech to complete mutism. These impairments of speech initiation may show different degrees of severity across the languages known by the subjects. For example, E.M., was no longer able to talk in her first language, but well in her L2. This might be due to a greater involvement of the limbic-striato-thalamo-cortical loop in organizing verbal initiation of L1 and/or any language which has been acquired with implicit strategies, as opposed to a language learned and mainly used with explicit strategies (Aglioti & Fabbro, 1993; Speedie et al., 1993; Paradis, 1994). In two other patients (C.B. and El.M..), however, speech initiation was equally impaired across lan-guages. This might be due to the fact that these 2 patients had a very good knowledge of all their languages, which were probably all related to implicit memory systems. The fourth patient, O.R., was equally fluent in both languages, possibly because his lesion involved not only subcortical structures, but also the cortex of the insula.

Lexical and semantic mistakes have been observed in all four patients. El.M. produced verbal paraphasias only in naming tasks, but not during spontaneous speech. Verbal and semantic paraphasias in aphasics with subcortical lesions corroborate the hypothesis that subcortical structures of the left hemisphere play a major role in monitoring semantic and lexical aspects of language (Wallesch & Papagno, 1988; Crosson, 1992).

Perseverations and echolalia were two further characteristic disorders presented by all subjects in all languages, which are probably the consequence of a deterioration of the mechanisms accounting for switching from one linguistic element of concatenated speech to the following one. In normal conditions, this switching function is generally subserved by the basal ganglia of the dominant hemisphere (Gray et al.,1991). In particular, in our opinion echolalia results from the inability of the speaker to inhibit the motor interiorization of verbal expressions produced by his/her interlocutor (Ojemann 1982; Di Pellegrino, Fadiga, Fogassi, Gallese, & Rizzolatti, 1992). All four patients made echolalic spontaneous translations (as previously reported in Veyrac, 1931; see also Perecman, 1984; De Vreese, Motta & Toschi, 1988). Not only did they repeat verbatim the interlocutor's expressions, but also immediately translated them in another language.

As to translation ability, only two patients showed a dissociation between two directions of translation. E.M. was no longer able to translate words and sentencesfrom her second language into her native language, a translation direction which is generally considered to be the easiest one to perform. This could depend on a severe impairment of initiation of verbal expression in L1. Similarly, C.B. could translate words from her L1 into her L3, but not vice-versa, although she perfectly understood the meaning of the words to be translated, since she correctly indicated the related objects (e.g. head, wall). Her spontaneous speech in L1 and L3 being fairly good, this impairment of word translation abilities from L3 into L1 clearly represents a selective disorder of a single component of the general translation system (Paradis, Goldblum & Abidi, 1982). This may be considered further evidence for the hypothesis that the cerebral systems underlying translation are at least partially independent, both with respect to the different languages known by the subject and the directions of translation (Paradis, 1984). Hence, it is possible that the basal ganglia of the dominant hemisphere play a major role also in some components of translation processes.

Conclusions

The neurolinguisitc analysis of these four multilingual aphasic patients with lesions mainly confined to the left basal ganglia gives a positive answer to the first question, namely, whether there are linguistic functions specific to the basal ganglia. Indeed, the basal ganglia of the left hemisphere apparently serve specific linguistic functions, since all our patients presented symptoms of agrammatism, verbal and semantic paraphasias, poor comprehension and echolalia. The only major difference between E.M., C.B., and El.M. on the one hand and O.R. on the other, was verbal fluency. Only O.R. was fluent, whereas the remaining three patients presented nonfluent speech. Most probably fluent speech in O.R. was due to a concomitant lesion to the cortex of the insula.

A lesion which is confined to the basal ganglia of the left hemisphere, thus, causes a particular syndrome, which is at an intermediate level between Transcortical Motor Aphasia characterized by nonfluent speech with good comprehension and good repetition, and Transcortical Sensory Aphasia characterized by fluent speech with poor comprehension but relatively good repetition. The language syndrome which shares most common features with aphasias due to lesions to the left basal ganglia is the Isolation of the Speech Area Syndrome, whose main characteristics are nonfluent speech with poor comprehension but good repetition.

The basal ganglia ought therefore to be considered as an essential structure for the link between the more automatic functions of language and the propositional, emotional and switching aspects of language, which are subserved by the so-called "frontal lobe system" (Rubens 1976, Wallesch & Papagno, 1988; Gray et al. 1991).

With respect to our second question, namely, whether all languages known to the patient show the same degree of impairment, our data demonstrate that, as with cortical aphasias, languages of a bilingual patient may be differentially affected by basal ganglia lesions.

The answer to our third question, whether there can be impairments in translation ability, is positive. Two patients exhibited an inability to translate from their second or third language into their first. Though both patients show a unidirectional impairment of translation toward their native language, more cases are needed before we can ascertain whether this directionality is exclusive.

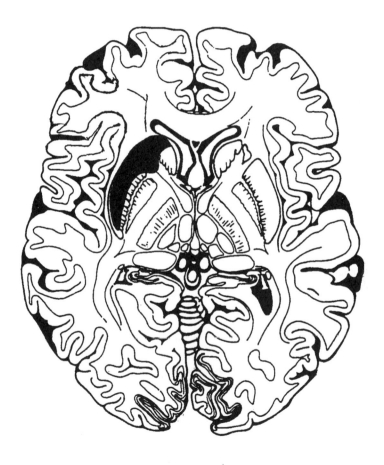

Figure 1. Patient E.M.: Line drawing of MRI showing a localized ischemic lesion to the left putamen and the body of the left caudate nucleus.

Table 1. Patient E.M.'s spontaneous speech in Venetan (L1) (23 minutes)

Number of utterances		346
Total number of words		1710
Mean length of utterance		4.94
Mean length of the 5 longest utterances		11.8
Number of different words		276
Type/token ratio		0.31
Number of neologisms		15
Number of phonemic paraphasias resulting in nonwords		38
Number of phonemic paraphasias resulting in words		1
Number of semantic paraphasias		6
Number of verbal paraphasias (unrelated words)		3
Morphosyntactic errors and percent in obligatory contexts	Number	Percent
Omission of free grammatical morphemes	68	8.6
Omission of full verbs	Ø	Ø
Substitution of inflectional morphemes	32	11.6
Substitution of free grammatical morphemes	15	1.9
Addition of grammatical morphemes in inappropriate contexts	6	0.7
Number of word-order errors		1
Number of verbs per utterance		0.40
Number of subordinate clauses		41
Number of intraphrasal pauses		64
Number of circumlocutions		Ø
Number of stereotypic phrases		Ø
Evidence of word finding difficulties		64
Detection of foreign accent (0: none; 5: very strong)	3	
Number of inappropriate foreign words	885	51.7
Number of semantically deviant sentences	13	
The discourse is cohesive	Yes	
The discourse is pragmatically sound	Yes	
Echolalia	Number	Percent
Partial or total repetitions of the examiner's questions	11	3.1
Self-repetitions	50	14.4
Words in echoed utterances	24	1.4
Words in self-repetitions	100	5.8
Total number of utterances repeated	61	17.6
Total number of words repeated	124	7.2

Table 2. Patient E.M.'s spontaneous speech in Italian (L2) (16 minutes)

	Number	Percent
Number of utterances	224	
Total number of words	1254	
Mean length of utterance	5.13	
Mean length of the 5 longest utterances	10.8	
Number of different words	250	
Type/token ratio	0.39	
Number of neologisms	9	
Number of phonemic paraphasias resulting in nonwords	20	
Number of phonemic paraphasias resulting in words	5	
Number of semantic paraphasias	1	
Number of verbal paraphasias (unrelated words)	6	

Morphosyntactic errors and percent in obligatory contexts	Number	Percent
Omission of free grammatical morphemes	58	9.6
Omission of full verbs	8	7
Substitution of inflectional morphemes	35	11.5
Substitution of free grammatical morphemes	12	1.9
Addition of grammatical morphemes in inappropriate contexts	11	1.8
Number of word-order errors	1	
Number of verbs per utterance	0.46	
Number of subordinate clauses	24	
Number of intraphrasal pauses	37	
Number of circumlocutions	Ø	
Number of stereotypic phrases	Ø	
Evidence of word finding difficulties	37	
Detection of foreign accent (0: none; 5: very strong)	2	
Number of inappropriate foreign words	55	
Number of semantically deviant sentences	3	
The discourse is cohesive	Yes	
The discourse is pragmatically sound	Yes	

Echolalia	Number	Percent
Partial or total repetitions of the examiner's questions	4	1.6
Self-repetitions	21	8.6
Words in echoed utterances	14	1.1
Words in self-repetitions	46	3.6
Total number of utterances repeated	25	10.2
Total number of words repeated	60	4.7

Table 3. Patient E.M.'s Aachener Aphasie-Test scores

	Italian (L2)		Venetan (L1)	
Token Test	36/50	72%	35/50	70%
Comprehension	52/60	86%	49/60	81.6%
Repetition	116/150	77%	112/150	74%
Naming	105/120	87%	63/120	52%

Table 4. Patient E.M.'s morphosyntactic errors and percentage of errors in obligatory contexts in Venetan (L1) and Italian (L2)

	L1		L2	
Omission of free grammatical morphemes		8.6%		9.6%
Prepositions	13	8.8%	7	6.9%
Conjunctions	5	2.4%	15	9.3%
Articles	12	11.6%	15	12.2%
Obligatory pronouns	20	8.9%	13	0.9%
Auxiliary verbs	18	15.6%	8	0.9%
Omission of full verbs	Ø	-	8	7.0%
Substitution of inflectional morphemes		11.6%		1.9%
Verbs	29	20.7%	27	23.6%
Adjectives	2	8.3%	7	11.6%
Nouns	1	0.9%	1	0.8%
Substitution of free grammatical morphemes		1.9%		11.5%
Prepositions	2	1.3%	1	0.9%
Conjunctions	Ø	-	2	1.2%
Articles	5	4.8%	3	2.4%
Obligatory pronouns	6	2.6%	6	4.5%
Auxiliary verbs	2	1.7%	Ø	–
Inappropriate addition of grammatical morphemes		0.7%		1.8%
Prepositions	2	1.3%	1	0.9%
Conjunctions	1	0.5	1	0.6%
Articles	Ø	-	5	4.0%
Obligatory pronouns	2	0.9%	3	2.2%
Auxiliary verbs	1	0.9%	1	1.1%

R   L

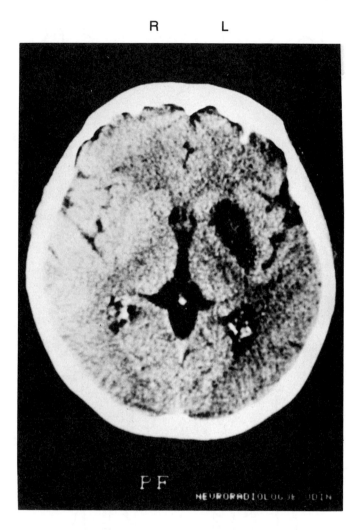

Figure 2. CT scan of patient C.B. showing left basal ganglia infarction (performed on 20 November 1993).

R   L

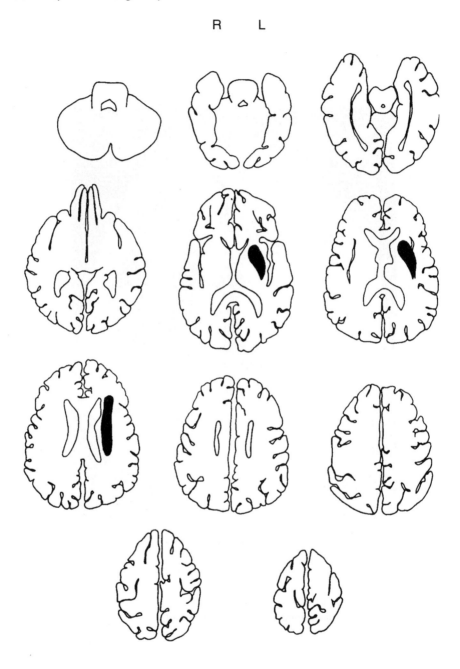

Figure 3. Patient C.B.: The templates following Damasio & Damasio (1989: 201) show the extent of the lesion. They represent an elaboration of the data from the first MRI scan.

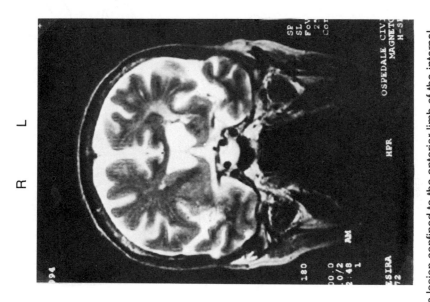

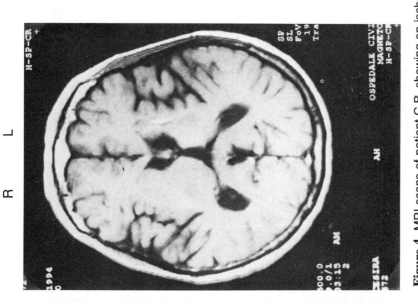

Figure 4. MRI scans of patient C.B. showing an ischemic lesion confined to the anterior limb of the internal capsule, to the head of the caudate nucleus, to the putamen of the left hemisphere (performed on 6 May 1994).

R   L

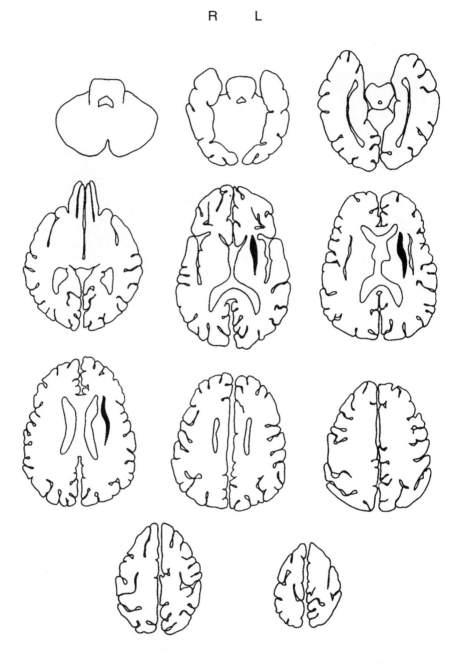

Figure 5. Patient C.B.: The templates following Damasio & Damasio (1989: 201) show the extent of the lesion. They represent an elaboration of the data from the second MRI scan (6 May 1994).

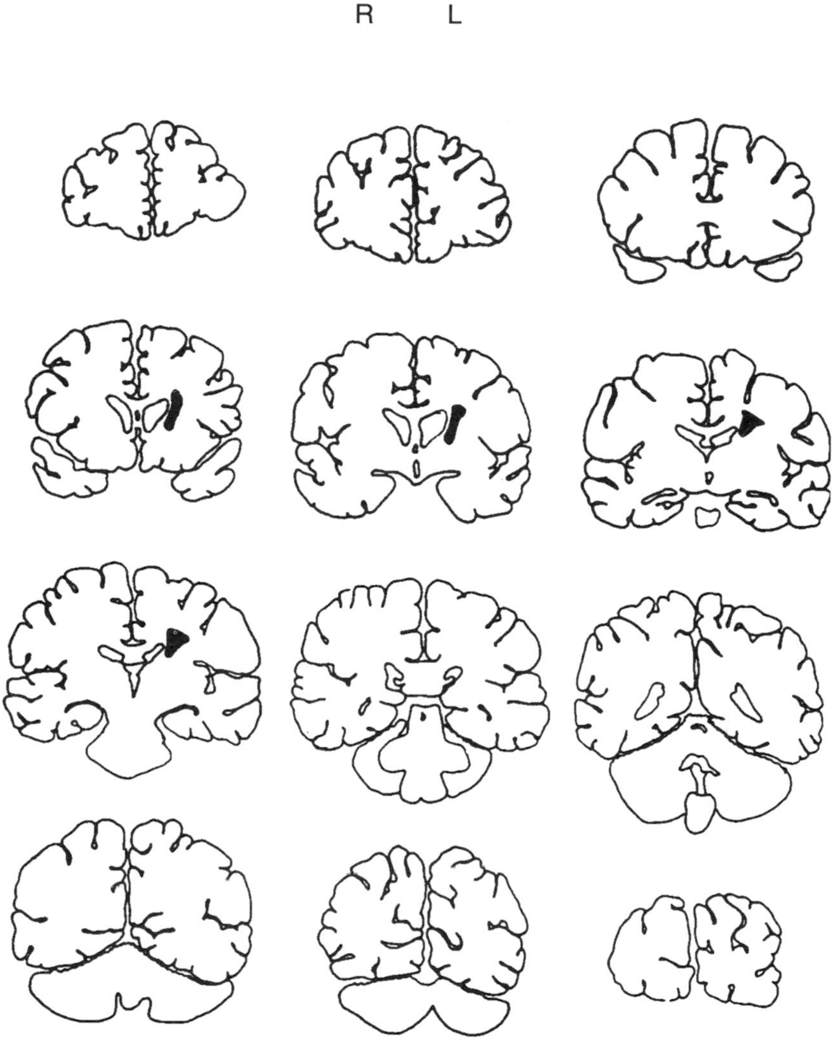

R   L

Figure 6. Patient C.B.: The templates following Damasio & Damasio (1989: 206) show the extent of the lesion. They represent an elaboration of the data from the second MRI scan (6 May 1994).

Table 5. Patient C.B.'s scores on the Friulian (L1), Italian (L2), and English (L3) Bilingual Aphasia Test

Friulian (L1)

Scores by linguistic level and skill

16/18	29/30	0/0	1/3	1/3	5/10	0/0	Phonlgy	52/64
0/0	0/0	0/0	12/23	12/23	0/0	0/0	Mrphlgy	24/46
62/117	7/7	5/10	1/3	10/17	7/20	0/5	Lexicon	92/179
40/63	29/30	24/30	31/56	1/3	9/20	0/15	Syntax	134/217
3/11	0/0	7/10	15/33	1/3	1/6	0/0	Smntics	27/63
Compre	Repet	Jdgmt	LexAcc	Propos	Readg	Writg		
121/209	65/67	36/50	60/118	25/49	22/56	0/20		

Decimal scores by linguistic level and skill

0.888	0.966	N/A	0.333	0.333	0.500	N/A	Phonlgy	0.812
N/A	N/A	N/A	0.521	0.521	N/A	N/A	Mrphlgy	0.521
0.529	1.000	0.500	0.333	0.588	0.350	0.000	Lexicon	0.513
0.634	0.966	0.800	0.553	0.333	0.450	0.000	Syntax	0.617
0.272	N/A	0.700	0.454	0.333	0.166	N/A	Smntics	0.428
Compre	Repet	Jdgmt	LexAcc	Propos	Readg	Writg		
0.578	0.970	0.720	0.508	0.510	0.392	0.000		

Italian (L2)

Scores by linguistic level and skill

10/18	29/30	0/0	1/3	1/3	8/10	0/0	Phonlgy	49/64
0/0	0/0	0/0	10/23	10/23	0/0	0/0	Mrphlgy	20/46
72/117	6/7	3/10	1/3	10/16	6/20	0/5	Lexicon	98/178
38/63	29/30	29/30	35/56	1/3	13/20	0/15	Syntax	145/217
8/11	0/0	3/10	19/33	1/3	4/6	0/0	Smntics	35/63
Compre	Repet	Jdgmt	LexAcc	Propos	Readg	Writg		
128/209	64/67	35/50	66/118	23/48	31/56	0/20		

Decimal scores by linguistic level and skill

0.555	0.966	N/A	0.333	0.333	0.800	N/A	Phonlgy	0.765
N/A	N/A	N/A	0.434	0.434	N/A/	N/A	Mrphlgy	0.434
0.615	0.857	0.300	0.333	0.625	0.300	0.000	Lexicon	0.550
0.603	0.966	0.966	0.625	0.333	0.650	0.000	Syntax	0.668
0.727	N/A	0.300	0.575	0.333	0.666	N/A	Smntics	0.555
Compre	Repet	Jdgmt	LexAcc	Propos	Readg	Writg		
0.612	0.955	0.700	0.559	0.479	0.553	0.000		

English (L3)

Scores by linguistic level and skill

8/18	30/30	0/0	1/3	1/3	5/10	0/0	Phonlgy	45/64
0/0	0/0	0/0	2/23	2/23	0/0	0/0	Mrphlgy	4/46
55/117	3/7	8/10	1/3	5/16	5/20	0/5	Lexicon	77/178
31/63	30/30	24/30	23/56	1/3	9/20	0/15	Syntax	118/217
7/11	0/0	7/10	7/33	1/3	4/6	0/0	Smntics	26/63
Compre	Repet	Jdgmt	LexAcc	Propos	Readg	Writg		
101/209	63/67	39/50	34/118	10/48	23/56	0/20		

Decimal scores by linguistic level and skill

0.444	1.000	N/A	0.333	0.333	0.500	N/A	Phonlgy	0.703
N/A	N/A	N/A	0.086	0.086	N/A	N/A	Mrphlgy	0.087
0.470	0.428	0.800	0.333	0.312	0.250	0.000	Lexicon	0.432
0.492	1.000	0.800	0.410	0.333	0.450	0.000	Syntax	0.543
0.636	N/A	0.700	0.212	0.333	0.666	N/A	Smntics	0.412
Compre	Repet	Jdgmt	LexAcc	Propos	Readg	Writg		
0.483	0.940	0.780	0.288	0.208	0.410	0.000		

Table 6.   Patient CB's spontaneous speech in Friulian (L1) (5 minutes)

Number of utterances		80
Total number of words		480
Mean length of utterance		6
Mean length of the 5 longest utterances		10.4
Number of different words		108
Type/token ratio		0.46
Number of neologisms		11
Number of phonemic paraphasias resulting in nonwords		18
Number of phonemic paraphasias resulting in words		3
Number of semantic paraphasias		2
Number of verbal paraphasias (unrelated words)		1
Morphosyntactic errors and percent in obligatory contexts	Number	Percent
Omission of free grammatical morphemes	42	23.7
Omission of full verbs	2	2.8
Substitution of inflectional morphemes	8	4.9
Substitution of free grammatical morphemes	1	0.5
Addition of grammatical morphemes in inappropriate contexts	1	0.5
Number of word-order errors	1	
Number of verbs per utterance	0.88	
Number of subordinate clauses	1	
Number of intraphrasal pauses	13	
Number of circumlocutions	1	
Number of stereotypic phrases	Ø	
Evidence of word finding difficulties	14	
Detection of foreign accent (0: none; 5: very strong)	Ø	
Number of inappropriate foreign words	7	
Number of semantically deviant sentences	Ø	
The discourse is cohesive	Yes	
The discourse is pragmatically sound	Yes	
Echolalia	Number	Percent
Partial or total repetitions of the examiner's questions	22	27.5
Self-repetitions	31	38.7
Words in echoed utterances	97	20.3
Words in self-repetitions	98	20.4
Total number of utterances repeated	53	66.2
Total number of words repeated	195	40.7

Table 7.   Patient C.B.'s spontaneous speech in Italian (L2) (5 minutes)

Number of utterances		79
Total number of words		394
Mean length of utterance		4.98
Mean length of the 5 longest utterances		9.8
Number of different words		83
Type/token ratio		0.44
Number of neologisms		2
Number of phonemic paraphasias resulting in nonwords		8
Number of phonemic paraphasias resulting in words		4
Number of semantic paraphasias		9
Number of verbal paraphasias (unrelated words)		Ø

Morphosyntactic errors and percent in obligatory contexts	Number	Percent
Omission of free grammatical morphemes	10	7.6
Omission of full verbs	1	1.6
Substitution of inflectional morphemes	3	2.0
Substitution of free grammatical morphemes	Ø	Ø
Addition of grammatical morphemes in inappropriate contexts	2	1.5

Number of word-order errors	Ø	
Number of verbs per utterance	0.77	
Number of subordinate clauses	2	
Number of intraphrasal pauses	17	
Number of circumlocutions	Ø	
Number of stereotypic phrases	Ø	
Evidence of word finding difficulties	17	
Detection of foreign accent (0: none; 5: very strong)	Ø	
Number of inappropriate foreign words	Ø	
Number of semantically deviant sentences	Ø	
The discourse is cohesive	Yes	
The discourse is pragmatically sound	Yes	

Echolalia	Number	Percent
Partial or total repetitions of the examiner's questions	21	26.6
Self-repetitions	22	27.8
Words in echoed utterances	68	17.2
Words in self-repetitions	83	21.1
Total number of utterances repeated	43	54.4
Total number of words repeated	151	38.3

Table 8.   Patient C.B.'s spontaneous speech in English (L3) (5 minutes)

Number of utterances	98
Total number of words	352
Mean length of utterance	3.59
Mean length of the 5 longest utterances	7.4
Number of different words	76
Type/token ratio	0.46
Number of neologisms	9
Number of phonemic paraphasias resulting in nonwords	18
Number of phonemic paraphasias resulting in words	Ø
Number of semantic paraphasias	4
Number of verbal paraphasias (unrelated words)	Ø

Morphosyntactic errors and percent in obligatory contexts	Number	Percent
Omission of free grammatical morphemes	20	17.7
Omission of full verbs	5	13.1
Substitution of inflectional morphemes	8	8.6
Substitution of free grammatical morphemes	6	5.3
Addition of grammatical morphemes in inappropriate contexts	3	2.6

Number of word-order errors	1
Number of verbs per utterance	0.38
Number of subordinate clauses	Ø
Number of intraphrasal pauses	18
Number of circumlocutions	Ø
Number of stereotypic phrases	Ø
Evidence of word finding difficulties	18

Detection of foreign accent (0: none; 5: very strong)	Ø
Number of inappropriate foreign words	9
Number of semantically deviant sentences	Ø
The discourse is cohesive	Yes
The discourse is pragmatically sound	Yes

Echolalia	Number	Percent
Partial or total repetitions of the examiner's questions	9	9.1
Self-repetitions	11	11.2
Words in echoed utterances	26	7.4
Words in self-repetitions	31	8.8
Total number of utterances repeated	20	20.3
Total number of words repeated	57	16.2

Table 9.   Patient C.B.'s morphosyntactic errors and percentage of errors in obligatory contexts in Friulian (L1), Italian (L2) and English (L3)

Omission of free grammatical morphemes	**L1** 23.7%		**L2** 7.6%		**L3** 17.7%	
Prepositions	2	5.5%	1	3.0%	3	7.8%
Conjunctions	2	17.5%	Ø	Ø	1	12.5%
Articles	2	7.1%	3	11.1%	4	18.2%
Obligatory pronouns	30	43.4%	3	10.3%	11	34.4%
Auxilary verbs	5	18.5%	3	10.0%	1	12.5%
Omission of full verbs	2	2.8%	1	1.6%	5	21.1%

Substitution of inflectional morphemes	**L1** 4.9%		**L2** 2.0%		**L3** 8.6%	
Verbs	4	5.6%	2	3.2%	8	21.1%
Adjectives	3	7.5%	1	2.2%	Ø	Ø
Nouns	1	1.9%	Ø	Ø	Ø	Ø

Inappropriate addn of gramm. morphemes	**L1** 0.5%		**L2** 0%		**L3** 8.6%	
Prepositions	Ø	Ø	Ø	Ø	1	2.6%
Conjunctions	Ø	Ø	Ø	Ø	Ø	Ø
Articles	Ø	Ø	Ø	Ø	Ø	Ø
Obligatory pronouns	1	1.4%	Ø	Ø	5	13.5%
Auxilary verbs	Ø	Ø	Ø	Ø	Ø	Ø

Substitution of free grammatical morphemes	**L1** 0.5%		**L2** 0%		**L3** 8.6%	
Prepositions	Ø	Ø	2	6.0	1	2.6%
Conjunctions	Ø	Ø	Ø	Ø	Ø	Ø
Articles	1	3.5	Ø	Ø	1	4.5
Obligatory pronouns	Ø	Ø	Ø	Ø	Ø	Ø
Auxilary verbs	Ø	Ø	Ø	Ø	1	12.5

Table 10.   Patient C.B.'s scores on the Bilingual Aphasia Test, Part C (specific to a given pair of languages) for Friulian-Italian (L1-L2)

Scores by section		
Word recognition L1 → L2	4/5	0.800
Word recognition L2 → L1	4/5	0.800
Translation of concrete words L1 → L2	4/5	0.800
Translation of abstract words L1 → L2	5/5	1.000
Translation of concrete words L2 → L1	3/5	0.600
Translation of abstract words L2 → L1	2/5	0.400
Translation of sentences L1 → L2	2/6	0.333
Translation of sentences L2 → L1	2/6	0.333
Grammaticality Judgments L1	14/16	0.875
Grammaticality Judgments L2	7/16	0.437

Scores by linguistic level and skill   L2 → L1

		L1 → L2	16/22	2/6	7/16	Morphosyntax	9/22
2/6	14/16	Morphosyntax	11/15	11/15	0/0	Lexicon	11/15
11/15	0/0	Lexicon	13/21			Translation	13/21
		Translation	14/16			Gram. judgm	7/16
		Gram. judgm					

Decimal scores   L2 → L1

		L1 → L2	0.727	0.333	0.437	Mrphosyntax	0.409
0.333	0.875	Mrphosyntax	0.733	0.733	n/a	Lexicon	0.733
0.733	n/a	Lexicon	0.619			Translation	0.619
		Translation	0.875			Gram.jdgmnt	0.437
		Gram. jdgmnt					

Table 11. Patient C.B.'s scores on the Bilingual Aphasia Test, Part C (specific to a given pair of languages) for Friulian-English (L1-L3)

Scores by section

Word recognition L1 → L3	3/5	0.600
Word recognition L3 → L1	4/5	0.800
Translation of concrete words L1 → L3	3/5	0.600
Translation of abstract words L1 → L3	3/5	0.600
Translation of concrete words L3 → L1	0/5	0.000
Translation of abstract words L3 → L1	0/5	0.000
Translation of sentences L1 → L3	0/6	0.000
Translation of sentences L3 → L1	0/6	0.000
Grammaticality Judgments L1	13/16	0.812
Grammaticality Judgments L3	7/16	0.437

Scores by linguistic level and skill

		L1 → L3				L3 → L1	
0/6	13/16	Morphosyntax	13/22	0/6	7/16	Morphosyntax	7/22
6/15	0/0	Lexicon	6/15	7/15	0/0	Lexicon	7/15
		Translation	6/21			Translation	7/21
		Gram. judgm	13/16			Gram. judgm	7/16

Decimal scores

		L1 → L3				L3 → L1	
0.000	0.812	Mrphosyntax	0.590	0.000	0.437	Mrphosyntax	0.318
0.400	n/a	Lexicon	0.400	0.466	n/a	Lexicon	0.466
		Translation	0.285			Translation	0.333
		Gram. jdgmnt	0.812			Gram.jdgmnt	0.437

Table 12. Patient C.B.'s scores on the Bilingual Aphasia Test, Part C (specific to a given pair of languages) for Italian-English (L2-L3)

Scores by section

Word recognition L2 → L3	4/5	0.800
Word recognition L3 → L2	5/5	1.000
Translation of concrete words L2 → L3	2/5	0.400
Translation of abstract words L2 → L3	1/5	0.200
Translation of concrete words L3 → L2	3/5	0.600
Translation of abstract words L3 → L2	0/5	0.000
Translation of sentences L2 → L3	0/6	0.000
Translation of sentences L3 → L2	0/6	0.000
Grammaticality Judgments L2	11/16	0.687
Grammaticality Judgments L3	6/16	0.375

Scores by linguistic level and skill

		L2 → L3				L3 → L2	
0/6	11/16	Morphosyntax	11/22	0/6	6/16	Morphosyntax	6/22
9/15	0/0	Lexicon	9/15	6/15	0/0	Lexicon	6/15
		Translation	9/21			Translation	6/21
		Gram. judgm	11/16			Gram. judgm	6/16

Decimal scores

		L2 → L3				L3 → L2	
0.000	0.687	Mrphosyntax	0.500	0.000	0.375	Mrphosyntax	0.272
0.600	n/a	Lexicon	0.600	0.400	n/a	Lexicon	0.400
		Translation	0.428			Translation	0.285
		Gram. jdgmnt	0.687			Gram.jdgmnt	0.375

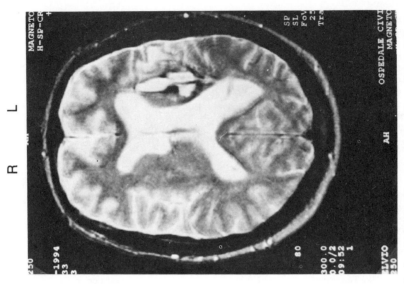

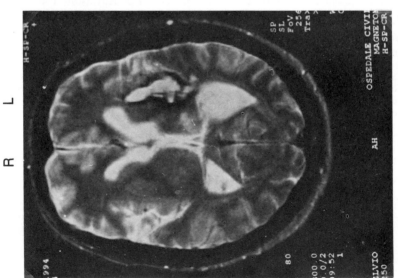

Figure 7. MRI scans of the patient El.M. showing a vascular lesion involving the caudate nucleus, the putamen, the globus pallidus and part of the thalamus of the left hemisphere (performed on 29 January 1994).

R   L

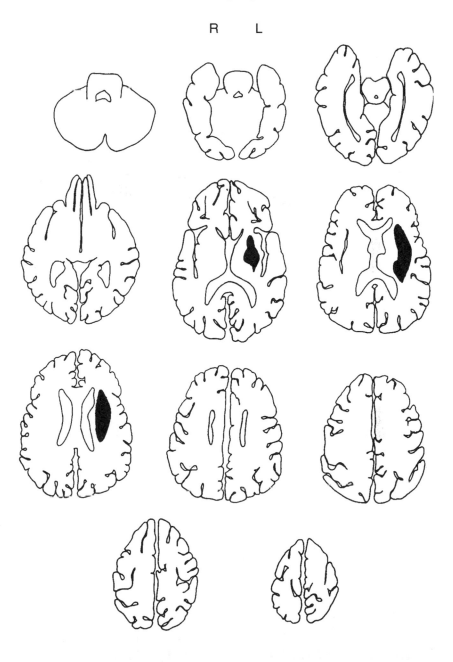

Figure 8. Patient El.M.: The templates following Damasio & Damasio (1989: 201) show the extent of the lesion. They represent an elaboration of the MRI performed on 29 January 1994.

R   L

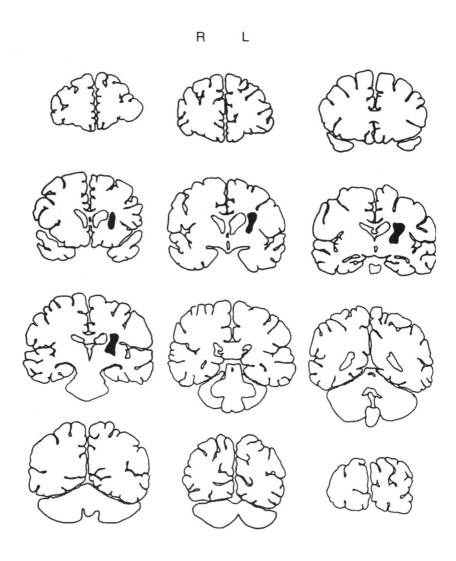

Figure 9. Patient El.M.: The templates following Damasio & Damasio (1989: 206) show the extent of the lesion. They represent an elaboration of the MRI performed on 29 January 1994.

Table 13. Patient El.M.'s scores on the Friulian (L1) Bilingual Aphasia Test

Scores by linguistic level and skill

13/18	28/30	0/0	1/3	1/3	8/10	0/0	Phonlgy	51/64
0/0	0/0	0/0	3/23	3/23	0/0	0/0	Mrphlgy	6/46
73/117	0/7	6/10	1/3	6/18	5/20	0/5	Lexicon	91/180
39/63	28/30	28/30	26/56	1/3	16/20	5/15	Syntax	143/217
5/11	0/0	9/10	15/33	1/3	0/6	0/0	Smntics	30/63
Compre	Repet	Jdgmt	LexAcc	Propos	Readg	Writg		
130/209	56/67	43/50	46/118	12/50	29/56	5/20		

Decimal scores by linguistic level and skill

0.722	0.933	N/A	0.333	0.333	0.800	N/A	Phonlgy	0.796
N/A	N/A	N/A	0.130	0.130	N/A	N/A	Mrphlgy	0.130
0.623	0.000	0.600	0.333	0.333	0.250	0.000	Lexicon	0.505
0.619	0.933	0.933	0.464	0.333	0.800	0.333	Syntax	0.658
0.454	N/A	0.900	0.454	0.333	0.000	N/A	Smntics	0.476
Compre	Repet	Jdgmt	LexAcc	Propos	Readg	Writg		
0.622	0.835	0.860	0.389	0.240	0.517	0.250		

Table 14. Patient El.M.'s scores on the Italian (L2) Bilingual Aphasia Test

Scores by linguistic level and skill

17/18	27/30	0/0	0/3	0/3	9/10	0/0	Phonlgy	53/64
0/0	0/0	0/0	16/23	16/23	0/0	0/0	Mrphlgy	32/46
72/117	1/7	8/10	0/3	6/18	14/20	0/5	Lexicon	101/180
45/63	27/30	21/30	32/56	0/3	19/20	5/15	Syntax	149/217
2/11	0/0	9/10	16/33	0/3	0/6	0/0	Smntics	27/63
Compre	Repet	Jdgmt	LexAcc	Propos	Readg	Writg		
136/209	55/67	38/50	64/118	22/50	42/56	5/20		

Decimal scores by linguistic level and skill

0.944	0.900	N/A	0.000	0.000	0.900	N/A	Phonlogy	0.828
N/A	N/A	N/A	0.695	0.695	N/A	N/A	Mrphlgy	0.695
0.615	0.142	0.800	0.000	0.333	0.700	0.000	Lexicon	0.561
0.714	0.900	0.700	0.571	0.000	0.950	0.333	Syntax	0.686
0.181	N/A	0.900	0.484	0.000	0.000	N/A	Smntics	0.428
Compre	Repet	Jdgmt	LexAcc	Propos	Readg	Writg		
0.650	0.820	0.760	0.542	0.440	0.750	0.250		

Table 15. Patient El.M. Analysis of 5 minutes of Friulian (L1) spontaneous speech

Number of utterances		77
Total number of words		360
Mean length of utterance		4.67
Mean length of the 5 longest utterances		7
Number of different words		70
Type/token ratio		0.30
Number of neologisms		Ø
Number of phonemic paraphasias resulting in nonwords		4
Number of phonemic paraphasias resulting in words		Ø
Number of semantic paraphasias		Ø
Number of verbal paraphasias (unrelated words)		Ø

Morphosyntactic errors and percent in obligatory contexts	Number	Percent
Omission of free grammatical morphemes	39	24.2
Omission of full verbs	5	16.1
Substitution of inflectional morphemes	Ø	
Substitution of free grammatical morphemes	7	4.3
Addition of grammatical morphemes in inappropriate contexts	Ø	
Number of word-order errors	2	
Number of verbs per utterance	0.40	
Number of subordinate clauses	Ø	
Number of intraphrasal pauses	53	
Number of circumlocutions	8	
Number of stereotypic phrases	7	
Evidence of word finding difficulties	61	
Detection of foreign accent (0: none; 5: very strong)	Ø	
Number of inappropriate foreign words	13	
Number of semantically deviant sentences	Ø	
The discourse is cohesive	Yes	
The discourse is pragmatically sound	Yes	

Echolalia	Number	Percent
Partial or total repetitions of the examiner's questions	2	2.5
Self-repetitions	25	32.5
Words in echoed utterances	5	1.3
Words in self-repetitions	62	17.2
Total number of utterances repeated	27	35.0
Total number of words repeated	67	18.6

Table 16.   Patient El.M. Analysis of 5 minutes of Italian (L2) spontaneous speech

Number of utterances	54	
Total number of words	167	
Mean length of utterance	3.1	
Mean length of the 5 longest utterances	5.6	
Number of different words	59	
Type/token ratio	0.55	
Number of neologisms	Ø	
Number of phonemic paraphasias resulting in nonwords	2	
Number of phonemic paraphasias resulting in words	Ø	
Number of semantic paraphasias	Ø	
Number of verbal paraphasias (unrelated words)	Ø	

Morphosyntactic errors and percent in obligatory contexts	Number	Percent
Omission of free grammatical morphemes	13	25.0
Omission of full verbs	4	25.0
Substitution of inflectional morphemes	1	1.8
Substitution of free grammatical morphemes	4	7.5
Addition of grammatical morphemes in inappropriate contexts	Ø	

Number of word-order errors	Ø	
Number of verbs per utterance	0.28	
Number of subordinate clauses	1	
Number of intraphrasal pauses	26	
Number of circumlocutions	3	
Number of stereotypic phrases	4	
Evidence of word finding difficulties	29	
Detection of foreign accent (0: none; 5: very strong)	Ø	
Number of inappropriate foreign words	15	
Number of semantically deviant sentences	1	
The discourse is cohesive	Yes	
The discourse is pragmatically sound	Yes	

Echolalia	Number	Percent
Partial or total repetitions of the examiner's questions	3	5.5
Self-repetitions	10	18.5
Words in echoed utterances	5	2.9
Words in self-repetitions	14	8.3
Total number of utterances repeated	13	24.0
Total number of words repeated	19	11.3

Table 17. Patient El.M.'s morphosyntactic errors and percentage of errors in obligatory contexts

	L1		L2	
Omission of free grammatical morphemes		24.6%		25.0%
Prepositions	6	15.7%	3	27.3%
Conjunctions	2	3.6%	1	6.6%
Articles	5	83.3%	7	29.1%
Obligatory pronouns	20	42.5%	Ø	
Auxiliary verbs	6	40.0%	2	100.0%
Omission of full verbs	5	16.1%	4	25.0%
Substitution of inflectional morphemes		Ø		1.8%
Verbs	Ø		Ø	
Adjectives	Ø		Ø	
Nouns	Ø		1	2.3%
Substitution of free grammatical morphemes	4.3%			7.5%
Prepositions	3	7.8%	3	27.3%
Conjunctions	Ø		Ø	
Articles	2	33.3%	1	4.1%
Obligatory pronouns	Ø		Ø	
Auxiliary verbs	2	13.3%	Ø	
Inappropriate addition of grammatical morphemes		Ø		Ø
Prepositions	Ø		Ø	
Conjunctions	Ø		Ø	
Articles	Ø		Ø	
Obligatory pronouns	Ø		Ø	
Auxiliary verbs	Ø		Ø	

Table 18. Patient El.M.'s scores on the Bilingual Aphasia Test, Part C (specific to a given pair of languages) for Friulian-Italian (L1-L2)

Scores by section

Word recognition L1 → L2	2/5	0.400
Word recognition L2 → L1	4/5	0.800
Translation of concrete words L1 → L2	4/5	0.800
Translation of abstract words L1 → L2	2/5	0.400
Translation of concrete words L2 → L1	5/5	1.000
Translation of abstract words L2 → L1	2/5	0.400
Translation of sentences L1 → L2	1/6	0.166
Translation of sentences L2 → L1	0/6	0.000
Grammaticality Judgments L1	5/16	0.312
Grammaticality Judgments L2	6/16	0.375

Scores by linguistic level and skill

		L1 → L2				L2 → L1	
1/6	5/16	Morphosyntax	6/22	0/6	6/16	Morphosyntax	6/22
11/15	0/0	Lexicon	11/15	8/15	0/0	Lexicon	8/15
		Translation	12/21			Translation	8/21
		Gram. judgm	5/16			Gram. judgm	6/16

Decimal scores

		L1 → L2				L2 → L1	
0.166	0.312	Mrphosyntax	0.272	0.000	0.375	Mrphosyntax	0.272
0.733	n/a	Lexicon	0.733	0.533	n/a	Lexicon	0.533
		Translation	0.571			Translation	0.380
		Gram. jdgmnt	0.312			Gram.jdgmnt	0.375

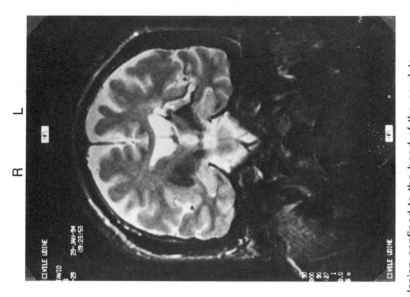

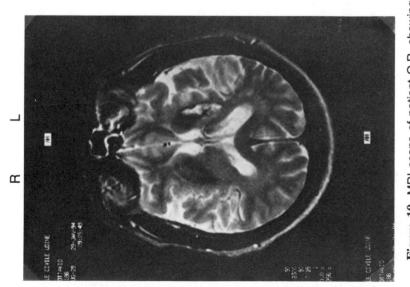

Figure 10. MRI scans of patient O.R. showing an ischemic lesion confined to the head of the caudate nucleus, the putamen and the cortex of the insula of the left hemisphere (performed on 29 January 1994).

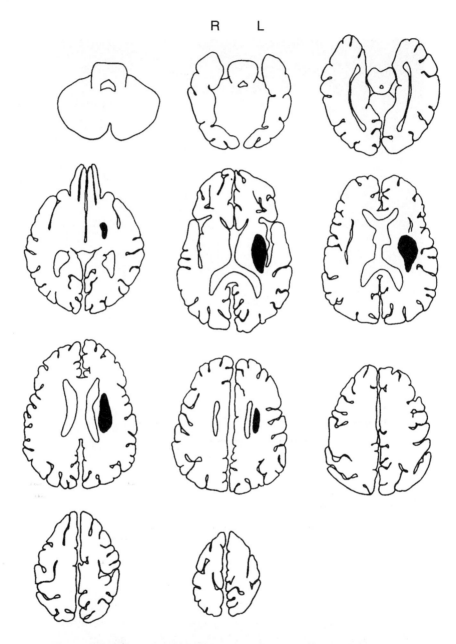

Figure 11. Patient O.R.: The templates following Damasio & Damasio (1989: 201) show the extent of the lesion. They represent an elaboration of the data from the second MRI scan (29 January 1994).

R   L

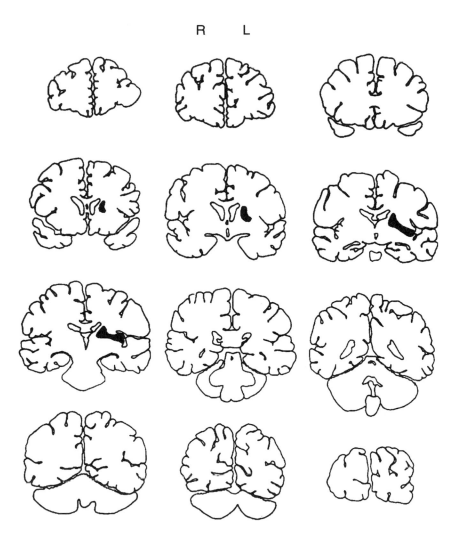

Figure 12. Patient O.R.: The templates following Damasio & Damasio (1989: 206) show the extent of the lesion. They represent an elaboration of the data from the second MRI scan (29 January 1994).

Table 19. Patient O.R.'s scores on the Friulian (L1) Bilingual Aphasia Test

Scores by linguistic level and skill

14/18	21/30	0/0	2/3	2/3	9/10	0/0	Phonlgy	48/64
0/0	0/0	0/0	10/23	10/23	0/0	0/0	Mrphlgy	20/46
69/117	2/7	5/10	2/3	10/18	8/20	0/5	Lexicon	96/180
41/63	21/30	24/30	26/56	2/3	16/20	8/15	Syntax	138/217
3/11	0/0	10/10	16/33	2/3	1/6	0/0	Smntics	32/63
Compre	Repet	Jdgmt	LexAcc	Propos	Readg	Writg		
127/209	44/67	39/50	56/118	26/50	34/56	8/20		

Decimal scores by linguistic level and skill

0.777	0.700	N/A	0.666	0.666	0.900	N/A	Phonlgy	0.750
N/A	N/A	N/A	0.434	0.434	N/A	N/A	Mrphlgy	0.434
0.589	0.285	0.500	0.666	0.555	0.400	0.000	Lexicon	0.533
0.650	0.700	0.800	0.464	0.666	0.800	0.533	Syntax	0.635
0.272	N/A	1.000	0.484	0.666	0.166	N/A	Smntics	0.507
Compre	Repet	Jdgmt	LexAcc	Propos	Readg	Writg		
0.607	0.656	0.780	0.474	0.520	0.607	0.400		

Table 20. Patient O.R.'s scores on the Italian (L2) Bilingual Aphasia Test

Scores by linguistic level and skill

12/18	28/30	0/0	2/3	2/3	6/10	0/0	Phonlgy	50/64
0/0	0/0	0/0	10/23	10/23	0/0	0/0	Mrphlgy	20/46
57/117	4/7	7/10	2/3	8/18	13/20	0/5	Lexicon	91/180
41/63	28/30	29/30	26/56	2/3	14/20	8/15	Syntzx	148/217
7/11	0/0	10/10	21/33	2/3	5/6	0/0	Smntics	45/63
Compre	Repet	Jdgmt	LexAcc	Propos	Readg	Writg		
117/209	60/67	46/50	61/118	24/50	38/56	8/20		

Decimal scores by linguistic level and skill

0.666	0.933	N/A	0.666	0.666	0.600	N/A	Phonlgy	0.781
N/A	N/A	N/A	0.434	0.434	N/A	N/A	Mrphlgy	0.434
0.487	0.571	0.700	0.666	0.444	0.650	0.000	Lexicon	0.505
0.636	N/A	1.000	0.636	0.666	0.833	N/A	Smntics	0.714
0.650	0.933	0.966	0.464	0.666	0.833	N/A	Syntax	0.682
Compre	Repet	Jdgmt	LexAcc	Propos	Readg	Writg		
0.559	0.895	0.920	0.516	0.480	0.678	0.400		

Table 21. Patient O.R. Analysis of 5 minutes of Friulian (L1) spontaneous speech

Number of utterances	88	
Total number of words	657	
Mean length of utterance	7.46	
Mean length of the 5 longest utterances	16.4	
Number of different words	137	
Type/token ratio	0.44	
Number of neologisms	23	
Number of phonemic paraphasias resulting in nonwords	16	
Number of phonemic paraphasias resulting in words	–	
Number of semantic paraphasias	4	
Number of verbal paraphasias (unrelated words)	5	

Morphosyntactic errors and percent in obligatory contexts	Number	Percent
Omission of free grammatical morphemes	53	17.9
Omission of full verbs	2	1.9
Substitution of inflectional morphemes	3	1.3
Substitution of free grammatical morphemes	1	0.3
Addition of grammatical morphemes in inappropriate contexts	4	1.3

Number of word-order errors	–	
Number of verbs per utterance	1.18	
Number of subordinate clauses	7	
Number of intraphrasal pauses	13	
Number of circumlocutions	–	
Number of stereotypic phrases	1	
Evidence of word finding difficulties	13	

Detection of foreign accent (0: none; 5: very strong)	Ø	
Number of inappropriate foreign words	15	
Number of semantically deviant sentences	13	
The discourse is cohesive	Yes	
The discourse is pragmatically sound	Yes	

Echolalia	Number	Percent
Partial or total repetitions of the examiner's questions	2	2.2
Self-repetitions	12	13.6
Words in echoed utterances	10	1.5
Words in self-repetitions	39	5.3
Total number of utterances repeated	14	15.9
Total number of words repeated	49	7.4

Table 22.   Patient O.R. Analysis of 5 minutes of Italian (L2) spontaneous speech

Number of utterances	119	
Total number of words	673	
Mean length of utterance	5.65	
Mean length of the 5 longest utterances	13.4	
Number of different words	143	
Type/token ratio	0.42	
Number of neologisms	27	
Number of phonemic paraphasias resulting in nonwords	18	
Number of phonemic paraphasias resulting in words	2	
Number of semantic paraphasias	Ø	
Number of verbal paraphasias (unrelated words)	4	

Morphosyntactic errors and percent in obligatory contexts	Number	Percent
Omission of free grammatical morphemes	15	6.7
Omission of full verbs	1	0.2
Substitution of inflectional morphemes	12	4.4
Substitution of free grammatical morphemes	7	3.1
Addition of grammatical morphemes in inappropriate contexts	2	0.8

Number of word-order errors	Ø	
Number of verbs per utterance	0.91	
Number of subordinate clauses	7	
Number of intraphrasal pauses	15	
Number of circumlocutions	Ø	
Number of stereotypic phrases	2	
Evidence of word finding difficulties	15	
Detection of foreign accent (0: none; 5: very strong)	Ø	
Number of inappropriate foreign words	15	
Number of semantically deviant sentences	24	
The discourse is cohesive	Yes	
The discourse is pragmatically sound	Yes	

Echolalia	Number	Percent
Partial or total repetitions of the examiner's questions	3	2.5
Self-repetitions	15	12.6
Words in echoed utterances	6	1.0
Words in self-repetitions	32	4.7
Total number of utterances repeated	18	15.1
Total number of words repeated	39	5.7

Table 23. Patient O.R.'s morphosyntactic errors and percentage of errors in obligatory contexts

	L1		L2	
Omission of free grammatical morphemes		17.9%		6.7%
Prepositions	3	4.8%	3	5.3%
Conjunctions	4	9.7%	Ø	
Articles	Ø		1	1.6%
Obligatory pronouns	31	29.5%	4	8.5%
Auxiliary verbs	13	26.0%	7	24.1%
Omission of full verbs	2	1.9%	1	0.2%
Substitution of inflectional morphemes		1.3%		4.4%
Verbs	3	2.8%	12	11.0%
Adjectives	Ø		Ø	
Nouns	Ø		Ø	
Substitution of free grammatical morphemes		0.3%		3.1%
Prepositions	1	1.6%	4	7.1%
Conjunctions	Ø		Ø	
Articles	Ø		2	0.3%
Obligatory pronouns	Ø		1	2.1%
Auxiliary verbs	Ø		Ø	
Inappropriate addition of grammatical morphemes		1.3%		0.8%
Prepositions	2	3.2%	1	1.7%
Conjunctions	1	2.4%	Ø	
Articles	1	2.6%	1	1.6%
Obligatory pronouns	Ø		Ø	
Auxiliary verbs	Ø		Ø	

Table 24. Patient O.R.'s scores on the Bilingual Aphasia Test, Part C (specific to a given pair of languages) for Friulian-Italian (L1-L2)

Scores by section

Word recognition L1 → L2	4/5	0.800
Word recognition L2 → L1	4/5	0.800
Translation of concrete words L1 → L2	5/5	1.000
Translation of abstract words L1 → L2	4/5	0.800
Translation of concrete words L2 → L1	3/5	0.600
Translation of abstract words L2 → L1	1/5	0.200
Translation of sentences L1 → L2	1/6	0.166
Translation of sentences L2 → L1	1/6	0.166
Grammaticality Judgments L1	6/16	0.375
Grammaticality Judgments L2	4/16	0.250

Scores by linguistic level and skill

		L1 → L2				L2 → L1	
1/6	6/16	Morphosyntax	7/22	1/6	4/16	Morphosyntax	5/22
12/15	0/0	Lexicon	12/15	9/15	0/0	Lexicon	9/15
		Translation	13/21			Translation	10/21
		Gram. judgm	6/16			Gram. judgm	4/16

Decimal scores

		L1 → L2				L2 → L1	
0.166	0.375	Mrphosyntax	0.318	0.166	0.250	Mrphosyntax	0.227
0.800	n/a	Lexicon	0.800	0.600	n/a	Lexicon	0.600
		Translation	0.619			Translation	0.476
		Gram. jdgmnt	0.375			Gram.jdgmnt	0.250

Table 25. Major Aphasic Symptoms in Bilingual Subcortical Aphasia

	Ester M L1 Ven	(F) L2 Ital.	C.B. L1 Fruil	(F) L2 Ital.	L2 Engl.	Elvio M. L1 Friul.	(M) L2 Ital.	O.R. L1 Friul.	(M) L2 Ital.
NONFLUENT SPEECH									
Reduction of spontaneous speech	complete	yes	yes	yes	yes	yes	yes	no	no
Hypophonia	yes	yes	yes	yes	yes	no	no	yes	yes
Foreign accent syndrome	yes	yes	no	no	no	no	no	no	no
NONFLUENT LANGUAGE									
Omission of free gramm morph	8.6%	9.6%	23.7%	7.6%	17.7%	24.2%	25%	17.9%	6.7%
Mean length of utterance	4.9	5.1	6.0	4.9	3.5	4.6	3.1	7.4	5.6
NEOLOGISMS	15	9	11	2	9	-	-	23	27
PHONEMIC PARAPHASIAS	39	25	21	12	18	4	2	16	20
SEMANTIC PARAPHASIAS	6	1	2	9	4	-	-	4	-
VERBAL PARAPHASIAS	3	6	1	-	-	-	-	5	4
COMPREHENSION	72%	70%	57.8%	61.2%	48.3%	62.2%	65%	60.7%	55.9%
REPETITION	77%	74%	97.8%	95.5%	94.0%	83.5%	82%	65.6%	89.5%
ECHOLALIA (partial or total repetition)									
repetitions of examiner's question	3.1%	1.6%	27.5%	26.6%	9.1%	2.5%	5.5%	2.2%	2.5%
self repetitions	14.4%	8.6%	38.7%	27.8%	11.2%	32.5%	18.5%	13.6%	12.6%
INAPPROPRIATE FOREIGN WORDS	51.7%	4.3%	1.4%	-	2.5%	3.6%	8.9%	2.2%	2.2%
TRANSLATION DISSOCIATIONS	L2 → L1 Impossible	L3 → L1 Impossible							

References

Aglioti, S., & Fabbro, F. 1993. Paradoxical selective recovery in a bilingual aphasic following subcortical lesions. *NeuroReport*, **4**, 1359-1362.

Alexander, M.P. 1989. Clinical-anatomical correlations of aphasia following predominantly subcortical lesions. In F. Boller & F. Grafman (Eds.) *Handbook of Neuropsychology*, Vol. 2. (Pp. 47-66). Amsterdam: Elsevier.

Blumstein, S.E., Alexander, M.P., Ryalls, J.H., Katz, W., & Dworetzky, B. 1987. On the nature of the foreign accent syndrome: A case study. *Brain and Language*, **31**, 215-244.

Crosson, B. 1985. Subcortical functions in language: A working model. *Brain and Language*, **25**, 257-292.

Crosson, B. 1992. *Subcortical functions in language and memory*. Guildford Press: New York.

Damasio, A.R., & Damasio, H. 1989. *Lesion analysis in neuropsychology*. New York: Oxford University Press.

Damasio, A.R., Damasio, H., Rizzo, M., Varney, N., & Gersh, F. 1982. Aphasia with nonhemorrhagic lesions in the basal ganglia and internal capsule. *Archives of Neurology*, **39**, 15-20.

Démonet, J.F., Puel, M., Celsis, P., & Cardebat, D. 1991. "Subcortical" aphasia: Some proposed pathophysiological mechanisms and their rCBF correlates revealed by SPECT. *Journal of Neurolinguistics*, **6**, 319-344.

De Vreese, L.P., Motta, M., & Toschi, A. 1988. Compulsive and paradoxical translation behaviour in a case of presenile dementia of the Alzheimer type. *Journal of Neurolinguistics*, **3**, 233-259.

Di Pellegrino, G., Fadiga, L., Fogassi, L., Gallese, V., & Rizzolatti, G. 1992. Understanding motor events: a neurophysiological study. *Experimental Brain Research*, **91**, 176-180.

Graff-Redford, N., Cooper W.E., Colsher P. 1986. An unlearned foreign "accent" in a patient with aphasia. *Brain and Language*, **28**, 86-94.

Gray, J.A., Feldon J., Rawlins J.N.P., Hemsley D.R., Smith A.D. 1991. The neuropsychology of schizophrenia. *Behavioral and Brain Sciences*, **14**, 1-84.

Gurd, J.M., Bessell N. J., Bladon R.A.W., Bamford, J.M. 1988. A case of foreign accent syndrome, with follow-up clinical, neuropsychological, and phonetic descriptions. *Neuropsychologia*, **26**, 237-251.

Luria, A.R. 1977. On quasi-aphasic speech disturbances in lesions of the deep structures of the brain. *Brain and Language*, **4**, 432-459.

Luzzati, C., Willmes, K., & De Bleser, R. 1992. *Aachener Aphasie-Test, Versione Italiana*. Firenze: Organizzazioni Speciali.

Ojemann, G.A. 1982. Models of the brain organization for higher integrative functions derived with electrical stimulation techniques. *Human Neurobiolgy*, **1**, 243-249.

Paradis, M. 1984. Aphasie et traduction. *Μετα, Translators' Journal*, **29**, 57-67.

Paradis, M. 1994. Neurolinguistic aspects of implicit and explicit memory: implications for bilingualism. In Ellis N. (Ed.) *Implicit and Explicit Learning of Languages* (Pp. 393-419). London: Academic Press.

Paradis, M. & Canzanella, M. 1990. *Test per l'afasia in un bilingue*. Hillsdale, NJ.: Lawrence Erlbaum Associates.

Paradis, M. & Fabbro, F. 1993. *Test pe afasie in tun bilingue*. Hillsdale, NJ.: Lawrence Erlbaum Associates.

Paradis, M., Goldblum M.C., Abidi R. 1982. Alternate antagonism with paradoxical translation behavior in two bilingual aphasic patients. *Brain and Language*, **15**, 55-69.

Paradis, M., Hummel, K., & Libben, G. 1989. *The Bilingual Aphasia Test*. Hillsdale, NJ.: Lawrence Erlbaum Associates.

Paradis, M., Libben G. 1987. *The assessment of bilingual aphasia*. Hillsdale, N.J.: Erlbaum.

Penfield, W. & Roberts, L. 1959. *Speech and brain-mechanisms*. Princeton: Princeton University Press.

Perecman, E. 1984. Spontaneous translation and language mixing in a polyglot aphasic. *Brain and Language*, **23**, 43-63.

Rubens, A.B. 1976. Transcortical motor aphasia. In Whitaker H. and Whitaker H.A. (eds) *Studies in Neurolinguistics*. Vol. 1 (Pp. 293-303). New York: Academic Press.

Speedie, L.J., Wertman E., Ta'ir, J., & Heilman, K.M. 1993. Disruption of automatic speech following right basal ganglia lesion. *Neurology*, **43**, 1768-1774.

Veyrac, G. 1931. Etude de l'aphasie chez les sujets polyglottes. Thèse pour le doctorat en médecine, Paris.

Wallesch, C.-W., & Papagno C. 1988. Subcortical aphasia. In F.C.Rose, R. Whurr & M.A. Wyke (Eds.) *Aphasia* (Pp. 257-287). London: Whurr Publishers.

11 Differential impairments and specific phenomena in 50 Catalan-Spanish bilingual aphasic patients

Carme Junqué, Pere Vendrell and Josep Vendrell

Introduction

When considering the acquisition of a second language, the most commonly used parameters are age of acquisition (Cziko, 1982), models of learning (Favreau, Melkin, Komoda & Segalowitz, 1980; Felix, 1981) and patterns of use (Brec'hed, 1980). All of them certainly have a remarkable value in the study of bilingual brain organization (Albert & Obler, 1978), but the most used and discussed parameter is the age of acquisition of the second language (L2). Lenneberg (1967), studying the data obtained from language deficits in brain-damaged children suggested that there is a critical period for language lateralization in the left cerebral hemisphere (and, consequently, for the adequate learning of L2).

The way in which languages are acquired and the specific patterns of their use gave rise to the distinction between coordinate and compound bilingualism. These two types of bilingualism (as well as "subordinative" bilingualism, counfounded with "compound" by Ervin & Osgood, 1954) were proposed by Weinreich (1953). This implies the division of bilinguals into two groups according to the structure and organization of the two languages in the storage system. The difference between these two groups originates, essentially, in the cultural and linguistic context in which the two languages are acquired.

The extreme compound bilingual would exhibit a total fusion of both languages. This prototypical individual would have learned single concepts for each experience in his/her life, each concept being assigned two labels, one for each language. This cerebral organization would originate from two different developmental possibilites. (1) Both languages have been used indistinctly and interchangeably from early childhood on by the subjects and their interlocutors. (2) After the subjects have fully acquired their first language, they learn the second language within the context of the first one, by translating and associating the words of L2 to the words and concepts of their L1. The extreme coordinate bilingual would independently store both languages at the phonological and semantic levels. The prototypical coordinate bilingual would be a person who acquires the second language in a context culturally different from the context where s/he has learned his/her first language. The coordinate system develops two different labels, each one with its own conceptual system (Gekoski, 1981).

In general, polyglot aphasics recover simultaneously all the languages that they spoke. The rate of recovery is proportional to previous degree of mastery. Neverthe - less, it is not infrequent to observe instances of differential impairment and recovery which cannot be explained by the premorbid degree of mastery or fluency of the languages. The study of such cases has elicited different theories on the brain organization in the bilingual aphasic and on the principles that determine differential recovery.

Aphasiology has shown a particular interest in polyglot aphasia phenomena, nearly from its origins (Lordat,1843; Pitres, 1895; Pick, 1903, 1913; etc.). Ribot (1882) assumed that in a polyglot aphasic the first language would be the most preserved and, therefore, the first to improve. Thus, language would follow the same mechanisms as memory, which would indicate that the first acquisitions would be the most resistant, less prone to impairment, or else, that the last acquisition would be the most vulnerable to deterioration or regression. This suggestion was subsequently often referred to as Ribot's law.

This law was not adequate to explain all cases of differential impairment of language in polyglot aphasia. Thirteen years later, Pitres (1895) proposed a second law, according to which the first language which recovers in polyglot aphasic is the most used during the period immediately preceding the aphasia, independently of the fact that this language would or wouldn't have been the first acquired.

Goldstein (1948), though he did not specifically address the issue of the order of language recovery, proposed a general mechanism to explain the selective or differential recovery. The incapacity or difficulty in using both languages at will would be a consequence of the general impairment of shifting capability that usually coexists with the aphasia and that is responsible for the impairment of abstract abilities.

Paradis (1977), in a survey of the literature on aphasia in polyglots, differentiates at least five basic patterns of restitution of the patients' various languages, namely, synergistic, antagonistic, successive, selective or mixed. Synergistic recovery occurs when progress in one language is accompanied by progress in another. The recovery is said to be parallel when both languages are similarly impaired and restored at the same rate. There is a differential recovery when impairment is of a different degree in each language and/or restitution occurs at a different rate. In antagonistic recovery, one language is seen to regress as the other is seen to progress. Recovery is said to be successive when one language does not begin to reappear until another has been restored. In selective recovery, the patient does not regain one or more of his/her languages. Finally, recovery is said to be mixed when the bilingual's two aphasic languages are intermingled.

Paradis and Lecours (1979) describe the possible factors influencing differential recovery in aphasia, namely, age of the patient, degree of automatism of the languages, their affectivity, visualizability, orthography, writing orientation, their context of acquisition, the severity of the aphasia, the relevance/appropriateness of the environment.

Other reports in the literature (Voinescu, Vish, Sirian & Maretsis, 1977; Watamori & Sasanuma, 1978; Siverberg & Gordon, 1979; Paradis, Goldblum & Abidi, 1982; Kraetschmer, 1982; Rapport, Tan & Whitaker, 1983) describe specific phenomena in single cases of polyglot aphasia.

The purpose of our study is to determine the presence and frequency of specific phenomena in bilingual aphasics. With this aim, we will carry out several quantitative measures to establish a comparison between the performance of both languages in a sample of 50 bilingual aphasic patients. We will analyze the clinical variables related to the differential recovery, i.e., linguistic variables (dominant language), neurological variables and personal variables. We will also pay special attention to the analysis of the specific phenomena in bilingual aphasia, i.e., dominance shifting, language mixing, and selective loss.

Methods

Patients

Fifty adult bilingual (Catalan/Spanish) aphasics were studied. The bilingual criterion established that the patient should be able to speak Catalan and Spanish fluently prior to the aphasia. Hence, the patients stating only a good oral comprehension or partial use of spoken Catalan were excluded.

All patients were examined in the Section of Neuropsychology of the Service of Neurology at the *Hospital de la Santa Creu i Sant Pau* (Barcelona). The 50 patients represent 64 % of the total number of aphasic patients seen during an 18 month period. The remaining 36 % consisted of unilingual Spanish aphasics.

Age of the sample ranges between 33 and 79 (Mean = 60.44; SD = 10.13). 36 (72 %) patients were males, and 14 (28 %) females. The greater incidence of aphasia is observed among patients in their fifties, accounting for 44 % of our sample. The next decade (sixties) accounts for 26 % (Table 1)

Table 1. Age

Ages	N	%	% Acc.
30-40	1	2	2
41-50	5	10	12
51-60	22	44	56
61-71	13	26	82
71-80	9	18	100

The history of the acquisition, use and dominance of both languages was determined through a questionnaire about the bilingualism of the patient, completed by the family. Thirty-four subjects (68 %) used only Catalan as the family language during their childhood; 14 subjects (28 %) used Spanish, and 2 (4%) used both languages. As for the current family language, 37 subjects (74%) used Catalan, 11 (22%) Spanish, and 2 (4%) both languages.

Among the 16 subjects for whom Catalan was not the first language, 4 had started to speak Catalan before the age of 5; 5 between 5 and 7; 3 before 12; and the other 4 between 12 and 20. Therefore, if we take the age of acquisition of L2 as a criterion for type of bilingualism (Lambert & Fillenbaum, 1959), only 4 patients present coordinate bilingualism. The other 46 are compound bilinguals.

The etiology of aphasia was stroke. Forty four with ischemic stroke, and 6 with haemorrhage (non-surgically treated). Every lesion was assessed through CT-scan. Forty nine were left hemisphere lesions, and one right hemisphere lesion (crossed aphasia).

The extent of lesion in Relative Units (RU) was estimated according to a procedure described elsewhere (Vendrell, Vendrell and Ibáñez, 1993). Figures obtained are valid for statistical comparison, although they do not express an absolute (directly size-related) value. The values obtained range between 405 RU and 15,552 RU. Mean =

4,480.2 RU; SD = 3,933 RU. The majority of lesions are small. Thirty one patients present a lesion of less than 4,000 RU. Only 4 patients present a lesion over 10,000 RU (Table 2).

Table 2. Distribution of lesions according its size

Lesion size	N	%	% Acc.
Less than 1000	8	16	16
1000-2000	8	16	32
2000-3000	7	14	46
3000-4000	8	16	62
4000-6000	7	14	76
6000-8000	4	8	84
8000-10000	4	8	92
More than 10000	4	8	100

Classification of patients was carried out according to the lesion localization through CT-scan and the Aphasia testing carried out at our Department of Neurology. For practical purposes, we have considered three broad types of aphasia: Motor, Sensory, and Global. Under the heading of Motor Aphasia, we include Broca's and Transcortical Motor Aphasia. Under Sensory Aphasia we include Wernicke's, Transcortical Sensory, Conduction, and Anomic Aphasia. Distribution of patients was 17 (34%) with Motor aphasia, 21 (42%) with Sensory aphasia, and 12 (24%) with Global aphasia.

Table 3. Distribution of patients according to sex, etiology and aphasia type.

	N	%
SEX		
Males	36	72
Females	14	28
ETIOLOGY		
Ischemic stroke	44	88
Non-neurosurgical bleeding	6	12
APHASIA TYPE		
Motor	17	34
Sensory	21	42
Global	12	24

Time of evolution from onset varies between 2 and 180 months ($\bar{X}$ = 21.1; SD = 41.2). Time of language rehabilitation ranges between 2 and 22 months ($\bar{X}$ = 6.61; SD = 4.44) (Table 4).

Table 4. Demographic variables

	Min.-Max.	$\overline{X}$	SD
Age	33 - 79	60.44	10.12
Time of evolution	2 - 172	21.12	41.21
Time of language rehabilitation	2 - 22	6.61	4.44
Extent of lesion	405 - 15,552	4,480.2	3.944

The time from aphasia onset until consultation is variable, from 2 months to 180 months (15 years). Mean = 21.1. Standard Deviation = 41.2 (Table 5).

The majority of patients asked for language rehabilitation two months post-onset, i.e., after the acute phase. Fifty-four percent consulted before three months post-onset, and in 74 % of the cases the consultation took place before one year had elapsed. Consultation after the first year was less frequent (4% during the second year, 8% during the third, 2% during the fourth, and 2% after five years post-onset).

Table 5. Time from onset

Months	N	%	% Acc.
2 months	25	50	50
3-6 months	6	12	62
6-12 months	6	12	74
12-24 months	2	4	78
24-36 months	4	8	86
36-48 months	1	2	88
More than 60 months	6	12	100

Control group

The control group comprised 20 subjects; 12 males, 8 females. The age ranged between 57 and 82 years ($\overline{X}$ = 7 0.25; SD = 6.4). Linguistic dominance was similar to that of the aphasic group. The selection criteria were absence of neurological or psychiatric abnormalities, social status comparable to that of aphasic patients. All subjects were volunteers, and, like the subjects of the aphasic group, were examined individually.

Testing procedure

NAMING TEST

Stimuli consisted of 24 colored pictures of common objects, representing basic words. Selection criteria established as little lexical similarity as possible between the two languages (Annex 1). Subjects were asked to name the pictures in each language. Pictures were presented one by one.

A naming test explores expressive aspects of language. It requires the visual identification of the picture, the association of the visual image/pattern to the verbal concept and from the verbal concept to the phonological pattern of each language and finally the verbal production involving a correct articulation and orderly sequencing of phonemes.

POINTING TEST

Stimuli consisted of the same 24 pictures used in the naming test. The pictures were presented simultaneously in two arrays containing 12 pictures each (Appendix 2).

Subjects were asked to point to the picture corresponding to the word uttered by the examiner. Words are presented in two groups of 24. The first group corresponds to the entire series of one language, and the second group to the other language.

The pointing task explores various aspects of language comprehension. It implies a process of phonemic decoding, identification of sound patterns, association to the verbal concept, association with the corresponding visual image and finally a motor response.

TRANSLATION TEST

20 words were selected, corresponding to the basic vocabulary of each language (Rosa Sensat, 1975). The meanings of words were different in each series. Lexical similarities were avoided as much as possible. Two different lists were constructed (instead of a single translated list) in order to avoid the facilitation provided by the order of presentation (Appendix 3).

Translation requires at the same time comprehension and production abilities. The first step consists of accoustical and conceptual word identification, the second step requires the translation task itself (to find the equivalent in the other language), and finally it is necessary to phonologically encode the equivalent. It constitutes the most complex task, as it implies the other two (comprehension and production), and the process of code switching at will.

Table 6. Language tests

Test	Stimuli	Analyzers	Response	Ling. process	Function
Naming	Visual	Visual	Verbal	Codification	Expression
Pointing	Verbal	Audit./Visual	Gestual	Decoding	Compr/Recept.
Translation	Verbal	Auditory	Verbal	Decod/Encoding	Compr/Express

Bilingualism Questionnaire

A questionnaire on the history of acquisition and use of each language was constructed (Appendix 4). The questionnaire inquired about type of bilingualism (coordinate or compound), first language, language used during early childhood, language used recently in the family setting, age of acquisition of the second language. These data would allow us to test the classical hypothesis of language recovery in bilingual aphasia (Pitres' and Ribot's laws), the hypothesis of bilingual cerebral organization according to age of acquisition of the second language (before or after 12, limit of cerebral plasticity) and finally the hypothesis of conceptual organization according to the type of bilingualism (coordinate or compound).

The family was asked about the eventual presence of specific bilingual aphasic phenomena, such as selective loss of one language, systematic and constant mixing of both languages, switching in the usual use of the language with family members, or the habitual trend to use preferably one language.

Additional testing

In addition, the Raven Coloured Progressive Matrices (RCPM) were administered to measure nonverbal reasoning.

Results

Linguistic variables

LANGUAGE DOMINANCE

History of acquisition, use and dominance of languages was assessed through the bilingualism questionnaire completed by the patient's family. Bilinguals are classified according to the early childhood family language (first language), currently used family language, and language used for language therapy.

The majority of our patients have Catalan as family language during their early childhood (68%) and as the current family language (74%). Table 7 compares the use of both languages along the personal history of subjects.

Table 7. Personal history of Catalan/Spanish use

	Developmental		Current familiar		Lang. rehabilitation	
	N	%	N	%	N	%
Catalan	34	68	37	74	30	66
Spanish	14	28	11	22	5	14
Bilingual	2	4	2	4	–	–

In general, the family use of one language is unilingual Catalan or Spanish. Only the 4% of the subjects utilize both languages. With respect to the change of language during the personal history of our subjects, one can see that change from Spanish to Catalan is more frequent than the reverse. Nevertheless, the more habitual situation is to maintain the same language.

COMPARISON WITH THE CONTROL GROUP

All aphasic patients perform significantly lower than the control group (Table 9). Differences are stronger in expression tests (naming, translation) than in comprehension tests. The control group scores 100 % on the pointing tests, 99% and 97% on the naming and translation tests respectively.

On comparing the aphasic's performance after treatment (N = 35) the differences are also statistically significant in both expressive tests (naming and translation) but not in pointing (Table 10). This is in accordance with the common clinical observation that aphasics tend to recover auditory word recognition.

RPCM scores (direct scoring) show no significant difference between the bilingual aphasics group and the age control group: t = 0.73; N.S.

Table 8. Changes of the use of developmental family language to current family language

Language	Subjects	%
Always Catalan	32	64
Always Spanish	8	16
From Catalan to Spanish	2	4
From Spanish to Catalan	5	10
From Bilingualism to Catalan	2	4
From Bilingualism to Spanish	0	0
From Spanish to Bilingualism	0	0
From Catalan to Bilingualism	1	2

Table 9. Comparison between aphasics and controls in the initial assessment

		$\overline{X}$	SD	t	p
Naming Catalan	Aphasics	8.82	9.11	-7.31	0.001
	Controls	23.80	0.62		
Naming Spanish	Aphasics	9.16	9.28	-11.11	0.001
	Controls	23.80	0.52		
Pointing Catalan	Aphasics	21.38	4.14	-2.82	0.001
	Controls	24.00	0.00		
Pointing Spanish	Aphasics	20.18	5.32	-3.19	0.002
	Controls	24.00	0.00		
Translation Catalan-Spanish	Aphasics	6.42	7.59	-12.25	0.001
	Controls	19.65	0.49		
Translation Spanish-Catalan	Aphasics	5.76	6.49	-14.70	0.001
	Controls	19.45	0.69		

Table 10. Comparison between aphasics and controls
in the final (after treatment) assessment

		$\overline{X}$	SD	t	p
Naming Catalan	Aphasics	14.97	8.77	-4.48	0.001
	Controls	23.80	0.14		
Naming Spanish	Aphasics	13.46	9.27	-4.97	0.001
	Controls	23.80	0.52		
Pointing Catalan	Aphasics	23.06	2.76	-1.52	0.135
	Controls	24.00	0.00		
Pointing Spanish	Aphasics	22.51	3.75	-1.76	0.084
	Controls	24.00	0.00		
Translation Catalan-Spanish	Aphasics	10.26	7.82	-5.34	0.001
	Controls	19.65	0.49		
Translation Spanish-Catalan	Aphasics	10.06	7.44	-5.61	0.001
	Controls	19.45	0.69		

Analysis of performance-related variables

Correlation between subject variables and language scores

Age only correlates with intelligence. The higher the age, the lower the performance in RCPM. This may be related to the senile regression associated with aphasia in some subjects in the sample. But there is no relationship between age and language scores. Therefore, anomic scores do not seem related to aging.

The time of evolution correlates weakly with the naming initial test ($r = 0.26$; $P < 0.01$). Bilingual aphasics for whom more time has elapsed since onset have access to more Catalan words. Time of evolution also correlates with the extent of lesion ($r = 0.42$; $P < 0.01$). Patients with large lesions need more attention and training, possibly because of the persistence of aphasic impairment.

Size of lesion correlates negatively with all other measures. The larger the lesion, the worst the language performance on the three tests. Expressive scores correlate more strongly in final than in initial tests (Tables 11, 12).

Finally, intelligence scores do not correlate with any of the three language tests nor with size of lesion. Deterioration does not seem to be related to the focal loss of encephalic mass.

Comparison between language tests performance according to subject variables

Comparison was established between subgroups, in order to control the possible difference between groups.

Sex: There is no difference between males and females in any of the language scores.

Table 11. Correlation between initial scores and subject variables

	Age	T. evol.	T. rehab.	Lesion	RCPM	NM CAT 1	NM SPA 1	PN CAT 1	PN SPA 1	TR CAT 1
TR SPA 1	-0.2093	0.1948	-0.0723	-0.3445**	0.1347	0.8470***	0.8739***	0.4725***	0.4453***	0.8800***
TR CAT 1	-0.1473	0.1171	-0.0318	-0.7788**	0.1278	0.8771***	0.5008***	0.5256***	0.8784***	
PN SPA 1	0.0295	0.0283	-0.0299	-0.4481**	0.1349	0.5008***	0.5530***	0.8800***		
PN CAT 1	0.0714	0.1477	-0.0374	-0.4930***	0.2465	0.5256***	0.8784***			
NM SPA 1	-0.1245	0.1746	-0.0451	-0.3536**	0.1265	0.5076***				
NM CAT 1	-0.1391	0.2625*	-0.0603	-0.2397*	0.1871					
RCPM	-0.2425*	0.0403	-0.1240	-0.0622						
Lesion	-0.1289	0.4201***	0.1768							
T. rehab.	0.1570	0.2726								
T. evol.	0.0577									

* P < 05
** P < 01
*** P < 001

Table 12. Correlation between final scores and subject variables

	Age	T. evol.	T. rehab.	Lesion	RCPM	NM CAT 1	NM SPA 1	PN CAT 1	PN SPA 1	TR CAT 1
TR SPA 1	0.0865	-0.2173	-0.0089	-0.6334***	0.1347	0.8813***	0.9166**	0.4743**	0.5317***	0.9493***
TR CAT 1	0.0398	-0.02214	-0.1170	-0.6093***	0.1278	0.8751***	0.9204***	0.4603**	0.5144***	
PN SPA 1	0.0186	-0.0457	-0.1197	-0.4523**	0.1349	0.6243***	0.5427***	0.8674***		
PN CAT 1	-0.0316	-0.0066	-0.1312	-0.6474***	0.2465	0.5835***	0.4982***			
NM SPA 1	0.1931	-0.1399	-0.0493	-0.5930***	0.1265	0.9345***				
NM CAT 1	0.1720	-0.0362	-0.1156	-0.6138***	0.1871					
RCPM	-0.2425*	0.0403	-0.1240	-0.0622						
Lesion	-0.1289	0.4201***	0.1768							
T. rehab.	0.1570	0.2726								
T. evol.	-0.0577									

* P < 05
** P < 01
*** P < 001

Etiology: Haemorrhagic patients perform badly in pointing in Spanish. The same test in Catalan shows the same trend, but differences have no statistical significance (Table 13). Expressive tests (naming, translation) do not show any difference of performance.

With the passing of time, pointing attains practically normal scores, and the final scores (second evaluation, after a rehabilitation period is elapsed) does not show any significant difference in scores (Table 14).

Comparison of performance between the two languages

INITIAL SCORES

There is no difference in performance between the two languages in any of the expressive tasks (Table 15). Naming and translation are similarly impaired in Catalan and Spanish (Naming: t = 0.53; gl = 49; N.S. Translation: t = 1.43; gl = 49; N.S.). However, pointing does show differences. Bilingual aphasics of our sample show a better pointing in Catalan than in Spanish (t = 3.28; gl = 49; P < 0.002).

FINAL SCORES

Final scores show differences between Catalan and Spanish for the naming task (Table 15). Bilingual aphasics who have undergone language rehabilitation name better in Catalan than in Spanish (t = 2.71; gl = 34; P < 0.01). Translation scores do not show significant differences (t = 0.48; gl = 34; N.S.).

These results are not surprising if we take into account that aphasia rehabilitation includes naming tasks, but not translation. Moreover, the language used during the rehabilitation of Catalan patients is Catalan.

Differences in pointing which were observed in the initial testing have disappeared now: pointing does not show differences between Catalan and Spanish in the final testing. This fact is related to practically total recovery of pointing in the majority of subjects, in agreement with Pitres' rule, according to which patients recover comprehension before production.

The control group does not show any difference of performance between Catalan and Spanish on any of the three tests.

Differential recovery of languages:

treated versus non-treated language

We have studied the evolution or improvement by comparing the initial and final performance on each test. There is a significant difference in Catalan and in Spanish between the initial and final performances, even though only one language has been systematically stimulated during language rehabilitation. Improvement is observed in all the tests, i.e., in naming, pointing and translation (Table 16).

Among the 35 treated subjects, 30 followed rehabilitation in Catalan and 5 in Spanish. Therefore, we will analyze only the subjects treated in Catalan.

Table 13. Etiology: comparison between ischemic (N=44) and haemorrhagic (N=6) stroke. Initial scores.

		$\overline{X}$	SD	t	p
Naming Catalan	Ischemic	9.32	9.07	1.05	0.300
	Haemorrhagic	5.17	9.43		
Naming Spanish	Ischemic	9.84	9.24	1.42	0.16
	Haemorrhagic	4.17	8.77		
Pointing Catalan	Ischemic	21.77	3.77	1.86	0.069
	Haemorrhagic	28.50	5.86		
Pointing Spanish	Ischemic	20.81	4.76	2.40	0.020*
	Haemorrhagic	15.50	7.29		
Translation Catalan-Spanish	Ischemic	6.80	7.60	0.95	0.349
	Haemorrhagic	3.67	7.61		
Translation Spanish-Catalan	Ischemic	6.05	6.50	0.84	0.406
	Haemorrhagic	3.67	6.65		

Table 14. Etiology: comparison between ischemic (N=44) and haemorrhagic (N=6) stroke. Final scores.

		$\overline{X}$	SD	t	p
Naming Catalan	Ischemic	16.14	8.41	1.78	0.083
	Haemorrhagic	9.33	8.98		
Naming Spanish	Ischemic	14.55	9.08	1.57	0.126
	Haemorrhagic	8.17	8.95		
Pointing Catalan	Ischemic	23.14	2.87	0.38	0.710
	Haemorrhagic	22.67	2.42		
Pointing Spanish	Ischemic	22.93	2.94	1.47	0.151
	Haemorrhagic	20.50	6.44		
Translation Catalan-Spanish	Ischemic	11.17	7.66	1.55	1.130
	Haemorrhagic	5.83	7.68		
Translation Spanish-Catalan	Ischemic	10.93	7.19	1.56	0.129
	Haemorrhagic	5.83	7.86		

ANCOVA (Covariance Analysis) was performed for each test (naming, pointing, translation), so as to be able to compare the recovery of the two languages, Catalan and Spanish, the treated and non-treated language respectively. The initial scoring has been considered as a concomitant variable (as it could influence the final recovery). Effectively, it has been observed that initial scoring (concomitant variable) does have influence on the recovery of the three abilities: Naming, $F(1,28) = 5.23$; $P < 0.05$. Pointing, $F(1,28) = 27.74$; $p < 0.005$. Translation, $F(1,28) = 98.57$; $P < 0.001$.

Table 15. Comparison of performance between the two languages. Initial and final scores.

	X̄	SD	t	p
INITIAL SCORES				
Naming Catalan	8.82	9.11	-0.53	0.599
Naming Spanish	9.16	9.28		
Pointing Catalan	21.38	4.14	3.28	0.002**
Pointing Spanish	20.18	5.32		
Translation Catalan-Spanish	6.42	7.59	1.43	0.159
Translation Spanish-Catalan	5.76	6.49		
FINAL SCORES				
Naming Catalan	14.97	8.77	2.71	0.010**
Naming Spanish	13.46	9.27		
Pointing Catalan	23.06	2.76	1.66	0.105
Pointing Spanish	22.51	3.75		
Translation Catalan-Spanish	10.26	7.82	0.48	0.633
Translation Spanish-Catalan	10.06	7.44		

** $p < 0.01$

Table 16. Comparison between initial and final scores.

		X̄	SD	t	p
Naming Catalan	Initial	9.06	9.03	-5.38	0.001
	Final	14.97	8.77		
Naming Spanish	Initial	9.00	9.26	-4.26	0.001
	Final	13.46	9.27		
Pointing Catalan	Initial	20.91	4.63	-4.25	0.001
	Final	23.06	2.76		
Pointing Spanish	Initial	19.77	5.76	-4.35	0.001
	Final	22.51	3.75		
Translation Catalan-Spanish	Initial	6.91	7.78	-3.56	0.001
	Final	10.26	7.82		
Translation Spanish-Catalan	Initial	5.86	6.60	-5.10	0.001
	Final	10.06	7.44		

After eliminating the influence of initial scoring, comparison between Catalan and Spanish recovery gives: Naming $F(1,28) = 10.24$; $P < 0.005$. Pointing $F(1,28) = 0.98$; N.S. Translation $F(1,28) = 1.06$; N.S. The only ability which shows a differential recovery is naming: it has improved more in Catalan than in Spanish. This is not surprising since translation or pointing are not tasks that are used during aphasia rehabilitation, while naming is a commonly used exercise.

Variables related to the differential performance

LANGUAGE DOMINANCE

FIRST LANGUAGE

According to Ribot's law, the first language is the most resistent to impairment and, in case of a selective impairment, it is the best preserved and the more easily recovered.

We have grouped the patients according to their early childhood language dominance. Analysis shows that each subgroup performs better in its first language. Initial scores show that pointing is better in Catalan for the Catalan subgroup (t = 3.47; p < 0.001) (Table 17) and naming is better in Spanish for the Spanish subgroup (t = -2.80; p < 0.01) (Table 18). The posttests also show that naming is better in Catalan for the Catalan subgroup (t = 3.23; p < 0.004) (Table 17).

Table 17. Comparison between the Catalan and Spanish performance for each test. Subgroup with Catalan as the first language.

	$\overline{X}$	SD	t	p
INITIAL SCORES (N=34)				
Naming Catalan	8.91	9.06	0.55	0.584
Naming Spanish	8.44	8.92		
Pointing Catalan	21.65	4.21	3.47	0.001***
Pointing Spanish	19.94	5.70		
Translation Catalan-Spanish	6.03	7.13	0.55	0.583
Translation Spanish-Catalan	5.71	6.36		
FINAL SCORES (N=23)				
Naming Catalan	14.78	8.53	3.23	0.004**
Naming Spanish	12.74	8.91		
Pointing Catalan	23.00	3.11	1.89	0.071
Pointing Spanish	22.13	4.51		
Translation Catalan-Spanish	9.65	7.64	0.69	0.498
Translation Spanish-Catalan	9.35	7.32		

** p < 0.01
*** p < 0.001

RECENT LANGUAGE

According to Pitres' law, the most familiar language at the time of insult is the less impaired and the first to recover in polyglot or bilingual aphasics.

Table 18. Differences between Catalan and Spanish performance
for each test. Subgroup with Spanish as first language.

	X̄	SD	t	p
INITIAL SCORES (N=14)				
Naming Catalan	9.86	9.56	-2.80	0.015**
Naming Spanish	12.14	10.01		
Pointing Catalan	21.29	3.89	0.37	0.720
Pointing Spanish	21.14	4.35		
Translation Catalan-Spanish	8.28	2.36	1.191	0.079
Translation Spanish-Catalan	6.71	1.89		
FINAL SCORES (N=10)				
Naming Catalan	16.10	9.17	-1.00	0.343
Naming Spanish	15.40	10.10		
Pointing Catalan	23.10	2.23	-1.00	0.343
Pointing Spanish	23.40	1.35		
Translation Catalan-Spanish	12.10	8.27	0.00	1.000
Translation Spanish-Catalan	12.10	7.56		

** p < 0.01

When grouping the patients according to their current family language (currently dominant language) we can observe that, if there is any performance difference between languages, the difference favours the current dominant language. Initial scores on pointing are better in Catalan for Catalan subgroup (t = 3.56; p < 0.001) (Table 19) and they are also better in the posttest (t = 2.05; p < 0.05), as are naming scores (t = 3.27; p < 0.01), while the Spanish subgroup show better initial scores on naming (t = −2.40; p < 0.05) (Table 20).

Therefore, differential impairment is seen to be related to the language dominance in each subgroup.

ANALYSIS OF THE COINCIDENCE OF ERRORS IN THE TWO LANGUAGES

As there is a common stimulus for two possible responses (one for each language) in the naming and pointing tasks, both responses may coincide (correct or incorrect in both languages) or not coincide (correct in one language and incorrect in the other). The possibilities are thus (1) correct in both languages, (2) incorrect in both languages, (3) correct in Catalan and incorrect in Spanish, and (4) correct in Spanish and incorrect in Catalan.

The analysis of error frequency will allow us to check a hypothesis on the bilingual's conceptual organization. In short, if the failure in naming (anomia) comes from not knowing the corresponding concept, the errors will coincide in both languages; however, if the problem is limited to the phonemic codification in each language, a selective anomia can be observed in one language.

Table 19. Differences between Catalan and Spanish performance for each test. Subgroup with Catalan as their current language.

	X̄	SD	t	p
INITIAL SCORES (N=34)				
Naming Catalan	9.35	9.50	1.69	0.100
Naming Spanish	8.43	9.09		
Pointing Catalan	21.27	4.24	3.56	0.001***
Pointing Spanish	19.62	5.65		
Translation Catalan-Spanish	6.38	7.59	1.71	0.095
Translation Spanish-Catalan	5.65	6.60		
FINAL SCORES (N=23)				
Naming Catalan	15.61	8.65	3.27	0.003**
Naming Spanish	13.57	9.09		
Pointing Catalan	23.14	2.84	2.05	0.050*
Pointing Spanish	22.36	4.13		
Translation Catalan-Spanish	10.25	7.82	0.69	0.496
Translation Spanish-Catalan	10.00	7.55		

  * $p < 0.05$
 ** $p < 0.01$
*** $p < 0.001$

Table 20. Differences between Catalan and Spanish performance for each test. Subgroup with Spanish as their current language (N=11).

	X̄	SD	t	p
INITIAL SCORES (N=34)				
Naming Catalan	6.36	7.28	-2.40	0.037*
Naming Spanish	9.09	9.16		
Pointing Catalan	21.27	4.22	-0.27	0.796
Pointing Spanish	21.36	4.25		
Translation Catalan-Spanish	5.64	7.42	0.74	0.477
Translation Spanish-Catalan	4.73	6.01		

* $p < 0.05$

On the other hand, regarding the theories on language organization in bilinguals, two conceptual models have been proposed depending on the bilingual type. In compound bilinguals, one single concept would correspond to two verbal labels, whereas for coordinated bilinguals there would be two different concepts with their corresponding verbal labels.

By analyzing the performance globally for each test the information on the coincidence or not of errors in both languages can be missed. In Table 21 we can see the two hypothetical examples. In both cases there are four errors in each language, one might conclude that there is no differential impairment in either language. Yet, in Case A there is no coincidence in any of the errors, whereas in Case B the errors coincide completely. In the first case, the subject knows the word in one language and not in the other, while in the second case the subject does not know the word in either language. The former would be compatible with the independence of both languages, both codes or both memory files, while the latter would be compatible with the interdependence of the two languages.

Table 21. Example of equal impairment of both languages, with two error types: asymmetric errors (A); coinciding errors (B).

Stimuli	Case A Response		Case B Response	
	Catalan	Spanish	Catalan	Spanish
1			E	E
2	E		E	E
3		E		
4	E		E	E
5		E		
6	E			
–				
–				
–				
–				
–				
–				
24		E	E	E
Total errors	4	4	4	4

E = error

TYPE OF ERRORS: COMMON VERSUS SELECTIVE

When comparing the mean of common errors in both languages with the selective errors in one language (asymmetric errors) we do not observe any difference in the naming tests, neither before nor after treatment (Table 22), that is to say that both forms of anomia (coincidence of errors in both languages and selective errors in one) are equally present. On the contrary, in the pointing tasks a greater number of asymmetric errors than common errors is observed, as much before ($t = 5.37$; $p < 0.001$) as after ($t = 4.71$; $p < 0.01$) treatment (Table 23). This would indicate that the identification of a word may depend more on the phonemic cues than on the semantic processing. Given that the phonological form of the words used for testing was different in each language, pointing probably resulted in more asymmetrical errors than naming because the pointing task involves phonological decoding.

Table 22. Comparison between common errors and asymmetrical errors in naming.

		$\bar{X}$	SD	t	p
Initial Naming	Asymmetrical	6.06	4.09	-0.77	0.447
	Common	7.22	7.32		
Final Naming	Asymmetrical	6.65	3.65	0.18	0.862
	Common	6.35	6.81		

Table 23. Comparison between common errors and asymmetrical errors in pointing.

		$\bar{X}$	SD	t	p
Initial Pointing	Asymmetrical	6.11	3.69	5.37	0.001
	Common	2.61	3.62		
Final Pointing	Asymmetrical	6.12	4.61	4.71	0.002
	Common	2.00	2.93		

Specific phenomena in bilingual aphasics

The term specific phenomena refers to those phenomena that appear only in bilingual aphasic patients. We will consider the following ones: Change of dominance of language, when, according to relatives, the bilingual aphasic tends to use a language other than the one currently used within his family. Erroneous mixing, when the bilingual patient mixes words or sentences from both languages in a constant and persistent way. Loss, when patients are incapable of speaking in one of the two languages they previously knew (according to the questionnaire of bilingualism, Appendix 1).

Specific phenomena have been observed in 15 patients, i.e., 30% of the sample. The distribution of those phenomena was the following: Seven patients (14%) presented a dominance shifting. Nine patients (18%) mixed inaccurately but regularly both languages. And four (8%) had lost the use of one of their two languages (Table 24).

Table 24. Specific phenomena in bilingual aphasia

	N	%
Change of dominance	7	14
Erroneous mixing	9	18
Selective loss	4	8
Total	15	30

Relationship between specific phenomena and linguistic variables

FIRST LANGUAGE

Among the aphasic patients who have Catalan as their native language (language of first use and used during chilhood within their family), 11 (32.35%) showed specific phenomena and 23 (67.65%) did not. Of the patients who have Spanish as their first language, four (28.57%) showed specific phenomena and ten (71.43 %) did not. The presence of specific phenomena was significantly different depending on whether the first language was Catalan or Spanish ($\chi^2 = 7.33$; gl = 1; P < 0.05, Yates correction).

RECENTLY ACQUIRED LANGUAGE

Within the group presently using Catalan as the familiar language, specific phenomena are observed in eight patients, while six patients present specific phenomena within the Spanish group. Analysis did not how statistically significant differences between the two groups as regards the presence of specific phenomena ($\chi^2 = 2.99$; gl = 1; NS).

Analysis of specific phenomena

SHIFTING

All the aphasic patients who have experienced shifting in the dominance of the language after the stroke have Catalan as their first language. No shifting was observed from Spanish to Catalan. Out of the seven patients showing a dominance shifting, two have Spanish as their everyday language and one lives in a continuous bilingual family environment. In four patients the change of dominance cannot be explained by a change of the language used within the family. In any case the rehabilitation training could be the origin of shifting, as Catalan was used as the rehabilitation language with all of them (Table 25).

Table 25.   Dominance shifting related to the linguistic variable of use of languages (N = 7)

	Catalan	Spanish	Bilingual
Native language	7	0	0
Current everyday language	4	2	1
Language of rehabilitation	4	0	0

ERRONEOUS MIXING OF LANGUAGES

Erroneous mixing appears in seven aphasics who had Catalan as their first language and in two who had Spanish. The seven Catalan patients continued to use Catalan as their everyday language. Therefore the mixing of both languages cannot be explained by their current family language. Only in one case a bilingual family situation could have increased the chances of erroneous mixing of both languages.

Table 26. Mixing of languages related to the linguistic variables.

	Catalan	Spanish	Bilingual
First language	7	2	0
Recently acquired language	7	1	1
Language of rehabilitation	6	1	0

SELECTIVE LOSS

All the patients who complain of selective loss of one language had Spanish as their current everyday language. Three of them claim to have lost Catalan and one of them Spanish. We shall examine the cases of selective loss one by one.

Study of cases with selective loss

We shall study one by one the cases of patients who present a selective loss of the current use of one of their two languages, and we shall compare the subjective complaints with the objective performances obtained on the bilingual tests.

Case 15 JSLL H.9994
Age: 69
Sex: female
Etiology: stroke
Aphasia: Motor. Broca.
Evolution time: 30 months
Sociolinguistic upbringing: born in the province of Huesca (Spanish speaking). At the age of seven, she moved to Lleida (Catalan speaking) and at 22 to Barcelona (Catalan speaking) where she has lived up until now.
Historical family language: she spoke Spanish with all her relatives.
Current family language: mixed. Spanish with her husband and Catalan with her children.
Learning age of the second language: at 7, in an informal manner with friends.

The language used after the stroke is Spanish. The couple live on their own and talk to each other in Spanish.

The language, at the time of exploration, is reduced, agrammatic and with multiple phonemic paraphasias. Nowadays the patient claims to be unable to speak Catalan any more, even with her children, with whom she usually spoke Catalan.

Test results:
Naming Catalan: 5/24   Naming Spanish: 12/24
Pointing Catalan: 23/24   Pointing Spanish: 24/24
Translation Catalan to Spanish: 0/24   Translation Spanish to Catalan: 0/24

In this case, the selective loss of Catalan could be explained by factors of automatism and lack of use of the language. The patient has, from her childhood and afterwards throughout her life, had a clear dominance of Spanish over Catalan. After the stroke her opportunities to speak Catalan have been almost nil; and at a receptive level Catalan has also been absent from her usual everyday life.

The tests carried out support the subjective complaints about the differential recovery of only one language: she correctly names 12 pictures (50%) in Spanish, whereas only 5 (21%) in Catalan. At a receptive level, the patient shows a similar performance in both languages. The unevenness of the impairment is only noticeable in word-finding tasks but not in the tasks of auditory recognition of the same words.

A remarkable feature is the total absence of translating ability in either direction. This disfunction may be interpreted as an impairment of her shifting abilities.

Case 28   JTN. H.17083
Age: 62
Sex: male
Etiology: stroke
Aphasia: crossed, anomic type.
Evolution time: 2 months
Sociolinguistic upbringing: born in Ribera de Cardós, Lleida (Catalan speaking). At the age of 14 he moved to Lleida (Catalan speaking). At the age of 18 he moved to Barcelona (Catalan speaking) where he has lived until now. He always spoke Catalan as a child with members of his family.
Native family language: Catalan only.
Current family language: married to a Spanish speaking woman, they have always spoken in Spanish. He has no children.

He says that during the first month following the stroke while he was still in the hospital ward, he was unable to talk in Spanish, whereas he had only slight difficulties in finding some words in Catalan. Even though his wife visited him daily and talked to him in Spanish, he always answered her in Catalan.

At the second month of evolution, he was already able to answer occasionally in Spanish, and after the first two months had elapsed, he was already able to select at will Spanish or Catalan. At the present time he has nominal aphasia in both languages.

Test results:
First examination:
Naming Catalan: 3/24   Naming Spanish: 1/24
Pointing Catalan: 24/24   Pointing Spanish: 23/24
Translation Catalan to Spanish: 7/24   Translation Spanish to Catalan: 14/24

Second examination:
Naming Catalan: 10/24   Naming Spanish: 6/24
Pointing Catalan: 24/24   Pointing Spanish: 24/24
Translation Catalan to Spanish: 14/24   Translation Spanish to Catalan: 15/24

The language used during the two months of rehabilitation was Catalan.

In this second case, the selective loss of one language was noticed only during the acute phase, and gradually disappeared afterwards. The first recovered language was not the last one used (against Pitres), but the first to have been acquired (in support of Ribot). The problem, in this case, seems to lie more in the voluntary access to one language rather than in a selective loss, as testing shows similar impairment of both languages at word-auditory-identification (pointing, receptive level) and word-finding (naming, expressive level), but word-translation from Catalan into Spanish is more difficult (7, 35%) than the reverse, from Spanish into Catalan (14, 70%). This would agree with Pitres' second law: the language which is not recovered is inhibited but not destroyed. Final scores show a greater naming improvement in the treated language, Catalan 10 (42 %) than in Spanish 6 (25 %). Translation ability has reached an equal level in both directions. At this time the patient was no longer complaining about specific difficulties in speaking Spanish. This observation again supports Pitres' second rule of initial inhibition of one language instead of a selective loss.

Case 35 CLH. H. 15.325
Age: 46
Sex: female
Etiology: stroke
Aphasia: nominal
Evolution time: 12 months
Sociolinguistic upbringing: born in Barcelona where she has lived ever since.
Native family language: Spanish with her parents and grandparents.
Current family language: Spanish with her husband and children.
Acquisition age of the second language: when she was about 5 and in an informal way among friends. Since then she has spoken Catalan with all her Catalan speaking friends and acquaintances.

She complains that she currently finds herself unable to speak Catalan because she cannot find the words and her communication is constantly hampered by fluency problems. On the other hand, when speaking Spanish she experiences fluency problems only occasionally .

Test results:
Naming Catalan: 21/24	Naming Spanish: 24/24
Pointing Catalan: 24/24	Pointing Spanish: 24/24
Translation Catalan to Spanish: 19/24	Translation Spanish to Catalan: 10/24

In this third case, the patient selectively recovered Spanish, her most commonly used everyday language which is also her first and current family language. The clear historical dominance of Spanish and scarce presence of Catalan within the most proximal environment after the stroke (the family context) would explain the greater anomia in Catalan and therefore its greater dysfluency and subsequent disuse. The tests show a slight naming difference: Catalan 21 (87.5%) and Spanish 24 (100%), and a greater difficulty in translating from Spanish into Catalan (10, 41.66 %) than the reverse (19, 79.17 %).

Case 44 RBP. H.6243
Age: 55
Sex: female

Etiology: stroke
Aphasia: global at the very beginning, evolved towards a motor aphasia with good
    recovery for current social use.
Evolution time: 172 months (14.3 years).
Sociolinguistic upbringing: born in Barcelona (Catalan speaking) where she lived until
    she was 19. Then she moved to Melilla (Spanish colony) where she lived until the
    age of 31. She has been living in Barcelona for 5 years now. She also speaks
    French.
Native family language: Catalan with all her relatives.
Current family language: mixed with Spanish dominance; mixed with her husband and
    Spanish with her children.
Language of common use after the stroke: Spanish.

Currently she complains that since her return to Catalonia, five years ago, she tries
to speak Catalan but cannot retrieve it.

Test results:

Naming Catalan:	18/24	Naming Spanish:	24/24
Pointing Catalan:	24/24	Pointing Spanish:	24/24
Translation Catalan to Spanish:	20/24	Translation Spanish to Catalan:	5/24

In this last case, the patient has selectively recovered the language that she used
last, the most commonly used during a long period of time premorbidly (in support of
Pitres) and also post onset. On the other hand, she did not recover the language first
acquired (against Ribot). The lost language had not been practiced for many years and
had been absent from her environment (the environment of her dayly life). The tests
carried out show, as in the previous cases, a slightly differential impairment, but not a
complete loss. Naming is 100% preserved in Spanish and 75% in Catalan. Pointing is
performed correctly in both languages and the patient can translate with good accuracy
from Catalan into Spanish, although only partially from Spanish into Catalan. These
results suggest the presence of selective anomic phenomena in Catalan, probably with
words that have not been used during the 14 years since the stroke.

Discussion

We have studied the performance on three linguistic tasks (naming, pointing and
word-translation) in a group of 50 bilingual Catalan-Spanish aphasic patients. Each
task was administered in both languages to every patient. Scores prior to the
rehabilitation period did not reveal significant differences between the two languages
in the expressive tasks. Before treatment, people with bilingual aphasia named and
translated similarly in both Catalan and Spanish. These results are in agreement with
previous reports on bilingual aphasia (Charlton, 1964; Lhermitte, Hécaen, Dubois,
Culioli, & Tabouret-Keller, 1971; Nair & Virmani, 1973; Fredman, 1975). On the
other hand, in the receptive task (pointing), we do notice uneven performances in the
two languages. Bilingual people with aphasia pointed better in Catalan than in
Spanish. When a differential impairment has been reported in single cases, a similar
comprehension performance but uneven expression results have been observed, which

is just the opposite of our results (Voinescu et al., 1977). This may be due to the fact that, in the exploration of single cases, simple commands are used as tasks of verbal comprehension, or else that the Token Test (De Renzi & Vignolo, 1962) is used when a quantitative measure is desired; this comprehension test, probably, assesses language structures different from those necessary for pointing. In our study we used a comprehension task of simple words. We thus use a purely "nominal" task that may depend on language aspects that can be affected in different ways in both languages. This dissociation may obtain particularly if both languages have been learned at separate times and in different social contexts (Paivio & Desrochers, 1980).

No differences between the translation from Catalan into Spanish and from Spanish into Catalan were noticed. Even though the translation is —like the naming task— an expressive task, it is not comparable to it as it has distinctive linguistic elements that, in the case of an aphasia, can be very clearly dissociated (Paradis, Goldblum & Abidi, 1982). Brec'hed (1980) claims that the switch from one language to the other is comparable to the ability of switching registers in the way of speaking in unilingual people, ability that in an aphasic person is particularly damaged (Goldstein, 1948). Moreover, it is necessary to remember that language therapy programmes include naming tasks and not translating ones.

The analysis of errors showed that defects in naming coincided in both languages but, in contrast, there were asymmetrical errors in pointing (patients did not obtain comparable scores in their two languages on the pointing task). These results indicate that probably in a naming task the patient uses more the conceptual/ semantic representation of words than the phonological strategies. In contrast, for the comprehension of words the patients used the phonological analysis rather than direct access to meaning.

The whole sample of bilingual aphasic patients is composed of two subgroups of bilinguals: the first in which Catalan is the historical family language, and the second, in which the family language is Spanish. These two subgroups thus have different linguistic dominance. Analyzing the two groups as a whole may have diminished the possible differences between Spanish and Catalan due to the mixing of the two types of dominance. Therefore, we have subdivided the bilinguals in accordance with their premorbid linguistic dominance. The reason for this double classification (developmental language and current everyday language) lies in the potential incidence of the age of second language acquisition (Lenneberg, 1967; Albert and Obler, 1978; Silverberg & Gordon, 1979), on the memory mechanisms which can be at work during senile decline (Ribot, 1882; Albert & Obler, 1978), or on the differential brain organization depending on the type of bilingualism (Lambert & Fillenbaum, 1959; Gekoski, 1980).

According to Ribot's law (1882), in case of differential impairment, the most preserved language is the first acquired. When we compared the performance of the Catalan and Spanish subgroups in both languages (classified according to which language was their first), we found that the subgroup with Catalan dominance initially understood Catalan words better than Spanish words and could name better in Catalan than in Spanish. From the beginning, the Spanish subgroup performed more poorly in Catalan on naming tasks.

It appears that for people with Spanish dominance, Catalan is more vulnerable to aphasia. Catalan speakers, on the other hand, do not show greater vulnerability in Spanish. Possibly, a bilingual person with Catalan dominance uses more Spanish

202 *Aspects of bilingual aphasia*

language than a person with Spanish dominance uses Catalan. The automatism factor (Paradis, 1977) has an undeniable influence on a bilingual person with aphasia.

In the classification according to the current use of languages we also observe different tendencies in the Catalan and Spanish subgroups. People in the Catalan subgroup show better recovery for Catalan on the naming task, i.e., they exhibit a greater anomia in Spanish. This is also the case in the pointing task. In the Spanish subgroup, scores on the naming task in Catalan are lower in the initial assessment. The reason why Catalan people do not name worse in Spanish, initially, may be due to their exposure to Spanish via the media. Both languages are present in a bilingual environment, with nevertheless a certain Spanish dominance.

To sum up, there were differences between both languages in the initial naming task and the final pointing task which were obscured by the mixture of the two groups with opposite dominance. These differences emerged after the subgroups had been analyzed separately. The only task where performance is kept equal in both languages is the translation task.

In all results the direction of the differences goes in favour of the premorbidly dominant language, that is to say, no paradoxical shifting in dominance, as reported in individual cases of bilingual or polyglot aphasics (Paradis & Lecours, 1979) is observed. Differences in performance between languages in this sample can be explained by language dominance.

Our results partially support both theories regarding the recovery of languages. The least impaired language is the first acquired and also the currently used everyday, but, in fact, these two cannot be dissociated, as, in the majority of our patients the first and the currently used language coincide, and only a small number of patients have changed their dominance during their lives. On the other hand, in Catalonia both languages are constantly present in the environment, and this situation does not promote the loss of words in any one language due to lack of use. Compound bilingualism (as is the case in the majority of our aphasic patients) tends to dilute the differences between languages. If we could obtain a sample of Spanish-dominant bilingual aphasics who had learned Catalan in their adulthood, the differences between languages would probably be even more remarkable. Only five of our fifty subjects had learned Catalan after the age of 12, which leads to a very strong fusion between both languages, even for the Spanish subgroup.

A surprising high incidence of specific bilingual aphasia phenomena was observed during this study. Thirty percent of the sample show some of the three specific phenomena studied: dominance shifting in 7 cases, erroneous mixing in 9 cases, selective loss in 4 cases.

These figures coincide with reported single cases (Paradis, 1977; Albert & Obler, 1978), although they were assumed to be rare and confined to coordinate bilinguals (Lambert & Fillenbaum, 1959). Systematic family questioning in our 50 cases confirms the presence of these phenomena and, moreover, with a relatively high frequency. We could argue that, when questioned on these matters, the family members could be prone to overemphasize the phenomena, but there is a high concordance between the questionnaire and the objective test results. Depending on the test, from 68% to 76% of subjects present similar impairment in both languages (differences of less than 3 words between the Spanish and Catalan tests); but the remaining patients present remarkable differences in performance. Sixteen percent of subjects, for example, name 25% more words in one of their two languages.

Catalan patients present more specific phenomena than Spanish patients. Subjects with Spanish as their first language can be assumed to be coordinate bilinguals, while subjects with Catalan as their first language could be assumed to be compound bilinguals, according to Ervin and Osgood's (1954) classification. Yet, Catalan patients exhibit more dominance shifting problems than Spanish-dominant patients. That is to say, they complain of finding words more easily in Spanish than in Catalan after the stroke, although their family language and the language commonly used every day premorbidly was Catalan. None of the Spanish speaking patients relate problems of this kind. Catalan patients also present more systematic mixing of both languages after the stroke. Both phenomena, dominance shifting and erroneous mixing, are probably related to the massive presence of Spanish in the mass-media, and the subsequent automatization of Spanish words which eventually causes interference phenomena. In the cases of selective loss of one language, Catalan is also the most frequently lost language. In only one case the selective loss of Spanish is observed during the acute period post-stroke, and it has proved to consist more in an access disturbance than a loss. In those cases of "selective loss", we could clearly see that prolonged lack of use of one language may determine, after a brain lesion, the loss of the ability to use it.

Conclusion

To sum up, our results demonstrate the existence of differential impairment of languages in bilingual aphasic patients, in both word recognition and word-finding tasks. In general, the better preserved is the dominant language, although in some isolated cases it is the non-dominant language. Specific phenomena (i.e., shift of dominance, mixing, and/or selective loss of access) are relatively frequent.

Given that our Catalan subjects could be considered compound bilinguals and our Spanish subjects coordinate, the results reported here are in contradiction with Lambert and Fillenbaum's (1959) prediction that there would be more cases of differential phenomena in coordinate than in compound bilinguals. On the other hand, our results are in agreement with those obtained by Ojemann (1983) using electrical stimulation. Ojemann and Whitaker (1978) found differential effects for the two languages in the arrest of naming produced by cortical stimulation. Other possible explanations of these results may be found in the theory about implicit versus explicit knowledge (Schacter, 1992) or the evidence of dissociation between declarative and non-declarative learning (Zola-Morgan & Squire, 1993). The differences in performance obtained in our study seem to support the idea that each bilingual type may be sustained by a different acquired pattern of cerebral organization. The second language probably involves a greater metalinguistic knowledge component and a more controlled cerebral function. In contrast, the first language is supported by an implicit and automatic competence (Paradis, 1994).

References

Albert, M., & Obler, L. 1978. *The bilingual brain*. New York: Academic Press.

Brec'hed, P. 1980. The language of bilingual children at play. BPS developmental section conference. Edinburgh.

Charlton, M. 1964. Aphasia in bilingual and polyglot patients. A neurological and psychological study. *Journal of Speech and Hearing Disorders*, **29**, 307-311.

Cziko, G.A. 1982. Language competence and reading strategies: a comparison of first and second language oral reading errors. *Language Learning*, **30**, 101-116.

De Renzi, E., & Vignolo, L. 1962. The token Test: A Sensitive test to detect receptive disturbances in aphasics. *Brain*, **85**, 665-678.

Ervin, S.M., & Osgood, C.E. 1954. Second language learning and bilingualism. *Journal of Abnormal and Social Psychology*, **49** (supplement), 139-146.

Favreau, M., Melkin, K., Komoda, F., & Segalowitz, N. 1980. Second language reading: implications of the word superiority effect in skilled bilinguals. *Canadian Journal of Psychology*, **34**.

Felix, S.W. 1981. The effect of formal instruction of second language acquisistion. *Language Learning*, **31**, 87-112.

Fredman, M. 1975. The effect of therapy given in Hebrew on the home language of the bilingual or polyglot adult aphasic in Israel. *British Journal of Disorders of Communication*, **10**, 61-69.

Gekoski, W.L. 1980. Language acquisition context and language organization in bilinguals. *Journal of Psycholinguistic Research*, **9**, 429-449.

Goldstein, K. 1948. *Language and language Disturbances*. New York: Grune & Stratton.

Kraetschmer, K. 1982. Forgotten cases of bilingual Aphasics. *Brain and Language*, **15**, 92-94.

Lambert, W., & Fillenbaum, S. 1959. A pilot study of aphasia among bilinguals. *Canadian Journal of Psychology*, **72**, 77-82.

Lenneberg, A. 1967. *Biological foundations of language*. New York: John Wiley.

Lhermitte, R., Hécaen, H. Dubois, J., Culioli, A., & Tabouret-Keller, A. 1966. Le problème de l'aphasie des polyglottes: remarques sur quelques observations. *Neuropsychologia*, **4**, 315-329.

Lordat, J. 1843. Analyse de la parole pour servir à la théorie de divers cas d'alalie et de paralalie. *Journal de la Société de médecine-pratique de Montpellier*, **7**, 426.

Nair, K.R., & Virmani, V. 1973. Speech and language disturbances in hemiplegics. *Indian Journal of Medical Research*, **61**, 1395-1403.

Ojemann, G.A. 1983. Brain organization for language from the perspective of electrical stimulation mapping. *Behavioral and Brain Sciences*, **6**, 189-230.

Ojemann, G.A., & Whitaker, H.A. 1978. The bilingual brain. *Archives of Neurology*, **35**, 409-412.

Paivio, A. & Desrochers, A. 1980. A dual coding approach to bilingual memory. *Canadian Journal of Psychology*, **34**, 388-399.

Paradis, M. Bilingualism and Aphasia. 1977. In: H. Whitaker & H. A. Whitaker (eds). *Studies in Neurolinguistics*, **3**, New York: Academic Press.

Paradis, M. 1994. Neurolinguistic aspects of implicit and explicit memory: implications for bilingualism and SLA. In N. Ellis (ed.), *Implicit and explicit learning of languages* (pp. 393-419). London: Academic Press.

Paradis, M., & Lecours, A.R. 1979. L'Aphasie chez les bilingues et les polyglottes. In R. Lhermitte & A.R. Lecours. *L'aphasie* (pp. 605-616). Paris: Flammarion.

Paradis, M., Goldblum, M.C., & Abidi, R. 1982. Alternate antagonism with paradoxical translation behavior in two bilingual aphasic patients. *Brain and Language*, **15**, 55-69.

Pick, A. 1903. Fortgesetzte Beiträge zur Pathologie der sensorischen Aphasie. *Archiv für Psychiatrie und Nervenkrankheiten*, **37**, 468-487.

Pick, A. 1913, Geheilte tuberkulöse Meningitis; zugleich ein Beitrag zur Aphasie bei Polyglotten. *Prager Medizinische Wochenschrift*, **38,** 254-285.

Pitres, A. 1895. Étude sur l'aphasie chez les polyglottes. *Revue de Médecine*, **15**, 873-899.

Rapport, R.L., Tan, C.T., & Whitaker, H.A. 1983. Language function and dysfunction among Chinese and English speaking polyglots: Cortical stimulation, Wada testing and clinical studies. *Brain and Language*, **18**, 342-366.

Ribot, T. 1882. *Diseases of Memory; An essay in the positive Psychology*. London: Paul.

Rosa Sensat (Ed.). 1978. *Vocabulario básico infantil*. Barcelona: Rosa Sensat.

Schacter, D.L. 1992. Understanding implicit memory. A cognitive neuroscience approach. *American Psychologist*, **47**, 559-569.

Silverberg, R., & Gordon, H. 1979. Differential aphasia in two bilinguals. *Neurology*, **29**, 51-59.

Vendrell, J.M., Vendrell, P., & Ibáñez, D. Interhemispheric participation in recovery from aphasia. In M. Paradis (ed.) *Foundations of Aphasia Rehabilitation* (pp. 379-410). Pergamon Press, Oxford, 1993.

Voinescu, I., Vish, E., Sirian, S., & Maretsis, M. 1977. Aphasia in a polyglot. *Brain and Language*, **4**, 165-176.

Watamori, T., & Sasanuma, S. 1978. The recovery processes of two English-Japanese bilingual aphasics. *Brain and Language*, **6**, 127-140.

Weinreich, U. 1953. *Languages in contact. Findings and Problems*. New York: Publica tion of the Linguistic circle of New York.

Zola-Morgan, S., & Squire L.R. 1993. Neuroanatomy of memory. *Annual Review in Neurosciences*, **16**, 547-567.

Appendix 1. Naming test. Actual recording form.

BILINGUISME: PROTOCOL DE DENOMINACION

Nom _____

N.Ha_____   Edat _____   Data Expl _____

CADIRA _____	SILLA _____
OCELL _____	PAJARO _____
TAULA_____	MESA _____
RAIM _____	UVA _____
S IVELLA_____	HEBILLA _____
DIT _____	DEDO _____
CIRERES _____	CEREZAS_____
ULL _____	OJO _____
GERRO_____ __	JARRON_____
GALLEDA _____	CUBO _____
PORC _____	CERDO _____
ESPELMA _____	VELA _____
FULLA _____	HOJA _____
CUC _____	GUSANO _____
GRANOTA_____	RANA _____
DONA_____	MUJER _____
FIL _____	HILO_____
ANEC _____	PATO _____
CLAU _____	LLAVE _____
BOLET _____	SETA_____
FINESTRA_____	VENTANA _____
MADUIXA _____	FRESA _____
GOS _____	PERRO _____
FORMATGE_____	QUESO _____

Appendix 2. Pointing test. Actual recording form.

BILINGUISME: PROTOCOL DE DESIGNACIO

Nom _____ _____

N.Ha _____   Edat _____   Data Expl _____

BOLET _____	SETA _____
OCELL _____	PAJARO _____
FINESTRA _____	VENTANA _____
DONA _____	MUJER _____
GRANOTA _____	RANA _____
MIADUIXA _____	FRESA _____
CIRERES _____	CEREZAS _____
FULLA _____	HOJA _____
FORMATGE _____	QUESO _____
DIT _____	DEDO _____
PORC _____	CERDO _____
SIVELLA _____	HEBILLA _____

GALLEDA _____	CUBO _____
CUC _____	GUSANO _____
FIL _____	HILO _____
RAIM _____	UVA _____
TAULA _____	MESA _____
GOS _____	PERRO _____
GERRO _____	JARRON _____
ESPELMA _____	VELA _____
ANEC _____	PATO _____
CADIRA _____	SILLA _____
CLAU _____	LLAVE _____
ULL _____	OJO _____

Appendix 3. Translation test. Actual recording form.

BILINGUISME: PROTOCOL DE TRADUCCION

Nom _____ _____

N.Ha_____   Edat _____   Data Expl _____

MIRALL _____	GRIFO _____
GABIA _____	NIEBLA _____
PAPALLONA _____	LECHUGA _____
SORRA_____	TENEDOR _____
RASPALL_____	RODILLA _____
FUSTA _____	COMEDOR _____
BOTIGA _____	AZUCAR _____
LLENÇOL _____	COLCHON _____
PERNIL _____	SERVILLETA_____
COTO _____	JABON _____
ULLERES_____	JUDIA_____
MOCADOR_____	NARANJA _____
POMA_____	ZAPATO _____
OLI _____	ALAMBRE _____
GEL _____	TRIGO _____
BEC _____	CUERNO _____
GANIVET_____	ALMOHADA _____
JUTGE _____	MEJILLA _____
FERRO _____	ABUELO_____
PRESSEC_____	GARBANZO_____

Appendix 4

BILINGUALISM QUESTIONNAIRE FOR APHASIC PATIENTS

Name..

lace of birth...

Number of years living in Catalonia. ....

Places where patient has lived and number of years in each place...........................

....

....

PRIOR TO APHASIA ONSET

Languages spoken:	Languages understood:
Catalan	Catalan
Spanish	Spanish
Other(s)................................	Other(s) ....

Language *used presently* in family setting (with wife/husband, children ...):

Only Catalan
Only Spanish
Catalan and Spanish

Language used in family setting during *early childhood*
(with parents, siblings, grandparents...):

Only Catalan
Only Spanish
Catalan and Spanish

Age of acquisition of the second language ....

AFTER APHASIA ONSET
Have you observed any of the following phenomena:
Selective *loss* of one language ....
Catalan
Spanish
Mixing of both languages ....
Change in the current use of one or both languages:
From Catalan to Spanish
From Spanish to Catalan

REMARKS

Epilogue: Bilingual aphasia 100 years later: consensus and controversies

Michel Paradis

We should now be in a better position to reflect on what we know, what we don't know, what remains controversial, and what can be inferred from the data reported in this volume. Let us first consider to what extent the traditional questions have been answered and to what extent new questions have emerged. We shall then examine which new data support which hypotheses and identify what areas remain contoversial and in need of further exploration.

Traditional questions and tentative solutions

Pitres (1895) asked four questions. The first three are explicitly stated at the end of his introductory paragrah. (1) Why these differences? (i.e., why do some patients simultaneously recover both languages to the same extent and other patients recover one language sooner and/or better than another? (2) what laws do they obey? (3) what is the mechanism responsible for the differences? The fourth question is not formulated explicitly, but much of the third and last part of his paper, the discussion section, is an attempt to answer it: (4) How are multiple languages represented in the cerebral cortex?

From the issues that Pitres discusses in the body of the paper, and construing the claims he makes as answers to his questions, the first is interpreted to mean "what determines the choice among different patterns of recovery?"; the second, "what is the systematic evolution of bilingual aphasia and which language is better recovered?"; the third, "what physiological process is responsible for selective or successive recovery?" or more generally, how are various patterns possible? (Note that Pitres only considered parallel, successive, selective and differential recovery, not antagonistic or pathological mixing that had not yet been reported in the scanty literature on the subject.)

To this day, the first question remains unanswered. What determines the occurrence of a particular recovery pattern in a given patient, rather than any of the other various possible ones, is unknown. While we may satisfactorily explain what phenomena produce the various patterns (including those not considered by Pitres), as will be seen below in the course of answering question (3), we do not know why it is that Patient A will undergo a parallel recovery whereas Patient B will exhibit alternating antagonism and not the reverse. No correlation has been found between pattern of recovery and neurological, etiological, experiential or linguistic parameters: not site, size or origin of lesion, type or severity of aphasia, type of bilingualism, language structure type, or factors related to acquisition or habitual use.

Question (2) can actually be subdivided, according to the two "laws" that Pitres seemed to have in mind: (2A) "what makes a patient preferably recover French over

Arabic, and not the reverse?", and (2B) "what are the steps in the systematic recovery of a patient's various languages". Question (2A) is probably the one that has received the greatest attention, that has been addressed by the largest number of authors over the years, and that has been the object of the most divergent explanations. Ribot (1881) had assumed that it was the language first acquired; Pitres (1895) proposed that it was the language most familiar to the patient at the time of insult; Minkowski (1927, 1965) suggested that it was the one with the strongest affective ties; Bay (1964) that it was the most useful post-onset. None of these variables account for a majority of cases (Paradis, 1977).

One tentative explanation, that might also serve as an answer to questions (3) and (4), hinted at by Scoresby-Jackson (1867), is that each language might be located in a different portion of the cortical language areas. Pitres strongly argued against this view of different loci for different languages. According to him, since there are several cortical areas subserving language (at least four centres: two sensory, for aural and written comprehension; and two motor, for speaking and writing) in order to result in the selective loss of only one language, each area would have to be selectively damaged only in the part subserving that language and not the other(s). Such a distribution of lesions is in itself close to impossible and could certainly not occur with the relatively high frequency characteristic of nonparallel recovery. From then on, and well into the seventies, most authors have continued to argue against the notion of separate loci for the various languages (Pötzl, 1925; Minkowski, 1927; Veyrac, 1931; Ombredane, 1951; Penfield, 1959; Gloning & Gloning, 1965).

More recently, however, some proposals have been put forward that might be interpreted as a form of different localization of the languages. First, the assertion that more of the second language is subserved by the RH can be construed as such a claim. We may consider that Albert and Obler's (1978) suggestion that there is a greater participation of the RH in the acquisition and use of a second language is true if we interpret the statement to mean that bilinguals rely to a greater extent on pragmatics to process utterances in their weaker language. However, the means by which this claim has been investigated experimentally suggest that the researchers had the language system in mind. Dichotic listening and visual half-field tachistoscopic presentation of digits, syllables, or single words could hardly be expected to tap pragmatic aspects of language use.

Ojemann & Whitaker's (1978) electrico-cortical stimulation study bears more directly on the issue. The authors report that in each of their two patients each language in part used different areas of brain. Similarly, Rapport, Tan & Whitaker (1983) interpret their data as being most compatible with the differential localization model of cerebral localization in bilingualism. The basic assumption is that both languages share the core areas of the classical language zone, the less automatized language is represented in additional areas at the periphery of the language area. Berthier, Starkstein, Lylyk and Leiguarda (1990) alleged to have found additional evidence in support of this notion, except that upon examination their findings, in keeping with their rationale, actually provide counter-evidence, since it is the stronger language that would be the one represented at the periphery. While the hypothesis remains attractive from a theoretical point of view, given that it is generally accepted that the cortical area that subserves a skill gets less extensive as the skill gets more automatized, nevertheless, for methodological reasons, the results cannot uncritically be interpreted as indicative of differential localization. One would first have to explain why, at some sites, languages were located only some of the time.

A third way in which the differential localization issue has been rekindled is in the context of age and manner of acquisition/learning of the second language. In contrast with Penfield's (1959) assertion that the mechanism that is developed in the brain is the same whether one, two, or more languages are learned, Lebrun (1971) entertains the possibility that different languages "may be stored differently in the brain or subserved by different cerebral circuits" (p. 181), especially if the languages are learned differently. These indeed may "rest on different neural organizations" (Lebrun, 1976, p. 102). It would appear that languages which are acquired differently "tend to be subserved by cerebral structures that are to some extent different" (Lebrun, 1971, p. 186). Event-related brain potential studies confirm that there is a difference in the way in which early and late bilinguals process their grammar in the left hemisphere (Neville, Mills & Lawson, 1992, Webber-Fox & Neville, 1992; Webber-Fox & Neville, 1994).

There is also some evidence that lesions in the temporo-parieto-occipital region tends to affect languages learned from reading to a greater extent than those acquired by ear, whereas the opposite is true with lesions in the temporal lobe that spare the parieto-occipital region (Hinshelwood, 1902; Lyman, Kwan & Chao, 1938; Halpern, 1949; Luria, 1956).

There is another sense in which one might argue that late bilinguals use, not so much different cerebral structures, but the same structures to a different extent, as they rely on metalinguistic knowledge and/or on pragmatic aspects of language use. But then, on the one hand, neither system is part of implicit linguistic competence, and on the other, both are part of unilinguals' verbal communicative system as well, even if possibly used to a considerably lesser extent.

Pitres' answer to question (2B) is his first conclusion, namely that polyglot aphasics will first recover comprehension of their most familiar language, then the ability to speak it, followed by the comprehension and subsequent ability to speak their other languages. We now know that this is not necessarily the case, that on the one hand patients may not recover their most familiar language, and on the other hand there are more than successive and selective recovery patterns, to which this evolution pattern does not apply, such as antagonistic recovery (Minkowski, 1933; Winterstein & Meier, 1939; Shubert, 1940; Chlenov, 1948; Wald, 1958; Paradis, Goldblum & Abidi, 1982; Nilipour & Ashayeri, 1989) pathological mixing (Pötzl, 1925; Gloning & Gloning, 1965; Perecman, 1984) or selective impairment of the patient's native as well as current language (Paradis & Goldblum, 1989), not to mention problems with translation (Paradis, Goldblum & Abidi, 1982, Fabbro & Paradis, this volume, Chapter 10). Nevertheless, the fact that many bilingual aphasic patients do recover their languages in this step-wise fashion is consonant with the activation threshold hypothesis which holds that comprehension is easier than production because its activation threshold is lower than that for production which, in addition, as Pitres underscores, necessitates the disinhibition (i.e., lowering of the activation threshold) of the kinesthetic and kinetic articulatory engrams. The linguistic system is easier to access when there is external stimulation than when it has to be self-activated.

It is also the case that comprehension precedes production because implicit linguistic competence is less essential for comprehension than for production, as pragmatic cues may compensate where syntax is not available. A good deal of comprehension need not involve linguistic decoding but can be inferred from the situational and paralinguistic context of the speech event. Production, on the other hand, necessarily relies on the linguistic system for encoding. For that reason comprehension skills precede production skills during the early stages of language development. Passive knowledge of a second language is more advanced than productive ability. When a language ceases to be practised, production deteriorates more quickly than comprehension. Thus at least two other factors, the involvement of the motor system and the availability of pragmatics, conspire with differential activation threshold to facilitate the recovery of comprehension over production.

In answer to question (3), Pitres argues in favour of functional impairment, i.e., inhibition, rather than destruction of the substrate (selective or otherwise), as evidenced by the transient nature of the phenomenon. This explanation is then deemed sufficient not to have to postulate different centres for each of the languages of a polyglot. His answer to question (4) is thus that languages are not represented separately in the cerebral cortex.

Another attempt at answering question (3) has been to postulate a switch mechanism that would syntonize one language or the other (Kauders, 1929), and that some authors localized in the Parietal-Temporal-Occipital junction area (Pötzl, 1930; Hoff & Pötzl, 1932; Leischner, 1948). At the time that Pötzl proposed a locus for the switch, several cases with switching problems had been reported without posterior lesions (Stengel & Zelmanowicz, 1933), as well as cases with lesions in the supramarginal gyrus area, the posterior part of the Sylvian fissure and adjacent parts of the parietal lobe without switching difficulty (Minkowski, 1927; Stengel & Zelmanowicz, 1933). More evidence followed (Gloning & Gloning, 1965; L'Hermitte, Hécaen, Dubois, Culioli & Tabouret-Keller, 1966; Schulze, 1968). The notion of a switch has perdured, although in a functional rather than anatomical form. Penfield (1953) refers to a switch mechanism that allows multilinguals to tune in and out of their various languages at will. Green's (1986) control mechanism is also very similar in function to the switch mechanism, as it distributes resources to the various language systems.

The answer to question (3) which Pitres (1895) himself proposed, namely inhibition, as amended by the notion of activation threshold (Paradis, 1984) and that of control of resources (Green, 1986) accounts for the way the various recovery patterns are possible (including those not considered by Pitres), but does not explain what is responsible for raising or lowering the activation threshold or for distributing resources evenly among the languages in some cases but not in others (which would be an answer to question (1).

Pitres' answer to question (4) seems to have wide acceptance today in one form or another. Multiple languages are generally thought to be represented in the same rather than separate anatomical areas. How they are organized, whether as an extended system, a dual system, a tripartite system, or a set of subsystems is a matter for further investigation. All of the normal and pathological data seem in agreement with the Subsystems Hypothesis (Paradis, 1987a).

The Extended System Hypothesis holds that languages are diffusely represented in the same cortical language areas. The bilingual speaker simply has more choices among elements of nonlinguistic competence that is undifferentiated with respect to specific languages. As a second language is acquired (concurrently with, or subsequently to, the first) additional phonemes (i.e., those of L2) are processed as allophones, used only in L2 environments; new syntactic rules are processed the way stylistic variations are processed within the same language. The speaker would thus have a larger stock of allophones, allomorphs and other allo-elements that would be used only in the context of their respective language.

The ease with which bilinguals can mix their languages intrasententially, with or without corresponding switches in phonology, is consistent with an extended system. Parallel recovery and blending of a patient's languages are also in agreement.

The Dual System Hypothesis assumes that elements of the various languages are stored separately, in underlying systems that are independent of each other. Different networks of neural connections subserve each language. Each linguistic system is thus represented separately in the brain. The hypothesis, however, does not necessarily imply differential localization at the macro-anatomical level. Both systems might be inextricably intertwined within the same square millimeter of cortical tissue.

The way bilinguals are able to speak one language at a time without interference from the other is easily accounted for by a dual system of language representation. So are successive and antagonistic recovery patterns, as well as selective loss, whether temporary or permanent, of one of a patient's languages.

The Tripartite Hypothesis supposes that those items that are identical in the two languages of a bilingual speaker are represented in a single neural substrate common to both languages. Only those elements that are different in each language have their own separate representation. This eliminates the redundancy of representation of whatever structural elements the two languages have in common.

Ojemann and Whitaker's (1978) proposal that there are sites common to both languages and sites specific to each is concordant with such a tripartite system. So are the findings of Sasanuma and Park (this volume) to the effect that the transfer of therapy benefits were confined to the areas where the two languages are similar. In other words, the structural distance effect on language therapy hypothesis (Paradis, 1993) is compatible with a tripartite system. The findings reported by Stadie, Springer, De Bleser and Bürk (this volume) to the effect that their multilingual patient made fewer interlingual errors between the two languages dissimilar in structure than between the two structurally similar languages are also congruent with such a hypothesis.

Data toward a consensus

Over the past decade, cognitive neuropsychology has focussed on the modularization of cognitive functions and the fractionation of complex cognitive tasks, identifying an ever increasing number of processing subcomponents of functions previously considered as a whole (Caramazza, 1984; Paradis, 1987b).

As already pointed out by Pitres one hundred years ago, memory is not a unitary function. Indeed there are many different types of memory, each susceptible of selective impairment. Even before him Gall (1819) had proposed multiple memory systems, from visuospatial memory to that responsible for music, and for arithmetic. In his own patients, Pitres independently tested musical memory, mental arithmetic, memory for places, faces, events, and rote memory. He also drew attention to the double dissociation that obtains between the various elements of language itself: each of the sensory and motor centres subserving the language function possesses its own memory independent of that of neighbouring centres and each of these memories can be selectively lost or impaired.

More recently, memory has been further subdivided into episodic (Tulving, 1972) or experiential (Penfield, 1959) and semantic; visuomotor (Milner, 1962), procedural and declarative (Winograd, 1975; Anderson, 1976; Cohen, 1984). Each type of memory contributes to the microgenesis of an utterance, that is, from the elaboration of a message to be communicated to its acoustic realization (or, in comprehension, from the analysis of the acoustic signal to the extraction of a nonlinguistic mental representation of the message), each subserving a different aspect. Short term memory deficits will reduce the ability to understand and produce long and/or complex sentences. Episodic and/or encyclopedic memory are necessary to understand the meaning of what is said as well as to have something to talk *about* (i.e, to elaborate the content of the message to be verbalized or to extract its meaning from the utterance). Procedural memory underlies the incidental acquisition and automatic use of implicit linguistic competence, and damage to that memory system is what causes aphasia proper. In addition, the speaker needs a pragmatic competence for the understanding and use of nonliteral meanings and for making inferences from situational context, discursive context, and general knowledge.

Thus, in bilingual aphasic patients, as suggested by Lebrun (this volume), it is quite possible that the language spoken in the patients' environment and used to interact with them may facilitate to a greater extent its recovery if it has been acquired incidentally than if it has been learned in a formal and conscious manner. Stimulation of the patient's partially inhibited implicit linguistic competence may help lower its activation threshold and thus improve its functioning in proportion to its premorbid automaticity relative to that of the later acquired language.

However, in the absence of spontaneous recovery, when implicit linguistic competence remains inhibited or has been permanently destroyed, patients may, as a compensatory strategy, rely on their metalinguistic knowledge which may very well be much more extensive in their second language, and thus give the impression of having paradoxically recovered the language they spoke the least well before insult. Assuming that aphasia interferes with the normal functioning of the procedural memory system that underlies implicit linguistic competence, metalinguistic knowledge, subserved by declarative memory, a neurofunctionally, neurophysiologically and neuroanatomically distinct system, remains available (Paradis, 1994).

The fact that the patient described by Sasanuma & Park (this volume), after therapy only in Korean, showed improvement in all modalities in both Korean and Japanese, except for writing in Japanese, tends to support the hypothesis that language therapy benefits transfer to the untreated language only to the extent that, and in the areas where, the two languages are similar in structure. At the same time, this is evidence in support of the neurofunctional modularity of the Japanese writing system (Paradis, 1987b).

Reports in this volume describe patients who have acquired both their languages at the same time in the same context and exhibit differential patterns of recovery (Junqué, Vendrell & Vendrell) as well as patients who have acquired their second language long after the first, in a different environment, and who show parallel recovery (Junqué, Vendrell & Vendrell; Sasanuma & Park). This is further evidence that type of bilingualism (coordinate/compound), based on age and/or context of acquisition, is a poor predictor of pattern of recovery. It does not speak in favour of a different cerebral organization for coordinate and compound bilinguals. In fact, there is PET evidence (Klein, Zatorre, Milner, Meyer & Evans, this volume) that there is no major difference in cerebral organization between unilinguals and bilinguals.

Before one can issue a diagnosis of differential aphasia (e.g., Broca's in one language and Wernicke's in the other) it is important to know (1) the surface manifestation of particular language impairments in specific languages, as illustrated by the different symptoms manifested in Farsi and English (Nilipour & Paradis, this volume), and (2) the relevant sociolinguistic variables, as illustrated by fluency and accuracy ratings between standard Japanese and Standard English in speakers of other dialects (Dronkers, Yamasaki, Ross & White, this volume). Moreover, the classification of a patient into a particular category may be an artefact of the rating scale of the test being used (Dronkers et al., this volume). In addition, some tests are more discriminating than others (De Luca, Fabbro, Vorano & Lovati, 1994)

Multiple languages in one brain are neurofunctionally independent, as evidenced by the various nonparallel recovery patterns, though not neuroanatomically separated, at least not at the gross anatomical level. What remains to be investigated is whether the "different cerebral circuits" referred to by Lebrun (1971) are anatomically indistinguishable, as part of the same corticothalamic mechanism, as proposed by Penfield, (1959), or occupy in part slightly different cortical locations, as suggested by Ojemann and Whitaker (1978). In any event, two languages are represented in the brain by two different systems or sets of traces, as must be different registers in unilinguals.

Penfield (1953) assumed that if the claim that injury to the dominant hemisphere has resulted in the loss of one language and the preservation of another were substantiated (as in fact it later was in Paradis & Goldblum, 1989), one would be forced to assume that one area of cortex was used for French and another for Spanish. He did not consider Pitres' proposal of functional impairment. Ironically, a few years after Penfield's retirement, a patient exhibiting alternating antagonism was seen at the Montreal Neurological Institute where Penfield himself had practised neurosurgery for over 40 years (Paradis, Goldblum & Abidi, 1982). The aphasia in this case was subsequent to surgical intervention in the left parietal area (for an arterovenous malformation) and caused by oedema of the language area, not physical destruction. Nonparallel recovery is thus not incompatible with a common neural substrate for all languages.

Translation also has been shown to be neurofunctionally independent of understanding and speaking two languages (Paradis, Goldblum & Abidi, 1982). Moreover, directionality of translation can be selectively impaired, as demonstrated by two additional patients for whom translation is spared from the first language into the second or third, but impossible from the second or third into the first (Fabbro & Paradis, Chapter 10, this volume).

Remaining controversies

Some psychologists still believe that, if only one were to look hard enough, with the appropriate instrument, one might yet be able to find, at least in some bilinguals, a difference in the asymmetry of language cerebral representation that has eluded them so far. In spite of all the contradictory evidence emanating from experimental studies over the past 20 years, and the total lack of clinical and neuropsychological evidence, instead of seriously questioning the validity of the experimental procedures used to determine laterality in individuals or small groups of individuals, against all odds, some authors continue to advocate that one multiply these experiments and continue to use dichotic listening and visual half-field tachistoscopic presentation of single words, or whatever else could have a chance of detecting differential asymmetry (Berquier & Ashton, 1992). And indeed, papers continue to appear, basing claims of greater right hemisphere participation on far-from-compelling data and without unilingual control subjects (Wuillemin, Richardson & Lynch, 1994—see Paradis, 1995 for an evaluation of the data).

Naming without comprehension (Kremin & De Agostini, this volume), like the ability to name kanji without comprehension (Hirose, 1949; Fujii & Morokuma, 1959; Kurachi & Takekoshi, 1977) is a dissociation in the context of connections between the phonological form of words, their lexical meaning, and their visual representation (in the case of naming), and their written representation (in the case of reading). This is not to be construed as evidence of the ability to use language, i.e., the ability to produce meaningful utterances appropriate to the situation, in the absence of comprehension of such utterances, except in cases of pure word deafness, as alluded to in Kremin's reference to Paradis (1989). (The rare cases of echolalia reported in the literature do not meet the appropriateness of use criterion.) Preserved picture naming in spite of severely impaired semantic comprehension of words that refer to the same stimuli speaks to the issue of naming pictures of objects (or the objects themselves) within a model for naming single words (or reading them, in the case of kanji or phonological dyslexia in general), not to the issue of the production of coherent utterances without comprehension referred to in Paradis (1989).

The remaining controversy here is between cognitive models of word recognition and word production (e.g., Morton, 1985; Riddoch & Humphreys, 1987; Lesser, 1989) and the dual pathway model to account for spared naming in the context of grossly impaired semantic comprehension of words (Kremin, 1986, 1994; Kremin, Beauchamp & Perrier, 1994; Kremin & De Agostini, this volume).

The reported dissociation between picture naming and comprehension may be considered further evidence for the differential status of words (with a non-negligeable declarative component) within the rest of implicit linguistic competence, which relies essentially on procedural memory (Paradis, 1994).

Of course, one may add to the rubric of remaining controversies any objection any reader may have to any of the viewpoints expressed in this volume.

Issues for further research

Pitres (1895) paved the way for the notion of inhibition/disinhibition of language systems, the activation threshold, the modularization of neurofunctional systems and their fractionation into subcomponents. Further research will continue to clarify these issues.

One issue worthy of further investigation is the critical period for the acquisition of a second language, and the subsidiary question as to whether languages acquired after a certain age are processed in ways that differ from those of the native language. The ERP studies (Neville, Mills & Lawson, 1992; Webber-Fox & Neville, 1992, 1994) speak to the issue. According to Penfield, multiple languages may be acquired perfectly, without physiological confusion, if they are acquired at the right age and with the right method, namely, according to him, the direct method (1959). ERP data seem to confirm Penfield's (1953) conviction that the brain passes through unalterable transitions and is especially adapted to the acquisition of language at early stages, but that after the ages of 10 to 14 (today we would say even earlier), gradually and inevitably the brain becomes rigid, slow, less receptive, and is soon senescent in regard to language.

PET evidence (Klein et al., this volume) supports Penfield's (1953) other claim, namely that "when more than one language is learned, the speech areas of the dominant hemisphere take them all on without geographical separation" (p. 208). Research in the next few years will examine the qualitative and quantitative differences involved in acquiring a second language after the age of six or seven, in the ways that implicit linguistic competence is organized in the brain, in the extent that compensatory mechanisms come into play and are subserved by the brain, and in how the additional effort involved in processing a weaker language impacts on cortical and subcortical structures. These will in turn help us design models of language rehabilitation for speakers of multiple languages.

Concluding remarks

Bilingualism is not just a rare, occasional occurrence in the language/speech pathology clinic (Wiener, Obler & Taylor Sarno, this volume) but a phenomenon every clinic must be prepared to cope with. An increasing percentage of the population everywhere speaks more than one language. All languages of an aphasic patient need to be assessed because it is impossible to predict on the basis of context of acquisition and/or use or relative degree of premorbid proficiency which language is best available to the patient and which one exhibits tell-tale symptoms that could not be observed in the other(s), because of either structural properties of the language or differential recovery. The subjective opinion of the patients themselves in that respect has been shown to be often unreliable. Given what we now know, it is no longer ethically acceptable to assess aphasic patients on the basis of the examination of only one of their languages.

References

Albert, M.L. & Obler, L.K. 1978. *The bilingual brain*. New York: Academic Press.

Anderson, J.R. 1976. *Language, memory, and thought*. Hillsdale, NJ.: Lawrence Erlbaum Associates.

Bay, E. 1964. General discussion. In A.V.S. De Reuck & M. O'Connor (eds.), *Disorders of language*. Boston: Little Brown.

Berquier, A., & Ashton, R. 1992. Language lateralization in bilinguals: more not less is needed. A reply to Paradis (1990)*Brain and Language*, **43**, 528-533.

Berthier, M.L. Starkstein, S.E., Lylyk, P. & Leiguarda, R. 1990. Differential recovery of languages in a bilingual patient: a case study using selective amytal test. *Brain and Language*, **38**, 449-453.

Caramazza, A. 1984. The logic of neuropsychological research and the problem of patient classification in aphasia. *Brain and Language*, **21**, 9-20.

Chlenov, L.G. 1948. Ob afazii u poliglotov. *Izvestiia Akademii Pedagogicheskikh NAUK RSFSR*, **15**, 783-790 [Translated in M. Paradis (ed.), Readings on aphasia in bilinguals and polyglots (pp. 446-454), Montreal: Marcel Didier.

Cohen, N. 1984. Preserved learning capacity in amnesia: evidence for multiple memory systems. In L.R. Squire and N. Butters (eds.), *The neuropsychology of human memory* (pp. 83-103). New York: Guilford Press.

De Luca, G., Fabbro, F., Vorano, L., & Lovati, L. 1994. Valutazione con il Bilingual Aphasia Test; (BAT) della rieducazione dell'afasico multilingue. Paper presented at the 4th Meeting, Disturbi cognitivi, comportamentali e della comunicazione nelle lesioni cerebrali acquisite, Ospedale di Medicina Fisica e Riabilitazione "Gervasutta", Udine, Italy, 1 July.

Fujii, K., & Morokuma, O. 1959. Gogi shitsogoshoo no ichi shoorei [A case of word-meaning (Gogi) aphasia]. *Seishin Igaku [Clinical Psychiatry]*, **1**, 431-435.

Gall, J.F. 1819. *Anatomie et physiologie du système nerveux et du cerveau en particulier*. T. IV, Paris: F. Schoell.

Gloning, I., & Gloning, K. 1965. Aphasien bei Polyglotten. Beitrag zur Dynamik des Sprachabbaus sowie zur Lokalisationsfrage dieser Störungen. *Wiener Zeitschrift für Nervenheilkunde*, **22**, 362-397. [Translated in M. Paradis (ed.), 1983. *Readings on aphasia in bilinguals and polyglots* (pp. 681-716). Montreal: Marcel Didier.]

Green, D.W. 1986. Control, activation, and resource: a framework and a model for the control of speech in bilinguals. *Brain and Language*, **27**, 210-223.

Halpern, L. 1949. La langue hébraïque dans la restitution de l'aphasie sensorielle chez les polyglottes. *Semaine des Hôpitaux de Paris*, **58**, 2473-2476. [Translated in M. Paradis (ed.), 1983. *Readings on aphasia in bilinguals and polyglots* (pp. 517-523). Montreal: Marcel Didier.]

Hinshelwood, J. 1902. Four cases of word blindness. Lancet, 1, 358-363.

Hirose, M. 1949. Kankakusei shitsugo no sai ni okeru shitsudoku [Dyslexia in the context of sensory aphasia] *Shinri [Psychology]*, **5**, 42-50.

Hoff, H., & Pötzl, O. 1932. Über die Aphasie eines zweisprechigen Linkshänders. *Wiener Medizinische Wochenschrift*, **82**, 369-373. [Translated in M. Paradis (ed.), 1983. *Readings on aphasia in bilinguals and polyglots* (pp. 339-349). Montreal: Marcel Didier.]

Kauders, O.. 1929. Über polyglotte Reaktionen bei einer sensorischen Aphasie. *Zeitschrift für die gesamte Neurologie und Psychiatrie*, **122**, 651-666. [Translated in M. Paradis (ed.), 1983. *Readings on aphasia in bilinguals and polyglots* (pp. 286-300). Montreal: Marcel Didier.]

Kremin, H. 1986. Spared naming without comprehension. *Journal of Neurolinguistics*, **2**, 131-150.

Kremin, H. 1994. Selective impairments of action naming: arguments and a case study. *Linguistische Berichte*, Sonderheft **6**, 62-82.

Kremin, H., Beauchamp, D., & Perrier D. 1994. Naming without picture comprehension? A propos the oral naming and semantic comprehension of pictures by patients with Alzheimer's Disease. *Aphasiology*, **8**, 291-294.

Kurachi, M. & Takekoshi, T. 1977. Shoji shoogai no keido na kankaku shitsugo—sokuhuku kekkoo no chomei na icherei [Sensory aphasia with relative preservation of writing ability: Collateral flow from the frontal to the middle cerebral artery]. *Noo to Shinkei [Brain and Neurology]*, **29**, 1085- 1091.

Lebrun, Y. 1971. The neurology of bilingualism. *Word*, **27**, 179-186.

Lebrun, Y. 1976. Recovery in polyglot aphasics. In Y. Lebrun & R. Hoops (eds.), *Recovery in aphasics* (pp. 96-108). Amsterdam: Swets & Zeitlinger.

Leischner, A. 1948. Über die Aphasie der Mehrsprachigen. *Archiv für Psychiatrie und Nervenkrankheiten*, **180**, 731-775. [Translated in M. Paradis (ed.), 1983. *Readings on aphasia in bilinguals and polyglots* (pp. 456-502). Montreal: Marcel Didier.]

Lesser, R. 1989. Some issues in the neuropsychological rehabilitation of anomia. In X. Seron & G. Deloche (eds.), *Cognitive approaches in neuropsychological rehabilitation* (pp. 65-104). Hillsdale, NJ.: Lawrence Erlbaum Associates.

L'Hermitte, R., Hécaen, H., Dubois, A., Culioli, A., & Tabouret-Keller, A. 1966. Le problème de l'aphasie des polyglottes: remarques sur quelques observations. *Neuropsychologia*, **4**, 315-329. [Translated in M. Paradis (ed.), 1983. *Readings on aphasia in bilinguals and polyglots* (pp. 727-743). Montreal: Marcel Didier.]

Luria, A. 1956. K voprosu o narushenii pis'ma i chteniia u poliglotov. *Fiziologicheskij Zhurnal*, **2**, 127-133.

Lyman, R., Kwan, S. & Chao, W. 1938. Left occipito-parietal brain tumor with observations on alexia and agraphia in Chinese and English. *Chinese Medical Journal*, **54**, 491-516.

Milner, B. 1962. Les troubles de la mémoire accompagnant des lésions hippocampiques bilatérales. In P. Passouant (ed.), *Physiologie de l'hippopcampe.* (pp. 257-272) Paris: C.N.R.S. [Translated as Memory disturbance after bilateral hippocampal lesions. In P.M. Milner & S. Glickman (eds.), *Cognitive processes and the brain.* (pp. 97-111). Princeton: Van Nostrand].

Minkowski, M. 1927. Klinischer Beitrag zur Aphasie bei Polyglotten, speziell im Hinblick aufs Schweizerdeutsche. *Schweizer Archiv für Neurologie und Psychiatrie*, **21**, 43-72. [Translated in M. Paradis (ed.), *Readings on aphasia in bilinguals and polyglots* (pp. 205-232). Montreal: Marcel Didier].

Minkowski, 1933. Sur un trouble aphasique particulier chez un polyglotte. *Revue neurologique*, **59**, 1185-1189 [Translated in M. Paradis (ed.), *Readings on aphasia in bilinguals and polyglots* (pp. 351-355). Montreal: Marcel Didier].

Minkowski, M. 1965. Considérations sur l'aphasie des polyglottes. *Revue neurologique*, **112**, 486-495 [Translated in M. Paradis (ed.), *Readings on aphasia in bilinguals and polyglots* (pp. 717-726). Montreal: Marcel Didier].

Morton, J. 1985. Naming. In S. Newman & R. Epstein (eds.), *Current perspectives in dysphasia* (pp. 217-230). Edinburgh: Churchill Livingston.

Neville, H.J., Mills, D.L., & Lawson, D.S. 1992. Fractionating language: different neural systems with different sensitive periods. *Cerebral Cortex*, **2**, 244-258.

Nilipour, R., & Ashayeri, H. 1989. Alternating antagonism between two languages with successive recovery of a third in a trilingual aphasic patient. *Brain and Language*, **36**, 23-48.

Ojemann, G.A. & Whitaker, H.A. 1978. The bilingual brain. *Archives of Neuro-ogy*, **35**, 409-412.

Ombredane, A. 1951. *L'aphasie et l'élaboration de la pensée explicite*. Paris: Presses Universitaires de France.

Paradis, M. 1977. Bilingualism and aphasia. In H. Whitaker & H.A. Whitaker (eds.), *Studies in neurolinguistics*, vol. 3 (pp.65-121). New York: Academic Press.

Paradis, M. 1984. Aphasie et traduction. Μετα, *Translators' Journal*, **29**,57-67.

Paradis, M. 1987a. Neurolinguistic perspectives on bilingualism. In M. Paradis & G. Libben, *The assessment of bilingual aphasia* (Chapter 1). Hillsdale, NJ.: Lawrence Erlbaum Associates.

Paradis, M. 1987b. The neurofunctional modularity of cognitive skills: evidence from Japanese alexia and polyglot aphasia. In E. Keller & M. Gopnik (eds.), *Motor and sensory processes of language* (pp. 277-289). Hillsdale, NJ.: Lawrence Erlbaum Associates.

Paradis, M. 1989. Bilingual and polyglot aphasia,. In F. Boller & J. Grafman (eds.), *Handbook of neuropsychology*, vol. 2 (117-140). Amsterdam: Elsevier.

Paradis, M. 1993. Bilingual aphasia rehabilitation. In M. Paradis (ed.), *Foundations of aphasia rehabilitation* (pp. 413-420). Oxford: Pergamon Press.

Paradis, M. 1994. Neurolinguistic aspects of implicit and explicit memory: implications for bilingualism and SLA. In N. Ellis (ed.), *Implicit and explicit learning of languages* (pp. 393-419). London: Academic Press.

Paradis, M. 1995. Another sighting of differential language laterality in multilinguals, this time in Loch Tok Pisin: Comments on Wuillemin, Richardson, and Lynch (1994). *Brain and Language*, **48**, in press.

Paradis, M., & Goldblum, M.C. 1989. Selected crossed aphasia in a trilingual aphasic patient followed by reciprocal antagonism. *Brain and Language*, **36**, 62-75.

Paradis, M., Goldblum, M.C. & Abidi, R. 1982. Alternate antagonism with paradoxical translation behavior in two bilingual aphasic patients. *Brain and Language*, **15**, 55-69.

Penfield, W. 1953. A consideration of the neurophysiological mechanisms of speech and some educational consequences. *Proceedings of the American Academy of Arts and Sciences*, **82**, 199-214.

Penfield, W. 1959. The learning of languages. In W. Penfield & L. Roberts, *Speech and brain-mechanisms*. Princeton: Princeton University Press.

Perecman, E. 1984. Spontaneous translation and language mixing in a polyglot aphasic. *Brain and Language*, **23**, 43-63.

Pitres, A. 1895. Etude sur l'aphasie chez les polyglottes. *Revue de médecine*, **15**, 873-899. [Translated in M. Paradis (ed.), *Readings on aphasia in bilinguals and polyglots* (pp. 26-48). Montreal: Marcel Didier].

Pötzl, O. 1925. Über die parietal bedingte Aphasie und ihren Einfluss auf das Sprechen mehrerer Sprachen. *Zeitschrift für die gesamte Neurologie und Psychiatrie*, **96**, 100-124. [Translated in M. Paradis (ed.), 1983. *Readings on aphasia in bilinguals and polyglots* (pp. 176-198). Montreal: Marcel Didier.]

Rapport, R.L., Tan, C.T., & Whitaker, H.A. 1983. Language function and dysfunction among Chinese- and English-speaking polyglots: cortical stimulation, Wada testing and clinical studies. *Brain and Language,* **18**, 342-366.

Ribot, T. 1881. *Les maladies de la mémoire*. 2e édition. Paris: Baillère.

Riddoch, M.J., & Humphreys, G.W. 1987. Picture naming. In G.W. Humphreys & M.J. Riddoch (eds.), *Visual object processing: a cognitive neuropsychological approach*. Hillsdale, NJ.: Lawrence Erlbaum Associates.

Schulze, H.A. 1968. Unterschiedliche Rückbildung einer sensorischen und einer ideo-kinetischen motorischen Aphasie bei einem Polyglotten. *Neurologie und medizinische Psychologie*, **20**, 441-445. [Translated in M. Paradis (ed.), 1983. *Readings on aphasia in bilinguals and polyglots* (pp. 753-760). Montreal: Marcel Didier.]

Scoresby-Jackson, R. 1867. Case of aphasia with right hemiplegia. *Edinburgh Medical Journal*, **12**, 696-706.

Shubert, A.M. 1940. Dinamika dvuiazychnoi aleksii i agrafii pri travme golovnogo mozga. *Trudy Tsentral'nogo Instituta Psikhologii*. Moskva. 169-175. [Translated in M. Paradis (ed.), 1983. *Readings on aphasia in bilinguals and polyglots* (pp. 399-417). Montreal: Marcel Didier.]

Stengel, E., & Zelmanowicz, J. 1933. Über polyglotte motorische Aphasie. *Zeitschrift für die gesamte Neurologie und Psychiatrie*, **149**, 292-311. [Translated in M. Paradis (ed.), 1983. *Readings on aphasia in bilinguals and polyglots* (pp. 356-375). Mont-real: Marcel Didier.]

Tulving, E. 1972. Episodic and semantic memory. In E. Tulving & W. Donaldson (eds.), *Organization of memory*. New York: Academic Press.

Veyrac, G.J. 1931. Etude de l'aphasie chez les sujets polyglottes. Thèse de doctorat en médecine, Université de Paris. [Translated in M. Paradis (ed.), *Readings on aphasia in bilinguals and polyglots* (pp. 320-338). Montreal: Marcel Didier].

Wald, I. 1958. Zagadnienie afazji poliglotow. *Postepy Neurologii Neurochirurgii i Psychiatrii*, **4**, 183-211 [Translated in M. Paradis (ed.), *Readings on aphasia in bilinguals and polyglots* (pp. 579-601). Montreal: Marcel Didier].

Webber-Fox, C.M., & Neville, H.J. 1992. Maturational constraints on cerebral specialization for language processing: ERP and behavioral evidence in bilingual speakers. Paper presented at the 22nd Annual Meeting of the Society for Neuroscience, Anaheim, 26 October.

Webber-Fox, C.M., & Neville, H.J. 1994. Sensitive periods differentiate neural systems for grammatical and semantic processing: ERP evidence in bilingual speakers. Paper presented at the Cognitive Neuroscience Society inaugural meeting, San Francisco, 28 March.

Winograd, T. 1975. Frame representations and the declarative-procedural controversy. In D. Dobrow & A. Collins (eds.), *Representations and understanding*. New York: Academic Press.

Winterstein, O., & Meier, J. 1939. Schäderltrauma und Aphasie bei Mehrsprachigen. *Der Chirurg*, **11**, 229-232 [Translated in M. Paradis (ed.), *Readings on aphasia in bilinguals and polyglots* (pp. 387-390). Montreal: Marcel Didier].

Wuillemin, D., Richardson, B., & Lynch, J. 1994. Right hemisphere involvement in processing later-learned languages in multilinguals. *Brain and Language*, **46**, 620-636.

Author Index

Subject Index